BODY BUILDERS

Gifts
to make
God's people
grow

David Petts

Published by :

Mattersey Hall
Mattersey
DN10 5HD
England

ISBN 1 873324 06 5

How much more will your Father in heaven give good gifts to those who ask him!
Matthew 7 :11

Try to excel in gifts that build up the church
1 Corinthians 14 :12

...so that the body of Christ may be built up
Ephesians 4 :12

Publisher's Note

Mattersey Hall is an international, evangelical Bible College with an emphasis that is distinctly charismatic. Students are drawn from a wide variety of nations, denominations, and fellowships. The College is owned by Assemblies of God, one of the world's largest Pentecostal groups. It is also a member of the Evangelical Alliance.

Courses offered lead to qualifications which include Certificate, Diploma, BA, MTh, and PhD. The College also offers a variety of Distance Learning courses.

As part of our commitment to assist in training for Christian service at a wide variety of levels, it has been decided that the essence of some of the courses taught at Mattersey Hall should be made available in book form. Such books will, therefore, normally be authored by the College tutor who teaches the course in question. This book is authored by Dr David Petts who teaches the College course on *Spiritual Gifts*.

As a matter of policy, our publications are written in a highly readable style without lacking academic integrity.

Body Builders – Gifts to make God's People Grow is published in 2002 to celebrate the author's 25th year as Principal of the College.

Mattersey Hall, Mattersey, DN10 5HD, England.

About the author

Dr David Petts has been Principal of Mattersey Hall since 1977. An international Bible teacher, he emphasises the work of the Holy Spirit in the Christian's life and has been instrumental in leading many into the experience of the Baptism in the Holy Spirit. He conducts seminars and Bible Studies in churches, colleges and universities.

David is an Assemblies of God minister and much of his ministry has been within the world-wide Pentecostal Movement. He has served as Chairman of the Executive Council of Assemblies of God for 15 years and in 2001 was elected to the Presidium of the Pentecostal World Fellowship.

He is married to Eileen who has been a strong support to his ministry for some 40 years. They have three children (who are all involved in the leadership of local churches) and seven grandchildren.

A former Exhibitioner of Brasenose College, Oxford, David's academic achievements include an MA, an MTh, and a PhD in Theology.

CONTENTS

Overview

There are several lists of gifts in the New Testament, but there are two that appear to be unique. The gifts in Ephesians 4:11 are *people* who are given to the church 'so that the body of Christ may be **built up**' (Ephesians 4:12) and those mentioned in 1 Corinthians 12:8-10 seem to be *supernatural* manifestations given to Christians in order to '**build up** the church' (1 Corinthians 14:12).

It is upon the gifts listed in these two passages that this book concentrates, although the Appendix deals briefly with some of the other gifts. I have assumed throughout, despite the views of the cessationists who argue that some of these gifts are not for today, that *all* the gifts mentioned in the New Testament are important for the church of the 21st Century. Like the Corinthians, we should not lack *any* spiritual gift as we wait for the coming of the Lord Jesus Christ (1 Corinthians 1:7).

Part One deals with the gifts of Christ to the church (Ephesians 4:11). The twelve **apostles** appointed by Jesus were in some respects unique, but later apostles like Paul, Barnabas, and James the Lord's brother provide interesting role-models for apostles today. **Prophets** in the New Testament, after Pentecost at least, fulfilled a rather different role from the prophets in the Old Testament, but Agabus serves as a good example of what we should expect of a prophet in the contemporary church situation. The only **evangelist** named in the New Testament is Philip and there is much that the modern evangelist can learn from the graphic description of his ministry offered to us in Acts 8.

The ministry of **pastors** (shepherds) will always be of great importance to the life of the church. There is some danger, however, that Christians today assume that they know what this ministry is, or should be, without considering what the Bible has to say on the subject. In this connection this book stresses the role of elders as those who in the New Testament formed the pastoral *team*. The ministry of the **teacher** may rightly be understood to be combined with that of pastor, but it may also function separately. Apollos serves as a good model of this, but it is Jesus himself who is the supreme example, as he is of all these gifts.

Part Two considers the gifts listed in 1 Corinthians 12:8-10. I argue that all nine are supernatural manifestations given by the Holy Spirit to individual Christians in order that the church might be built up. I have not dealt with these in the order in which Paul lists them but have chosen to leave the more controversial gifts until last. From the early days of the Pentecostal Movement there has been a measure of disagreement as to the nature of '**a word of wisdom**' and '**a word of knowledge**'. And we cannot say with absolute certainty what Paul meant by '**discerning of spirits**'. In the chapters that deal with these gifts I have tried to evaluate various views before expressing an opinion of my own.

With regard to the other gifts in the list, in my view there is little room for disagreement. The meaning of '**tongues**', '**interpretation**', and '**prophecy**' seems to be self-evident as is that of '**the working of miracles**' and '**gifts of healing**'. It also seems reasonably clear that when Paul talks about '**faith**' in the context of spiritual gifts he is referring to the supernatural faith that can move mountains (cf. 1 Corinthians 13:2).

In discussing these gifts, therefore, I have concentrated less on their definition and more on their value and use. However, in most cases the chapter that deals with the gift in question addresses a wider area than the gift itself. For example, the chapter on healing deals with the subject of healing in general, not just the specific spiritual gift of healing. Finally, I have wherever possible illustrated the use of these gifts by examples from my own personal experience or that of people I know. I have done so deliberately as a testimony to the reality of these gifts today.

INTRODUCTION

Establishing a Biblical Basis

The Bible tells us very clearly that God is a *giving* God. He loved the world so much that he *gave* his one and only Son (John 3:16). Those who put their trust in him receive the *gift* of eternal life (Romans 6:23). He also *gives* us his Holy Spirit (Luke 11:13, Acts 2:38). And all this despite the fact that we don't deserve it! We didn't deserve Jesus to die for us, we don't deserve eternal life, and we don't deserve to receive his Spirit! Everything we receive from God is because of his undeserved kindness to us. The Bible calls it God's *grace*.

And there are many other gifts that God graciously showers upon his people. Some of these gifts are *natural* talents we were born with, others are *supernatural* gifts like prophecy and healing and miracles. Other gifts are *people* like apostles and prophets, evangelists, pastors and teachers, who are given to the church to build it up and prepare God's people to serve him. But whatever kind of gift it might be, it comes from God's grace, his undeserved kindness towards us.

It's because of this that the apostle Paul in his letters uses a special word to describe these gifts. He calls them *charismata*, which means 'gifts of grace'. (It's from this, of course, that we get our English word 'charismatic'). In this book we're going to consider some of these gifts, what they are, and how to receive them and use them. But first it will be helpful to take a more detailed look at how Paul uses the word *charismata* in the New Testament. Then we'll examine various lists of gifts we find in the New Testament and decide how best to approach our study of them.

Paul's Use of *Charismata*

In the Greek language in which the New Testament was written, the word *charis* means 'grace'. So a *charisma* is a gift which comes from God's grace and 'gifts' (plural) are *charismata*. Paul uses this word in five main ways. We'll briefly outline them here, but it is the gifts in the last group that we'll be mainly concerned with in this book.

First, Paul uses the word in a general way to refer to *any* gift that comes from God. Since all that we have and are is a result of God's grace it follows that all God's gifts are *charismata*. That's why Paul can use the word to refer to marriage and celibacy as gifts from God (1 Corinthians 7:7) and how he can speak of his deliverance from danger as a result of the Corinthians' prayers as a *charisma* (2 Corinthians 1:11).

Secondly, in Romans 11:29, when talking about God's gracious dealings with Israel, Paul tells us that God does not change his intentions with regard to his gifts (*charismata*) and calling.

Thirdly, as we have already seen, the gift of eternal life is a *charisma* (Romans 6:23), and closely connected with this, the gift of righteousness (justification) is seen as a gracious *charisma* from God in Romans 5:15-16.

Fourthly, in 2 Timothy 1:6 Paul refers to the gift Timothy received through the laying on of Paul's hands as a *charisma*. This was probably the gift of the Holy Spirit himself (cf. v 7), sometimes described as the baptism in the Spirit. In the New Testament this was closely connected with the charismatic gift of speaking in tongues.

Finally, the word is used to refer to a variety of gifts (natural or supernatural) which God gives to Christians. These are the gifts that we will consider in this book. In the next section you will find the main passages where a number of different gifts are listed.

Lists of Gifts

The table below summarises the five main lists of gifts found in the New Testament. The description of each gift follows the NIV translation, but I have abbreviated some gifts to save space.

Romans 12:6-8	1 Corinthians 12:8-10	
prophesying serving teaching encouraging contributing to the needs of others leadership showing mercy	message of wisdom message of knowledge faith gifts of healing miraculous powers prophecy distinguishing… spirits different kinds of tongues interpretation of tongues	

1 Corinthians 12:28-30	1 Corinthians 13:1-3	Ephesians 4:11
apostles prophets teachers workers of miracles gifts of healing gifts of administration those able to help others different kinds of tongues interpretation of tongues	tongues prophecy knowledge faith *giving to the poor?* *martyrdom?* (These are probably not intended to be understood as gifts. See my comment on the next page).	apostles prophets evangelists pastors teachers

In addition to these, there are also brief references in Romans 1:11, 1 Corinthians 1:7, 7:7, and 1 Timothy 4:14.

A quick glance at the five lists in the table immediately shows us that

- All the lists are different
- Some gifts occur in more than one list
- One list (Eph. 4:11) is made up entirely of *people*
- Some gifts appear to be supernatural (1 Cor.12:8-10)
- Others appear to be quite natural (1 Cor.7:7)
- It is not always clear where the list ends (e.g. 1 Cor. 13:1-3).

In addition to these rather obvious features, it is probably helpful to point out that in some cases a different description may be used to refer to what is essentially the same gift. For example, *prophesying* in the Romans 12 list is exactly the same as *prophecy* in the 1 Corinthians 12 list. The English translators have just translated the same Greek word in two slightly different ways.

This is why it is virtually impossible to answer such questions as *How many gifts are there?* It's not entirely clear to what extent one gift overlaps another, and indeed, we can't be sure that everything in these lists is intended to be understood as a gift. For example, you will see that I have placed a question mark against *giving to the poor* and *martyrdom* (surrendering one's body to the flames). I see no reason in the context to assume that these are gifts[1]. I've included them simply because other writers sometimes do so. However, if martyrdom *is* a gift, you could clearly only use it once!

Despite these difficulties, however, certain things are clear:

---

[1] Gordon Fee clearly shares my view on this.
See: Fee, G.D., *The First Epistle to the Corinthians,* Grand Rapids Mich., Eerdmans, 1987, p. 633.

1. The list in Ephesians 4:11 is unique because it is a list of *people* who are given by Christ to his church.

2. The list in 1 Corinthians 12:8-10 may well be unique too, in that it appears to be made up entirely of *supernatural* gifts[2].

3. The other lists are largely a mixture of these two types of gift.

Because of this, we will concentrate in this book on the gifts listed in 1 and 2 above. **Part One** will deal with the gifts in Ephesians 4:11 and **Part Two** will consider the gifts listed in 1 Corinthians 12:8-10.

As far as the other lists are concerned, you will notice that many of the gifts mentioned are dealt with because they are also included in the two lists we will be considering. This way, most of the gifts will be covered. The few remaining gifts will be dealt with in a brief Appendix.

---

[2] Although this may not be immediately obvious, I will give my reasons for saying this later in the appropriate section of this book. It is perhaps sufficient to mention here that Paul calls these gifts *pneumatika* (spiritual) as well as *charismata*. Therefore they may well be a special category of gift. All God's gifts are *charismata* because they all come from his grace, but not all are *pneumatika*. Some, like marriage, appear to be entirely natural.

PART ONE

Gifts of Christ to the Church
Ephesians 4:11

CHAPTER ONE

Gifts of Christs to the Church

As we mentioned in the Introduction, **Part One** of this book will deal with the gifts listed in Ephesians 4:11 (to which from now on I shall refer simply as the 4:11 gifts). The gifts Paul mentions here are:

- Apostles
- Prophets
- Evangelists
- Pastors
- Teachers.

These may conveniently be described as *Gifts of Christ to the Church*. We will devote a chapter to each of these in turn, but before doing so it will be helpful to look at the context in which the gifts are mentioned in Ephesians 4. In this introductory chapter, therefore, we will briefly consider:

- The overall teaching of Ephesians 4:1-16
- The nature of the 4:11 gifts
- The purpose of the 4:11 gifts
- Are all God's people ministers?

Ephesians 4:1-16

The overall theme of this wonderful letter is probably best summarised by Paul's statement in Ephesians 5:32, *I am talking about Christ and his church*. The theme of the first part of Chapter

4 is, as the NIV heading rightly indicates, *Unity in the Body of Christ.*

Paul begins by urging his readers to live lives worthy of their calling as Christians (v.1). This will mean being *humble and gentle, patient,* and *bearing with one another in love* (v.2). The fact that he encourages them to do this and to *make every effort to keep the unity of the Spirit* (v.3) suggests that maintaining unity in the local church is something that needs to be worked at. It doesn't come automatically!

One reason for this is that people are so different. Despite our differences, however, there is much that unites us. The Ephesian church was a mixture of people some of whom were Jewish and others Gentile by background, but who were all now one in Christ (Ephesians 2:11-22, esp. v.15). Paul stresses this unity in vv.4-6:

There is **one** body and **one** *Spirit* – just as you were called to **one** hope when you were called – **one** *Lord*, **one** faith, **one** baptism; **one** God and *Father* of **all**, who is over **all** and through **all** and in **all**.

Notice the seven references to the word **one** and the four references to the word **all** in this passage. Notice, too, the reference to the Trinity, *Spirit... Lord... Father.* Whatever differences there may be among us as Christians, we **all** through faith and baptism into the name of the **one Lord** Jesus Christ have become members of his body and serve **one** God, Father, Son, and Holy Spirit.

Yet although we have all these things in common, we are all very different, and that, says Paul, is how God intended it to be. This is indicated in v. 7 where he says:

But to each one of us grace has been given as Christ apportioned it.

The differences between us are God-given! By 'grace' here Paul does not mean the grace by which we have all been saved (cf. Eph. 2:8) – that's something we all have in common – but, as v. 8 makes clear, he is referring to the various *gifts* Christ has given (cf. vv.11-16). Whatever gift we may have (or be) it is God who has given it, and he has given it so that the church, which is Christ's body, might be built up and edified (vv. 12, 16).

Paul develops this theme in much greater detail in 1 Corinthians 12, to which we will turn in PART TWO of this book, but it is interesting here to note the great similarity in his teaching to both the Corinthian and the Ephesian churches. This can be seen very easily from the table below:

	1 Corinthians	Ephesians
The body	12:12-27	4: 4, 12-16
Love	13:1-13	4: 2, 15, 16
Unity	12:13-27	4: 3, 13
Diversity	12:4-11	4: 7, 11, 16
The Trinity	12:4-6	4: 4-6
Edification	14:1-5, 12, 26	4: 12, 16

So in both passages Paul teaches that the church is the body of Christ and that its members, though very different from one another, must seek to be united by showing their love for each other by building one another up with the gifts God has given them. The reference to the Trinity in both passages may well reflect the idea that, just as there is diversity and yet unity within the Godhead, so too there is to be diversity and yet unity within the body of Christ.

Despite these similarities, however, there appear to be several differences between the 4:11 gifts and those mentioned in 1

Corinthians 12:8-10. We will consider these as we now turn to examine the nature of the 4:11 gifts.

The Nature of the 4:11 Gifts

The table below, which compares the 4:11 gifts with those of 1 Corinthians 12:8-10, will provide a useful starting point for our discussion of the nature of the 4:11 gifts.

	1 Cor. 12:8-11	Ephesians 4:11-12
Who gives these gifts?	**The Holy Spirit** (vv. 8, 9, 10, 11)	**Christ** (v. 11, cf. v. 7)
To whom are they given?	**Individuals** (vv. 8, 9, 10, 11)	**The Church** - the body of Christ (vv. 12 &16)
What are these gifts?	**Supernatural abilities** e.g. Healings Miracles Tongues etc.	**People** Apostles Prophets Evangelists etc.

This shows us that whereas the gifts listed in 1 Corinthians 12:8-10 are supernatural *abilities* given to individual *Christians* by the *Holy Spirit*, the 4:11 gifts are *people* given to *the church* by *Christ*. Indeed, the contents of the two lists are completely different[3].

---

[3] The only similarity between the contents of the two lists appears to be that *prophecy* is mentioned in one and *prophets* are mentioned in the other. We will discuss this in greater detail in Chapter 3.

In fact, so great does the difference between the two lists seem to be that my students have sometimes challenged me as to why I have included a discussion of the 4:11 gifts in a course on charismatic gifts, especially in the light of the added fact that the word *charismata* does not appear in Ephesians 4. My response to this is that the 4:11 should be regarded as *charismata* for the following reasons:

1. As we saw in the Introduction, everything God gives us comes because of his grace and may, therefore, rightly be described as a *charisma*.
2. Although *charisma* is not used in Ephesians 4, the word *charis* (grace) is used in v. 7 with much the same meaning. This identifies the gifts that are mentioned as gifts from God's grace.
3. The gifts in Romans 12 and 1 Corinthians 12:8-10 are called *charismata*. These include *teaching* and *prophecy*. We may therefore say that a teacher has the *charisma* of teaching and a prophet the *charisma* of prophecy. Because of the flexibility of Paul's general use of the word *charisma* (see 1 above), there is no reason to see any conflict between a prophet *having* the gift (*charisma*) of prophecy and at the same time *being* a gift (*charisma*) that God has given to the church.
4. In the light of the striking similarities we have already noticed in Paul's teaching in both 1 Corinthians 12-14 and Ephesians 4, it is difficult to see how the apostle would not have viewed the 4:11 gifts as *charismata*. At all events, they are certainly *good gifts* which God gives to his church, and are therefore a suitable topic of study for this book.

A detailed study of each of the 4:11 gifts will be found in Chapters 2 to 6. It is sufficient now to note that these gifts are people given by the ascended[4] Christ to his church for the purpose of preparing God's people for works of service (v.12). But that is the subject of the next section.

The Purpose of the 4:11 Gifts

To understand the purpose of the 4:11 gifts we must first understand God's purpose for the church. This is expressed in vv. 12-16 by the use of two closely related metaphors. God wants his church to *be built up* (vv. 12, 16) and he wants it to *grow up* (v.15). These two expressions mean basically the same thing. Paul has already used the illustration of a *building* to describe the church (cf. 2:19-22). He also describes it as a *body* (1:23, 4:4, 16).

He now combines these two ideas and applies them to the church as the body of Christ. The body must grow, and it must grow strong. It must reach maturity. This involves:

- doctrinal understanding (v.14), and
- working relationship (v.16).

Paul calls this *attaining to the whole measure of the fulness of Christ* (v.13) and *growing up into Christ* (v.15). This is God's purpose for his church.

This will only be achieved, says Paul, *as each part does its work* (v.16). The church will only be what God wants it to be as the individual members find their place in the body of Christ and lovingly help and support each other.

---

[4] The connection with the Ascension (vv.8-10) is noteworthy in that it may well indicate that, although Paul refers to the 4:11 gifts as coming from Christ, he also has the ministry of the Holy Spirit very much in mind. The coming of the Spirit at Pentecost was a direct result of Christ's Ascension (Acts 2:33-34).

But that leads us to the purpose of the gifts mentioned in v.11. The apostles, prophets, evangelists, pastors and teachers are not there to do all this work. They are God's gifts to his church to *prepare God's people for works of service* (v.12). For too long too many of God's people have been mere 'pew-fillers' expecting the 'minister' or (a little better, but not much) 'the ministry team' to do the work. To be fair, this has hardly been their fault. Too many 'ministers' have seen 'the work of the ministry' as their sole responsibility. But these verses clearly teach that every saint must be prepared or equipped for service, and that equipping is the responsibility of those gifted as apostles, prophets, evangelists, pastors and teachers. But that leads us to the interesting question, *Are all God's people ministers?*

Are all God's People Ministers?

The short answer to this question is *Yes and No*. The word 'minister' really means 'servant' and a ministry is a form of service. Clearly then, in the light of what we have seen, all God's people have a role to play in building up the body of Christ. Christ has apportioned grace to every one of us (v.7). In that sense we all have a ministry.

On the other hand, it would be a mistake to think that everybody is gifted to be one of the 4:11 gifts. It is clear from v.11 and from 1 Corinthians 12:29ff that only *some* are apostles or prophets or teachers etc. However, as we shall see later, though we may not all be prophets, we can all eagerly desire to prophesy! In other words, all God's people should expect to receive one or more of the spiritual gifts listed in 1 Corinthians 12:8-10, though not all will be one of the 4:11 gifts. In the next chapter we will begin our study of the first of those gifts, that of the apostle.

CHAPTER TWO

Apostles

In the last chapter we considered the overall context of Ephesians 4:11 in which Paul speaks of five gifts which Christ has given to the church. We now turn our attention to each of those gifts in detail and in this chapter we will be considering *apostles*. This is a subject over which there has been a great deal of misunderstanding, as many Christians think of apostles as the twelve disciples appointed by Jesus. However, as we shall see, the New Testament uses the word much more widely than this and clearly indicates that we should expect to see apostles at work in the church today. To help us understand this we will consider the subject under the following headings:

- The meaning of the word *apostle*
- Apostles in the New Testament
- Apostles today.

The meaning of the word *apostle*

The New Testament was written in Greek. This was the universal language of the then-known world (rather like English is very widely spoken and understood throughout the world today). Our English word *apostle* comes from the Greek word *apostolos*. (This comes from the verb *apostello* which simply means *I send*). So *apostolos* means *someone who is sent* or *a messenger*. This is made very clear from the simple table over the page.

Greek	English
Apostello	I send
Apostolos	someone who is sent, a messenger.

It is interesting that both these Greek words are used in Mark 3:14 where we read that Jesus appointed twelve, designating them apostles (*apostolos*), that he might send (*apostello*) them out to preach. So the first twelve people that Jesus sent out to preach were called *apostles*, but that doesn't mean that every time *apostello* or *apostolos* is used in the New Testament that the person referred to is an apostle!

For example, in Mark 6:27 we read that King Herod sent an executioner to behead John the Baptist. The word *apostello* is used here, but the executioner wasn't an apostle. It is used again in Matthew 27:19 when Pilate's wife sends a messenger to warn her husband to have nothing to do with Jesus because he was an innocent man. But the messenger was not an apostle.

Because of examples like this we need to bear in mind that the basic meaning of *apostolos* is simply *someone who is sent.* That's why it can be translated in any of the following ways:

- Apostle
- Messenger
- Delegate
- Representative
- Ambassador.

Of course, in the examples I gave it was obvious that John the Baptist's executioner and Pilate's wife's messenger were not apostles. But there are other examples in the New Testament where the meaning is not so clear. Epaphroditus is described as an *apostolos* in Philippians 2:25. However, although it is possible that he was one of the later apostles like Paul or Barnabas, we know little of his ministry and the context in Philippians 2 suggests that the word *apostolos* is being used here simply in the sense of *messenger* or *representative*.

Another example of the use of the word *apostolos* to mean *messenger* or *representative* is to be found in 2 Corinthians 8:23. In verse 19 Paul talks of how Titus had been chosen by the churches to accompany Paul as he carried an offering for the poor. Now Paul is sending him to Corinth along with certain other brothers who are described in verse 23 as *representatives of the churches*. Although the word used here is *apostolos* there is no need to assume that these people were apostles like Paul or Barnabas. It simply means that they were people chosen and sent by the churches to fulfil a particular task.

I have given these examples to show that we must not jump to the conclusion that wherever the words *apostolos* and *apostello* are used there is a reference to an apostle. We simply can't be sure that people like Epaphroditus or the brothers who accompanied Titus were apostles. All we can do is to examine the context and ask ourselves what the writer most probably intended us to understand.

However, there are people named as apostles in the New Testament about whom we can be sure and it is to these that we now turn our attention.

Apostles in the New Testament

Apart from the examples mentioned in the last section, the word *apostolos* is used in the New Testament in three main ways:

1.   Uniquely, to refer to **Jesus** who was *sent* into the world by God (Hebrews 3:1, John 3:17, Luke 4:18)
2.   Specifically, to refer to **the Twelve** appointed and *sent* out by Jesus (Matthew 10:1ff, Mark 3:14)

3.   More generally, to refer to **later apostles** who emerged after the Twelve and who were *sent* out by the Holy Spirit (Acts 13:1-4).

We will consider each of these in turn.

Jesus, the unique apostle

We do not usually think of Jesus as an apostle, but in Hebrews 3:1 we are told to fix our eyes on Jesus *the apostle* and high priest whom we confess. The use of the word *apostle* here probably simply reflects the fact that Jesus was *sent* by God. In his Gospel, for example, John uses *apostello* 17 times (e.g. John 3:17) to tell us that God *sent* his Son into the world. And of course the purpose for which God did this was to save us from our sins. That is why I have called Jesus the *unique* apostle. He came to die for our sins. In that respect his mission was unique because no other apostle could have fulfilled it. God *sent* Jesus to die for the sins of the world. No-one else could have done that. Clearly, Jesus' apostles were not sent into the world to die for our sins but to proclaim the message that Jesus had done so.

Despite this important difference, however, Jesus did say that he had sent his apostles into the world in much the same way that the Father had sent him. In John 17:18 he says:

As you sent (*apostello*) me into the world, I have sent (*apostello*) them into the world.

This clearly indicates that at least some comparison can be drawn between Jesus' mission as the apostle sent by the Father and the mission of the apostles sent by Jesus. To illustrate this it will be helpful to look at Luke 4:18. Here Jesus is in the synagogue at Nazareth and reading from the scroll of the prophet Isaiah. The passage he reads from is Isaiah 61:1-2 which is recorded in Luke 4:18-19 as follows:

The Spirit of the Lord is upon me, because he has anointed me to preach good news to the poor. He has *sent* me to proclaim freedom for the prisoners and recovery of sight for the blind, to release the oppressed, to proclaim the year of the Lord's favour.

It is noteworthy here that the word *sent* in verse 18 is *apostello*. Part of Jesus' apostolic mission from the Father was to do the things listed in these verses. He was to *preach* or *proclaim*:

- Good news to the poor
- Freedom for the prisoners
- Recovery of sight for the blind
- Release for the oppressed
- The year of the Lord's favour.

He was able to accomplish this because of the anointing of the Spirit resting upon him (cf. Acts 10:38). As we turn now to consider the ministry of the twelve apostles appointed by Jesus we will see that their mission was very similar.

The Twelve appointed by Jesus
In Mark 3:13-15 we read:

Jesus went up into the hills and called to him those he wanted, and they came to him. He appointed twelve – designating them apostles – that they might be with him and that he might send them out to preach and to have authority to drive out demons.

This event is recorded more fully in Matthew 10. Jesus calls his twelve disciples to him and gives them authority to

drive out evil spirits and to cure every kind of disease and sickness (v.1).

25

Then the names of the twelve apostles are listed (vv. 2-4) and the instructions given by Jesus take up the remainder of the chapter. The passage makes clear that the mission of the first apostles was parallel to his own. This is summarised in vv. 7-8 where Jesus says:

As you go, preach this message: 'The kingdom of heaven is near'. Heal the sick, raise the dead, cleanse those who have leprosy, drive out demons. Freely you have received, freely give.

The table below compares Jesus' apostolic ministry (recorded in Luke 4:18) with the commission he gave the Twelve (Matthew 10:1-8, Mark 3:13-15).

Jesus	The Twelve
Sent by the God the Father	**Sent by God the Son (Jesus)**
Heb. 3:1, Jn. 3:17, Luke 4:18.	Matt. 10:1-8, Mk. 3:13-15
Empowered by God	**Empowered by Jesus**
He has anointed me to preach	*He gave them authority*
Luke 4:18 (cf. 3:21-22)	Matt. 10:1 (cf. Luke 9:1)
God anointed Jesus of Nazareth	*He appointed...them to have*
Acts 10:38	*authority* (cf. Mk. 3:13-15)
Sent to preach good news	**Sent to preach good news**
To preach good news to the poor...	*Preach this message: 'The*
to proclaim the year of the Lord's	*kingdom of heaven is near'.*
favour Luke 4:18-19	Matt. 10:7 (cf. Luke 9:2)
Sent to bring deliverance	**Sent to bring deliverance**
Freedom for the prisoners	*Heal the sick, raise the dead,*
Recovery of sight for the blind	*cleanse those who have leprosy,*
Release for the oppressed	*drive out demons*
Luke 4:18-19	Matt.10:8 (cf. Mk. 3:14-15)

The similarities are very clear. The apostle was sent and empowered by God to preach good news and to bring deliverance. However, although this summarises the role of the apostles *before* Jesus' death, resurrection, and ascension into heaven, it was *afterwards* that the most important purpose of their apostolic calling began. They were now to be **witnesses of the resurrection** (Acts 1:22, 2:32, 3:15 etc.) and to do so they needed to be empowered by the Spirit at Pentecost (Acts 1:1-8, 2:1-4)[5].

Yet despite this added responsibility, the apostolic role remained essentially the same. The message was still the good news of the kingdom manifested in healing, release and deliverance. The year of God's favour had come because Jesus had atoned for the sins of mankind and his resurrection from the dead demonstrated that he was both Lord and Christ (Acts 2:36). The kingdom which had come near with the presence of Christ on earth was now being manifested through the power of the Spirit in the ministry of the church.

Indeed they were no longer to go only to the people of Israel (Matthew 10:5-6). The good news was to be preached to all nations (Matthew 28:19-20, Mark 16:15ff). And the book of Acts tells us how they did it. They testified to the fact that Jesus was alive in Jerusalem, in Judea and Samaria, and to the ends of the earth (Acts 1:8). They had not only *seen* him after he had risen from the dead,

---

[5]The question is sometimes asked why the apostles needed to receive power at Pentecost when they had already been used in working miracles during Jesus' earthly ministry. The answer lies in the fact that the authority with which Jesus empowered his disciples in Matthew 10:1 was only for the time he was personally with them. They worked those miracles under *his* delegated authority. But he taught them in John 14-16 that he was to go away and that the Holy Spirit would come to take his place. From Pentecost on, their empowering would come from the Spirit.

but they provided evidence that he was still alive by the miracles they performed in his name.

But this leads us naturally to the subject of certain other apostles, referred to in Acts, who were not part of the Twelve. Their ministry was to be very much the same.

Later apostles

The most obvious example of someone the New Testament calls an apostle, but who was not one of the original Twelve, is the apostle **Paul**[6]. He is first described as an apostle in Acts 14:14, but it is noteworthy that **Barnabas** is also called an apostle in the same verse. Paul also refers to **James the Lord's brother** as an apostle alongside Peter (Galatians 1:18-19).

To these names we could possibly add **Epaphroditus** (Philippians 2:25) and **Andronicus** and **Junias** (Romans 16:7). However, with regard to Epaphroditus NIV translates *apostolos* as 'messenger' rather than 'apostle' and this seems to be the clear meaning in the context of the passage as I suggested earlier. Furthermore, the understanding that Junias[7] and Andronicus were apostles is a little uncertain. Their apostleship is sometimes questioned because the Greek text could mean that they were well-known *by* the apostles. However, in my view the more natural translation is that they were 'eminent *among* the apostles'.

---

[6] Some people think that Paul was God's intended replacement for Judas Iscariot after Judas had betrayed Jesus. However, Acts 1 records how Matthias was appointed to take the place of Judas and nowhere does the New Testament suggest that the disciples were wrong to appoint Matthias or that Paul was God's intended replacement. The theory is really based on the assumption that there could only be 12 apostles, but, as we shall see, Paul was by no means the only person to be called an apostle. In my view it is better to think of Paul as one of these later apostles rather than to include him as one of the 12.

[7] Or *Junia*, in which case this person would have been a woman.

Nevertheless, since their apostleship is in dispute, and since we know considerably more about the ministries of Paul, Barnabas and James, we will confine our attention to them. Inevitably this will mean that by far the greatest emphasis will be on Paul's ministry because of the vast amount of material about him. However, where appropriate we will refer to the work of Barnabas and James. This will be important in showing that not all apostolic ministry need be modelled on the example of Paul. Moreover, since the existence of these apostles forms a major part of the basis for our belief in apostles for today, we can expect an examination of what the New Testament tells us about their ministries to reveal valuable information as to what we might expect of apostles today. For this reason we will leave further discussion of the ministries of Paul, Barnabas and James until the next section.

Apostles today

Now that we have considered various types of apostle in the New Testament we are in a position to discuss the question of apostles today. We'll begin by explaining why it is reasonable for us to expect apostles in the church today. Then we'll consider the role of apostles today by examining the ministries of Paul, Barnabas and James.

Why we should expect apostles today

As we saw earlier, the first apostles were chosen to be witnesses of Christ's resurrection. This raises an important question. Is it essential to have seen the risen Christ in order to be an apostle, and if so, how is it possible for us to speak of people as apostles today? The thought underlying this question is based largely on Acts 1:21-22 where the replacement for Judas was to be one who could be *a witness of Christ's resurrection*.

On this basis some Christians stumble over the idea of there being apostles today, but there really is no need to. The answer is quite simple if we bear in mind the following facts:

First, the replacement for Judas was not only to be someone who had seen the risen Christ, but also who had been someone who had been with the other apostles, in the words of Peter,

> the whole time the Lord Jesus went in and out among us, beginning from John's baptism to the time when Jesus was taken up from us (Acts 1:21-22).

Since this requirement would have disqualified even the apostle Paul, it clearly related to the choice of an apostle for that particular occasion only (to make up the complement of the Twelve), and cannot be used as evidence that there were to be no further apostles later.

Secondly, as we have already seen from Mark 3:14, the Twelve were apostles *before* ever Jesus died and rose from the dead! It is, therefore, clearly possible to be an apostle without having witnessed the resurrection.

Thirdly, the problem with this doctrine is that it restricts the ministry of the apostle to the first few decades of the history of the church and makes Ephesians 4:11ff meaningless for today as far as the apostle is concerned. The New Testament nowhere states that the gift was to be withdrawn.

Finally, since, as we have already seen, the New Testament actually mentions by name[8] apostles who were not part of the Twelve, the clear solution to the problem is to draw a distinction between these later apostles and those known as the Twelve. Membership of the Twelve was dependent on the conditions stated

---

[8] See, for example, Acts 14:14 where Barnabas is called an apostle. Cf. Galatians 1:19 where Paul refers to James the Lord's brother as an apostle.

by Peter in Acts 1:21-22. Later apostles, like Paul[9], by the very nature of the case, could not, and were not expected to, fulfil them[10]. It is clear, therefore, that since in the New Testament apostles were recognised who emerged later than the Twelve, similar apostles might well arise today.

The role of apostles today

Having established, therefore, that it is both reasonable and biblical for us to expect and believe for apostolic ministry in the church today, we must now determine which New Testament apostles might serve as suitable role-models. Since the role of Jesus was clearly unique[11], as was also that of the Twelve[12], we will take as examples Paul and Barnabas and James, the Lord's brother. But we'll begin by making a brief comparison between the role of these later apostles and that of the Twelve.

---

[9] The fact that in 1 Corinthians 9:1 Paul appeals to his Damascus Road experience (Acts 9) as evidence of his apostleship need not be taken to mean that he was claiming membership of the Twelve. He is simply vigorously defending his apostleship to a church where some people were doubting its validity. Nowhere does the NT suggest that the disciples were wrong to appoint Matthias in Acts 1 as a replacement for Judas. Indeed, he is one of the eleven others who, with Peter, stood up to preach the gospel on the Day of Pentecost (Acts 2:14).

[10] The idea of the uniqueness of the Twelve may also be supported by passages such as Matthew 19:28 and Luke 22:29-30 where Jesus promises the Twelve that they will sit on 12 thrones judging the twelve tribes of Israel. Such a promise is not made to later apostles. However, I.H.MacDonald suggests that this is intended to mean that the Twelve were the nucleus of a new Israel composed of those who accepted Jesus as the Messiah. See MacDonald, I.H., *Apostle* article in Ferguson, S.B., & Wright, D.F. (eds.),*New Dictionary of Theology,* Leicester, IVP, 1988, p.40.

[11] Since he alone could die for our sins.

[12] Since they were with Jesus from the beginning (Acts 1:21-22).

Later apostles compared with the Twelve

As we have already pointed out, the work of the Twelve after Pentecost continued to be much the same as their work before Pentecost. To this was added the preaching that Christ had now died for man's sin and the testimony that God had raised him from the dead. This was accompanied by amazing miracles of healing and deliverance.

It is not surprising, therefore, that the ministry of later apostles like Paul should follow a similar pattern. The ministry of people like Peter and John who were undoubtedly the most outstanding among the Twelve, is described mainly in the first twelve chapters of Acts. But from Acts 13 onwards the same message is proclaimed with the same power by later apostles such as Paul and Barnabas. In fact Paul could later (2 Corinthians 12:12) refer to **signs, wonders and miracles** as the things that mark an apostle[13]. Paul's message, therefore, like Peter's, was that Christ had died for our sins and risen again and the miracles they performed in his Name were an evidence of this. It seems clear, therefore, that the ministry of an apostle today should be evidenced by similar signs and wonders. These, as we have seen, not only accompanied the ministry of Jesus and of the original Twelve, but also of later apostles, and it is on this basis that we should certainly expect them to do so today[14].

However, an apostle's ministry is not just a matter of preaching the gospel with signs following. As we will see in a later chapter, that is the main role of an *evangelist*. As we now turn to consider

---

[13] Cf. Romans 15:18-20. Note, however, that not all those who work miracles are apostles. Acts tells us of Stephen (Acts 6:8) and Philip the evangelist (8:6-7) performing miracles.

[14] However, an apostle's ability to perform signs and wonders may be limited by unbelief in the local community. See, for example Mark 6:5-6 where even Jesus 'could not do any miracles there'.

the work of Paul, Barnabas and James, it will become clear that an apostle's work is even greater than that.

Paul

Much of Paul's ministry is described for us in the Book of Acts and he himself teaches us a number of things about the work of an apostle in his letters. In addition to the signs and wonders already mentioned, this includes planting churches, laying a foundation for them, exercising authority over them, receiving financial support from them and training others for works of service. It also may involve travelling to deal with important matters on behalf of the churches.

Paul's **church planting** ministry is mainly described in Acts (e.g. Acts 13-14, 16-20). In fact 1 Corinthians 9:2 tells us that the existence of the church at Corinth was the 'seal' (or proof) that Paul was an apostle. Perhaps this highlights the difference between the apostle and the evangelist. The apostle does more than win people for Christ. He forms them into a church and establishes a leadership there (Acts 14:21-23, 15:41-16:5). By the nature of their ministry apostles are people who move on once the church has been planted[15]. It was therefore important that they engage in **training others** for works of service[16] (Ephesians 4:12).

Obviously closely connected with church-planting is the apostolic role of **laying a foundation** for the church. Ephesians 2:20 tells us that the church is built upon the foundation of the apostles and prophets. However, there are two senses in which apostles are seen as doing this. The first apostles clearly laid a

---

[15] Although this is clearly the case with the apostle Paul, it is not so obviously true of the apostle James who appears to have been based in Jerusalem somewhat permanently (cf. Acts 15:4,13; 21:17; Galatians 1:18-19).

[16]This is almost certainly one of the reasons why Paul took travelling companions with him on his missionary journeys in Acts.

foundation for the church universal by receiving through the Spirit the completed revelation of the word of God (John 16:12-15, Ephesians 2:20, 3:5). Obviously no later apostle can be a foundation-layer in this sense. However Paul also talks of having laid the foundation of the local church in Corinth (1 Corinthians 3:10) and this is certainly applicable to later apostles including apostles today.

Paul also clearly exercised **authority over the churches** he had founded. This authority was not forced, but spontaneous and natural. He saw himself as a father-figure (1 Corinthians 4:15, Galatians 4:19, cf. 1 Corinthians 9:1). He made no claim of authority over churches he had not founded (Romans 15:20, 2 Corinthians 10:16). He did, however, **travel to deal with important matters that affected the whole church** as when he accompanied Barnabas to Jerusalem to discuss the vital issue of circumcision (Acts 15).

Finally, it is clear that Paul considered that as an apostle he was entitled to **financial support** from the churches. 1 Corinthians 9:1-18 indicates that although Paul and Barnabas had chosen voluntarily to work for their living (v.6) it was their right as apostles to receive food and drink from the churches and, like Peter, to take along a wife as a travelling companion (v.5). In what is probably a reference to Matthew 10:10 he points out that

The Lord has commanded that those who preach the gospel should receive their living from the gospel (v.14).

Paul's example and teaching on the role of an apostle may therefore be summarised as follows:

− Preaching accompanied by miraculous signs
− Planting churches
− Laying a foundation for them

- Exercising authority over them
- Receiving financial support from them
- Training others for works of service
- Travelling to deal with important matters on behalf of the churches.

From this it would seem reasonable to assume that the ministry of modern apostles might be expected to follow a similar pattern. However, we need to consider the examples of Barnabas and James before coming to a final conclusion.

Barnabas

According to Acts 4:36 Barnabas was a Levite from Cyprus. His name was Joseph, but the apostles called him Barnabas (which, Luke tells us, means Son of Encouragement[17]). This suggests that part of Barnabas' ministry was that of encouraging his fellow-Christians. A brief outline of what Acts tells us about him will help to identify the nature of his role as an apostle.

Firstly, it was Barnabas who introduced Paul to the apostles despite their mistrust of this new convert (Acts 9:26-27; cf. Galatians 1:18).

A little later he was sent by the Jerusalem church to take care of the growing company of believers at Antioch and his ministry was highly successful there (Acts 11:19-24). By this time Paul had gone home to Tarsus, but Barnabas, feeling the need of help with the growing work at Antioch, went in search of Paul to help him. Together they taught the people for a year (Acts 11:25-26) before travelling to Jerusalem with famine-relief. (vv.27-30). It was probably here that their call to Gentile missionary work was recognized (Galatians 2:9).

---

[17] More literally, however, Son of Prophecy – but 1 Corinthians 14:3 mentions encouragement as part of the purpose of prophecy.

When they returned to Antioch, during a time of worship and fasting with other church leaders, the Holy Spirit spoke specifically that it was time for Barnabas and Paul to be set apart for the work to which they had been called (Acts 13:1-4). As a result of this, together they planted churches in Pisidian Antioch, Iconium, Lystra and Derbe (Acts 13-14) before returning to their home-church in Antioch.

Finally, in Acts 15:1-29 Barnabas was appointed with Paul to bring the circumcision question before the Jerusalem Council.

From this brief summary of Barnabas' ministry as outlined in the Book of Acts, it is evident that his apostolic role was closely akin to that of the apostle Paul. Like Paul, Barnabas was involved in planting churches and like Paul he refused the financial support to which he was entitled (1 Corinthians 9:6). In the same way that Paul was later to see potential in young men like Timothy and bring them alongside for experience in ministry, Barnabas saw the potential in Paul when others were suspicious of him and he brought him alongside to help in the ministry at Antioch. And he travelled with Paul on the same important mission to Jerusalem to debate with other church leaders the important subject of circumcision.

All this seems to suggest that there is nothing more that we can learn from Barnabas about the role of an apostle than we have already discovered in the ministry of Paul. However, there is one other important factor that needs to be mentioned. Barnabas not only *planted* churches, but at Antioch he went and **took over a church which had already started.** It was not planted by an apostle, but had come into being simply because ordinary Christians had spread the good news about Jesus (Acts 11:19-21). Perhaps we could say that Barnabas laid the foundation (cf. Paul in 1 Corinthians 3:10), but the fact that Barnabas did not plant the church should at least alert us to the fact that apostolic ministry is not all church planting. It can involve taking over the leadership of a church which has already started. But that leads us naturally to the subject of James, the Lord's brother.

James, the Lord's brother

We know little of James, the Lord's brother except that he was one of Jesus' brothers (Matthew 13:55) and that he does not seem to have accepted Jesus' authority until after the resurrection (Mark 3:21, John 7:5) when the risen Jesus appeared to him (1 Corinthians 15:7).

He eventually became a 'pillar' in the church at Jerusalem (Galatians 2:9) and at the Council of Jerusalem, which discussed the issue of the circumcision of Gentile Christians, he made a vital contribution (Acts 15:19-23). Indeed, verses like Acts 12:17 and 21:18 seems to indicate that he was the senior leader of that church. In Galatians 1:19 Paul refers to him as an apostle.

What is interesting about this is the fact that, although he is called an apostle, there is no record of James ever planting a church. He certainly did not plant the Jerusalem church or lay its foundation. It began spontaneously at Pentecost and was initially led by the Twelve (Acts 1:13-26, 2:14, 42 etc.). James emerges later in Acts as a leader among a group of elders (Acts 15:6-13, 21:18). And it would be wrong to assume that he may have planted churches elsewhere later, simply to justify the theory that an apostle is a church-planter. The weight of evidence both from the Bible and from church history is against this[18].

There is, therefore, at least one apostle mentioned in the New Testament who was not a church-planter. This must be borne in mind as we seek to draw a conclusion on the role of apostles today.

---

[18] 'A few years later James suffered martyrdom by stoning at the instigation of the high priest Ananus during the interregnum after the death of the procurator Festus in AD 61 (Josephus, *Ant.* 20. 9)'. See *James* article in *The New Bible Dictionary*, Wheaton, Tyndale House, 1962.

Conclusion

In this chapter we have seen that the word *apostle* comes from the Greek word *apostolos* which means *someone who is sent*. It is used of Jesus, who was sent by the Father, of the Twelve who were sent out by Jesus, and of later apostles who were sent out by the Holy Spirit.

These later apostles, like Paul and Barnabas and James the Lord's brother, not only give us a basis for believing that the ascended Christ is still giving apostles to his church today (Ephesians 4:11), but also serve as role-models for modern apostles.

As we look at the similarities and the differences between their ministries, we can safely conclude that an apostle is a person who is sent by God to fulfil a special task. Their apostolic gifting will normally be recognised by such features as:

- Preaching accompanied by miraculous signs
- Planting churches
- Laying a foundation for local churches
- Having authority over those churches
- Training others for works of service.

Apostles are entitled to receive financial support from the churches to enable them to fulfil their God appointed task, which may also include travelling on behalf of the churches and taking responsibility for a church which has already started.

This does not mean that a person who fulfils any one of these is an apostle, nor does it mean that an apostle will fulfil *all* of these functions. In my view we should not hesitate to refer to people as apostles if they broadly fulfil the range of ministries listed above, but in the final analysis it is probably not so important that we give people a title but that we recognise their ministry and allow them to function.

CHAPTER THREE

Prophets

We saw in the last chapter that *apostles* are a vitally important gift for the church today. We now turn to the subject of *prophets* which Paul mentions immediately after apostles, not only in Ephesians 4:11, but also in passages like 1 Corinthians 12:28 and Ephesians 2:20. This strongly suggests that Paul considered prophetic ministry to be highly significant and it is clearly important that we understand what it is and how this gift should function in the church today. To help us to do that, we will consider the subject under the following headings:

- The meaning of the word *prophet*
- Prophets in the Old Testament
- Prophets in the New Testament
- Prophets today.

The meaning of the word *prophet*

In the English language the word *prophet* is usually used to refer to someone who foretells the future. This reflects the Greek use of the word *prophetes* which has its origin in two other Greek words, *pro* (which means *before*) and *phemi* (which means *I speak*). So one meaning of the word *prophet* is someone who speaks beforehand what is going to happen.

However, as we shall see, this is not the only way in which *prophet* is used in the Bible. In both Old and New Testaments it can also mean *someone who speaks on behalf of another.* A good illustration of this can be found in Exodus 7: 1-2. Here the Lord says to Moses:

See, I have made you like God to Pharaoh, and your brother Aaron will be your prophet. You are to say everything I command you, and your brother Aaron is to tell Pharaoh to let the Israelites go…

Aaron is called Moses' prophet because he is going to speak on his behalf. Understood this way, prophets are people who hear from God and then pass on to others what he has said. They speak on behalf of God. This is in fact the *main* way the word *prophet* is used in the Bible. Of course, because God knows the future, prophets may foretell the future (if that is what the Lord reveals to them), but most of the time they speak on God's behalf to the people of their own generation. So as we come to examine prophets in both the Old and the New Testaments it is important to bear in mind that the word *prophet* has two main meanings:

1. *Forthteller* – one who *proclaims* God's truth
2. *Foreteller* – one who *predicts* the future.

Prophets in the Old Testament

Since the main purpose of this book is to consider the function of spiritual gifts in the church *today*, we will concentrate in this chapter mainly on the role of prophets in the New Testament. However, since the New Testament can only be correctly understood in the light of the Old, it is important to look at least briefly at what the Old Testament has to say on the subject. A comparison of the role of prophets in the Old Testament with those in the New will also help us answer the important question as to whether we should expect prophets today to fulfil a similar function to those of the Old Testament.

As we begin to think about prophets in the Old Testament, immediately names like Moses, Elijah, Isaiah, Jeremiah, and Ezekiel come to mind. Of course the Old Testament mentions many more prophets than these, but a brief look at the ministry of these

40

men of God will provide a convenient overview of the role of prophets in the Old Testament. Consider the table below:

OT PROPHETS	MOSES	ELIJAH	ISAIAH	JEREMIAH	EZEKIEL
Called by God	✓	✓	✓	✓	✓
Moved by the Spirit	✓	✓	✓	✓	✓
Heard God's voice	✓	✓	✓	✓	✓
Spoke God's word	✓	✓	✓	✓	✓
Foretold the future	✓	✓	✓	✓	✓
Performed miracles	✓	✓			
Led the nation	✓				
Involved in national affairs	✓	✓	✓	✓	
Spoke to foreign nations/leaders	✓	✓	✓	✓	✓
Wrote God's word	✓		✓	✓	✓

Space forbids detailed scripture references in support of the information in the above table – in some cases there are far too many! A reading of the relevant OT books will verify its accuracy! However, what this simple table does show us is that at least some of the OT prophets were people of great power and influence, proclaiming God's word and manifesting his power to Israel and to the nations beyond.

But these were not the only type of prophet described in the Old Testament. The word *prophet* was sometimes used of people who prophesied when the Spirit of the Lord suddenly came upon them. One example of this is the passage in Numbers 11:24-29 when the Spirit came on the seventy elders and then on Eldad and Medad enabling them to prophesy. When Joshua protested, Moses replied:

> I wish that all the Lord's people were prophets and that the Lord would put his Spirit on them (v.29).

Here the word *prophet* seems to be used of people who prophesied in a temporary capacity as a result of the Spirit's activity. Their role can by no means be considered comparable with that of Moses himself or with that of the great prophets we mentioned earlier. It seems, therefore, that there are different levels of prophet referred to in the Old Testament, and this distinction may prove helpful as we come to consider the role of prophets in the New Testament.

Prophets in the New Testament

To understand the nature of the prophetic gift after the coming of Jesus we need first to appreciate the significance of what happened at Pentecost (Acts 2). Until then the Holy Spirit was given to relatively few people, but at Pentecost Moses' prayer was answered and Joel's prophecy that God would pour out his Spirit on all people began to be fulfilled (Joel 2:28, Acts 2:16-17).

This meant that Acts 2 was in a very real sense a turning point in human history. The real dividing-line in God's dealings with mankind is not the break between Old and New Testaments, but the seven weeks that started with Christ's death and resurrection and that culminated with the outpouring of the Spirit at Pentecost. From then on the Holy Spirit was available to all and all God's people are in a sense 'prophets' (Acts 2:16-18).

This means that people referred to as prophets in the New Testament before Pentecost should be considered in the same category as the Old Testament prophets. This is well illustrated by the example of **John the Baptist** who was the last in the line of Old Testament prophets. Jesus himself made this clear when he said:

> For all the Prophets and the Law prophesied until John (Matthew 11:13).

In saying this Jesus revealed the continuity of the prophetic line from Moses right through to John for, until Jesus came, all prophetic ministry pointed forward to him. But what was the purpose of prophetic ministry after Jesus had come? There clearly was to be a change of emphasis and we must not be surprised if certain differences appear in the role of the prophet after Pentecost.

As we look at prophets in the New Testament we discover that there are at least three different levels at which the word *prophet* may appropriately be used:

1. There is a sense in which all God's people are prophets (Acts 2:16-18)
2. Prophecy as a spiritual gift is given to some Christians, but not all. Such people may be referred to as prophets (1 Corinthians 12:8-11)

3. Prophets are given to the church to equip God's people for works of service (Ephesians 4:11-12).

The purpose of this chapter is to deal with the prophets referred to in (3). To do so we will need to consider (1) and (2) first.[19]

All God's people are prophets

As we saw earlier in this chapter, a prophet is a person who speaks on behalf of God. Understood this way it is easy to see how, in a sense, all God's people are called to be prophets. We are all called to speak on his behalf. As the children of God it is our privilege to be led by the Spirit of God (Romans 8:14) and the purpose of the Spirit's coming at Pentecost was that we might receive power to be witnesses (Acts 1:8). The Spirit was poured out so that all God's people could prophesy – sons and daughters, young and old, servants, men and women (Acts 2:16-18).

This does not mean that all Christians will be prophets in the Ephesians 4:11 sense, or even that we will all exercise the gift of prophecy as it is described in 1 Corinthians 12-14. But it does mean that God has made his Spirit available to all so that we can all speak on his behalf. Acts 8:1 tells us how, because of the persecution that had broken out against the church in Jerusalem, all the Christians (except the apostles) were scattered throughout Judea and Samaria. Verse 4 tells us that these people *preached the word wherever they went*. As a result many people turned to Christ and the great church at Antioch was founded (Acts 11:19-21).

These people were not called to be 'preachers' in the way we tend to use the word today, nor were they prophets like John the Baptist, but they had received God's Spirit and they did speak out on his behalf, and in that sense they were both preachers and

---

[19] Although our main discussion of (2) will be left until we consider the gift of prophecy in Part Two of this book.

44

prophets! In short, all God's people are called to speak up for him. All God's people are prophets.

The gift of prophecy

In 1 Corinthians 12:8-11 Paul lists nine spiritual gifts. One of these is prophecy. 1 Corinthians 12:10-11 says:

> ...to *another* prophecy... he (the Spirit) gives them to each man just as he determines (my italics).

This strongly suggests that this gift is not given to everybody and Romans 12:6 backs this up by saying:

> We have *different* gifts according to the grace given us. *If* a man's gift is prophesying, let him use it in proportion to his faith (my italics).

We will deal with this gift in greater detail in Part Two of this book when we come to consider each of the nine gifts listed in 1 Corinthians 12:8-10. For the time being it is enough to note that this gift is given by the Spirit to individual Christians in order to speak words of encouragement and edification to the church (1 Corinthians 14:3-4). Although all Christians are to 'prophesy' in the general sense of speaking on God's behalf, not all will exercise this gift. Furthermore, not all who exercise this gift will be prophets in the Ephesians 4:11 sense. In short:

- All God's people should prophesy (speak on his behalf)
- Not all will receive the spiritual gift of prophecy (to edify the church)
- Not all these will be prophets in the Ephesians 4:11 sense.

But what are these Ephesians 4:11 prophets and how is their ministry different from that of those who exercise the simple gift of prophecy?

The ministry of the prophet

Perhaps the best way to explain the difference between the gift of *prophecy* (1 Corinthians 12:10) and the gift of *prophet* (Ephesians 4:11) is to remind ourselves of what we said in Chapter One. The 1 Corinthians 12 gifts are supernatural *abilities* given to individual *Christians* by the *Holy Spirit*. The Ephesians 4:11 gifts are *people* given to *the church* by *Christ*. In fact the two lists are completely different, apart from the fact that *prophecy* is mentioned in one and *prophets* are mentioned in the other. So are the Ephesians 4:11 prophets simply people who exercise the gift of prophecy or are they something more?

To answer this question it will be helpful to look at some of the people who are named as prophets in the Book of Acts[20]. These are Agabus (Acts 11:27-28, 21:10), Judas and Silas (Acts 15:32), and some or all of those mentioned in Acts 13:1-2 (Barnabas, Simeon, Lucius, Manaen, Paul). The difficulty here is that it is not clear whether they were all 'prophets and teachers' or whether some were prophets and some were teachers.

Of all those mentioned in the previous paragraph, we know nothing more of Simeon, Lucius, Manaen, and Judas. Barnabas and Paul were also apostles and so it is difficult to distinguish their apostolic ministry from their prophetic ministry. Silas 'said much to encourage and strengthen the brothers' (Acts 15:32) and preached that Jesus was the Christ, the Son of God (2 Cor.1:19-20).

---

[20] Anna (Luke 2:36), John the Baptist (Matthew 11:9), and the Lord Jesus (John 4:19), all exercised their ministry *before Pentecost*. Although the epistles mention certain OT prophets they refer to no post-Pentecost prophet by name. This means that the only examples of Ephesians 4:11 prophets named in the NT are to be found in Acts.

We know little else of his ministry except that he accompanied Paul on his second missionary journey[21].

This leaves Agabus of whom we know rather more. He clearly spoke with great revelation from the Spirit (Acts 11:27-28, 21:10) including the accurate prediction of certain future events. His prophecy about a widespread famine is a well-known example of this (Acts 11:27-30) as is his prediction of Paul's captivity in Jerusalem (Acts 21:11).

From this it is clear that his ministry involved more than the simple gift of prophecy which need not contain any element of prediction[22]. However, there is no suggestion that he fulfilled a role similar to that of OT prophets like Moses, Elijah etc. who spoke prophetically to national leaders[23].

This may well point to the conclusion that though the prophets referred to in Ephesians 4:11 exercised a greater ministry than the simple gift of prophecy, they are by no means the equivalent of the great prophets of the Old Testament or of John the Baptist in the New. And that understanding must surely influence any conclusion we may wish to draw about the role of prophets today.

Prophets today

So far we have looked briefly at the role of prophets in both the Old and New Testaments. Our purpose in doing so was to establish

---

[21] For further discussion of Silas, see:
Kay, WK, *Prophecy,* Mattersey, Mattersey Hall, 1991, pp 38 & 45.
[22] See 1 Corinthians 14:3 which speaks of prophecy as 'strengthening, encouraging and comforting'. It does not mention prediction.
[23] Indeed, we must always remember that in the Old Testament God's people were a single nation, whereas in the New Testament the people of God are a multi-national church. After Pentecost there is no New Testament equivalent of a prophet speaking to a nation. Prophets speak to the church, for the church is now the people of God.

precisely what kind of gift is referred to in Ephesians 4:11. Our findings may be summarised as follows:

The prophets referred to in Ephesians 4:11 are **not the same as**

- the prophets of the Old Testament
- NT prophets before Pentecost
- the simple gift of prophecy (1 Cor. 12:10).

Therefore, to discover the role of prophets today, we must examine:

- Any NT examples of the ministry of prophets after Pentecost (and we have noted that Agabus is the only clear example)
- Specific verses in Paul's letters which relate to the ministry of Ephesians 4:11 prophets.

We will deal with each of these in turn.

Agabus

We find references to the ministry of Agabus first in Acts 11 and then later in Acts 21. In Acts 11:27-28 we read that some prophets came to Antioch. One of them, named Agabus

> stood up and predicted that a severe famine would spread over the entire Roman world.

We are then told not only that this came to pass (v.28), but also what the disciples decided to do about it and how they did it. They decided that they would provide help for the brothers living in Judea (v.29) and they did so by sending a gift by Barnabas and Saul (v.30).

Two things are important here. First, Agabus' prediction came to pass. If it had not done so it would have been a false prophecy according to the principles laid down in Deuteronomy 18:21-22. Clearly if a prophetic revelation comes from God it will come to pass. Secondly, it is noteworthy that *the prophet did not tell the disciples what to do*. Agabus simply gave them information as to what would happen. There is no suggestion here, therefore, that the prophet gives direction to the church or to individuals.

But this is something which becomes even clearer when we consider the later passage in Acts 21 where we read:

> ... a prophet named Agabus came down from Judea. Coming over to us he took Paul's belt, tied his own hands and feet with it and said, "The Holy Spirit says, 'In this ways the Jews of Jerusalem will bind the owner of this belt and will hand him over to the Gentiles'" (vv.10-11).

The disciples then pleaded with Paul not to go to Jerusalem (v.12), but Paul answered that if needs be he was ready to die in Jerusalem for the name of the Lord Jesus (v.13). Seeing that they could not persuade him, the disciples replied, "The Lord's will be done" (v.14).

Again we see clearly that *the prophet does not give direction* to Paul. Agabus tells Paul that he will go to Jerusalem and that he will be captured by the Jews and handed over to the Gentiles. He does not tell him not to go. It is the disciples in the following verses who plead with Paul not to go. They put their own interpretation on the prophecy. But Paul knew that they were misunderstanding what God was saying, for he himself knew what God wanted him to do.

To help us understand this we need to go back to Acts 20. Paul is on his way to Jerusalem, hoping to get there in time for the feast of Pentecost (v.16). He reaches Miletus and sends to Ephesus for the elders of the church (v.17). In his farewell address to them he says

And now, compelled by the Spirit, I am going to Jerusalem, not knowing what will happen to me there. I only know that in every city the Holy Spirit warns me that prison and hardships are facing me. However, I consider my life worth nothing to me, if only I may finish the race and complete the task the Lord Jesus has given me... (Acts 20: 22-24)

Three things are significant here. First, it is clear that prophetic ministry was common at that time. *In every city* Paul was receiving prophetic words. Secondly, these prophetic words were testifying to the same thing. Paul would be imprisoned in Jerusalem. Thirdly, despite all this Paul was convinced that God wanted him to go for he was *compelled by the Spirit* to do so.

It is very important to understand this when we come to Acts 21:4 which says that *through the Spirit* the disciples at Tyre *urged Paul not to go on to Jerusalem.* This apparently completely contradicts Paul's own statement that he was *compelled by the Spirit* to go (20:22). However, the passage about Agabus (vv. 10-14) sheds light on this. The disciples at Tyre made the same mistake as those at Caesarea. They received a revelation from the Spirit as to Paul's future imprisonment, but they wrongly understood that this meant that Paul was not to go.

To summarise all this, we can say that the ministry of Agabus teaches us that Ephesians 4:11 prophets may receive revelation from the Holy Spirit with regard to the future. However, it is not their role to tell the church or individual Christians what to do. They do not give direction. They impart to us information from the Spirit which helps us decide in advance what to do (Acts 11) or may encourage us that we are still in the will of God even when we are called to pass though hardship and difficulty (Acts 20-21).

But don't Ephesians 4:11 prophets do more than this? To answer this we must now turn to certain specific verses in Paul's letters which refer to the ministry of prophets.

Prophets in Paul's letters

It is clear from Paul's writings that he considered the ministry of prophets of great importance. He not only mentions them alongside apostles in Ephesians 4:11, but also on three other occasions – 1 Corinthians 12:28 (cf. 14:29-32), Ephesians 2:20, and 3:5. We will look at each of these passages briefly and seek to apply them, where possible, to the role of prophets today.

1 Corinthians 12:28

In 1 Corinthians 12:28 Paul tells us that

> ... in the church God has appointed first of all apostles, second prophets, third teachers, then workers of miracles etc.

It is interesting that the first three in the list are in the same order as they appear in Ephesians 4:11 and this may indicate something of the importance that Paul gave to these gifts. It also strongly suggests that the prophets referred to here are of the same kind as those in Ephesians 4:11. Paul clearly states that God has appointed them *in the church*. This, along with the fact that they are mentioned *after* apostles, indicates that Paul is not referring to Old Testament prophets here. This means that they are the kind of prophets we may expect in the church today.

Although the role of prophets is not described here, a brief passage two chapters later gives us considerable insight into their ministry.

1 Corinthians 14:29-32

In a chapter in which Paul is stressing the importance of order in the church and the need for the exercise of spiritual gifts to be regulated in such a way that people are edified rather than confused, Paul gives brief instructions with regard to the ministry of prophets:

29 Two or three prophets should speak and the others should weigh carefully what is said. 30 If a revelation comes to someone who is sitting down, the first speaker should stop. 31 For you can all prophesy in turn so that everyone may be instructed and encouraged. 32 The spirits of prophets are subject to the control of prophets.

This shows us that:

- A prophet's message comes from a revelation (v.30)
- This may well come spontaneously while someone else is speaking (v.30)
- The revelation may include instruction and encouragement (v.31)
- Prophets are not out of control (v. 32) – they are capable of stopping! (v.30)
- Prophets are accountable for what they say (v.32)
- The prophet's message is not infallible and needs to be weighed carefully (v.29) – cf. 1 Thessalonians 5:20-21
- The number of such messages is limited to two or three[24].

Finally, it is noteworthy that in verse 37 Paul adds

> If anybody thinks he is a prophet or spiritually gifted, let him acknowledge that what I am writing to you is the Lord's command.

This may mean that Paul considered his apostolic authority to be greater than that of the prophet. However, the clear relevance of this verse for prophets today is that no prophetic revelation can supersede the authority of what is written in Scripture.

Ephesians 2:20

In this verse prophets are listed with apostles in forming a foundation for the church. It has often been suggested that the prophets referred to here are the OT prophets. Understood this way the verse means that the church is founded on the revelation of both Old and New Testaments (written mainly by prophets and apostles respectively). Although at first sight this may seem an attractive idea, it should probably be rejected for two main reasons. First, if this were the correct understanding, we would have expected Paul to have mentioned the prophets before the apostles (as the OT came before the NT). Secondly, and probably more importantly, wherever Paul uses the phrase *apostles and prophets* elsewhere, the prophets referred to are clearly the prophets of the Christian church (see especially Ephesians 3:5).

But if prophets as well as apostles form the foundation of the church, in what sense do they do so? In our attempt to answer this question it will be helpful to remember what we said about apostles in this connection. In the last chapter we argued that there were two senses in which apostles like Paul laid a foundation for the church. They laid a foundation for the *church universal* by receiving through the Spirit the completed revelation of the word of God (John 16:12-15, Ephesians 2:20, 3:5). But Paul could also claim to have laid the foundation of the *local church* at Corinth because it was he who had planted it (1 Corinthians 3:10). We said that although apostles today cannot claim to be the foundation of the universal church, they can claim to lay foundations for local churches.

But how does this relate to prophets? Paul certainly saw the early Christian prophets along with the apostles as a foundation for the church universal, but is there any evidence that he saw them as

---

[24] v.31 appears to contradict this unless Paul did not expect there to be more than 2 or 3 prophets in the church. This seems quite likely.

part of the foundation of the local church? The answer is no. With the possible exception of Silas (who is called a prophet in Acts 15:32) there is no clear NT example to show that a prophet's role is church-planting. Admittedly, Silas accompanied Paul on part of his second missionary journey (Acts 15:40), but there is no suggestion that he did so in his capacity as a prophet any more than Mark who accompanied Barnabas in the previous verse.

Furthermore, the verses that link prophets with apostles as a foundation for the church do so in the context of the church universal, not the local church. The discussion in Ephesians 2 centres around the inclusion of the Gentiles along with the Jews as part of God's people. The Gentiles are now *no longer foreigners and aliens, but fellow citizens with God's household, built upon the foundation of the apostles and prophets* (vv.19-20). This is clearly a reference to the universal church as is also Ephesians 3:5 to which we will now turn our attention.

Ephesians 3:4-6

Here again Paul refers to prophets alongside the apostles:

> In reading this then you will be able to understand my insight into the mystery of Christ, 5 which was not made known to men in other generations as it has now been revealed by the Spirit to God's holy apostles and prophets. 6 This mystery is that through the gospel the Gentiles are heirs together with Israel, members together of one body, and sharers together in the promise in Christ Jesus.

As we have already pointed out, this passage is clearly a reference to the role of prophets in the universal church. The prophets referred to cannot be the OT prophets because Paul explicitly states that the mystery of Christ was not made known to other generations. Neither can they be the prophets of today, for Paul says that the mystery '*has* now been revealed' to them. The prophets referred to, therefore, must be the Christian prophets of Paul's generation. It is upon these prophets that the church is founded, for it is founded on the revelation of the mystery of Christ.

In my view, therefore, verses like Ephesians 2:20 and 3:5 have no direct bearing on the role of prophets today. But that is not to say that there are no prophets today. Far from it. The prophets of Paul's generation fulfilled a unique role as part of the foundation of the universal church because it was to them, along with the apostles, that the mystery of the gospel of Christ was first revealed. But *in all other respects* prophets today may expect to fulfil an identical role to that of the Christian prophets of the New Testament period. They will bring words of revelation from the Spirit to the church and in so doing will share in the ministry of equipping God's people for works of service (Ephesians 4:11-12).

Conclusion

The ministry of the Christian prophet is to bring words of revelation from God to his people. This may at times involve predicting future events (Acts 11:28, 21:11) but at others it will be a revelation of encouragement or instruction (1 Corinthians 14:31). There is, however, no basis for the view that prophets are to bring direction to God's people[25].

Since no prophecy (other than that of Scripture) is infallible, all prophecy must be judged in the light of Scripture. Where Scripture sheds no clear light on the content of a prophecy (e.g. cases such as Agabus' prophecy that Paul would be imprisoned in Jerusalem) it must be 'weighed' by those it affects. For this reason it is advisable

---

[25] Where an element of direction appears to be present it should at best be a confirmation of what God has already said to the individual concerned. In Acts 13:1-3, for example, the Holy Spirit confirms a call which Barnabas and Paul have already received.

that prophetic words are spoken in a context where Christians are gathered together so that more than one person can weigh what is being said.

Finally, in the light of the importance placed on prophets both in Acts and in the writings of Paul, it is clear that the Christian church of the 21st century needs to make greater room for this ministry. In order to weigh prophecy correctly, we need to know the Bible better, and we need to learn to hear more clearly what God the Holy Spirit is saying. We need to encourage God's people to desire eagerly the spiritual gift of prophecy (1 Corinthians 12:10). Some will be so used in that gift that we will begin to recognise in them the ministry of the prophet.

CHAPTER FOUR

Evangelists

In this chapter we will look at what the New Testament teaches us about the important work of evangelists. But first we need to realise that most of us have preconceived ideas about what an evangelist is. These are usually based on our experience of the ministry of a particular evangelist and, although much of our understanding may be correct, we must recognise that only the New Testament itself can teach us what this gift is and how it should operate. So, to help us be sure that our approach is biblical, we will consider the subject under the following headings:

–   The meaning of the word *evangelist*
–   *Evangelism* in the New Testament
–   Evangelists today.

The meaning of *evangelist*

In the Greek language in which the New Testament was written the word *euaggelistes* (evangelist) is closely connected with two other Greek words, *euaggelion* and *euaggelizo*. *Euaggelion* literally means *good news* but is often translated *gospel*. From this we also have the English word *evangel* which is just another word for *gospel* or *good news*. Similarly, the verb *euaggelizo* literally means *bring good news* but is often translated *preach the gospel* or *evangelize*. So the basic meaning of the word *euaggelistes* is:

–   someone who brings good news
–   preacher of the gospel
–   evangelist.

Evangelism in the New Testament

The word *evangelist* occurs only three times in the New Testament. Apart from its use in Ephesians 4:11, we find it in 2 Timothy 4:5 (where Timothy is told to *do the work of an evangelist*), and in Acts 21:8 (where Philip is described as *Philip the evangelist*). However, the verb *euaggelizo* occurs much more frequently. Before Pentecost[26] it is used of:

- the angels who proclaimed the good news of Christ's birth (Luke 1:19, 2:10)
- John the Baptist's preaching (Luke 3:18)
- the Twelve apostles who were sent out by Jesus (Luke 9:6)
- Jesus himself (Matthew 11:5, Luke 4:18, 44, 7:22, 8:1, 20:1).

After Pentecost *euaggelizo* is used of:

- the apostles
- Philip the evangelist
- everybody else doing so as well!

We will consider each of these briefly in turn.

Apostles preach the gospel

Of course, an apostle is more than an evangelist, but apostles need to evangelise in order to fulfil their ministry of planting churches. Indeed, evangelism seems to have been the habitual

---

[26] Please note what we said in the last chapter about the significance of the day of Pentecost (Acts 2) as a turning point in human history. Whereas we can undoubtedly learn much from the example of the Lord Jesus and the first twelve apostles, there is a sense in which their ministry was unique. The ministries of people after Pentecost, however, may clearly serve as models for ministry today.

activity of the early apostles. We read in Acts 5:42 that *day after day... they never stopped* teaching and proclaiming the good news.

It is clear that they took every opportunity to spread the word. Peter and John, on their way back from Samaria to Jerusalem, preached the gospel in many Samaritan villages (Acts 8:25). Likewise Paul and his companions *continued to preach the good news* everywhere they went (Acts 14:7, 15, 21, cf. 15:35, 16:10, 17:18).

Evangelists preach the gospel

Acts 21:8 describes Philip as *Philip the evangelist*. It is not surprising, therefore, that in Acts 8, where his ministry is described in some detail, we read that Philip *preached the good news* of the kingdom of God (Acts 8:12, cf. v. 40). We will deal with this in greater detail in the final section of this chapter when we consider evangelists today. This is because Philip is the only person clearly named as an evangelist in the New Testament, and Acts 8 is the only description we have of his ministry. This means that the only clear NT model we have for evangelists today is that of Philip in Acts 8. It will be convenient, therefore, to deal with it then, rather than now.

Everybody preaches the gospel

But not only did apostles and evangelists preach the gospel. Others were expected to do so too. Timothy who was probably not an evangelist[27] is told to do the work of one (2 Timothy 4:5). And Acts 8:1-4 makes it clear that there is also a sense in which every believer may do the work of an evangelist. In verse 1 we read that

... all except the apostles were scattered thoughout Judea and Samaria.

---

[27] See next section.

However, in verse 4 we are told that

those who had been scattered preached the word (*euaggelizo*) wherever they went.

Putting these two verses together it is clear that *everybody went everywhere preaching the gospel!* Of course, this does not mean that everyone is called or gifted to be an apostle or an evangelist, but every Christian may – and should – evangelise. In fact, so effective was this evangelistic activity of those ordinary Christians that at Antioch *a great number of people believed and turned to the Lord* (Acts 11:19-21) and so was founded the great missionary church that was eventually to send out Paul and Barnabas on their first apostolic mission.

This shows us very clearly that even if we are not gifted as evangelists in the Ephesians 4:11 sense, we still have a responsibility (and the privilege) to preach the gospel. The only qualification needed to do this is to be a believer in Jesus (Mark:16:15ff).

Was Timothy an evangelist?

Before leaving this section on evangelists in the New Testament it is appropriate to ask whether Timothy was an evangelist or not. The relevant verse here is 2 Timothy 4:5 where Paul encourages Timothy to *do the work of an evangelist*. Some have argued from this that Timothy must have been an evangelist on the grounds that Paul could not have required Timothy to do the work of an evangelist if he was not one.

However, as we have seen, it is the responsibility of all Christians to evangelise, even if they are *not* gifted as evangelists. So Timothy was to do his best to evangelise even if that was not his main area of gifting. Indeed, if he had been an evangelist, we might have expected Paul to tell him to *fulfil his ministry as an evangelist* rather than to *do the work of* one.

On balance, therefore, it seems best to understand the verse to mean that Timothy was not an evangelist. But if we are right in drawing this conclusion, it does mean that Philip is the only person named as an evangelist in the New Testament, and if so, he is the only NT example given us to serve as a model for the ministry of evangelists today.

Evangelists today

Because, as we have said, Philip appears to be the only example of an evangelist offered to us in the New Testament, we will consider his ministry in Acts 8 as a basis for the role of evangelists today. Having said that, we should beware of trying to squeeze every evangelist into the same mould! Nevertheless, the chapter does teach us certain important principles. It tells us about:

- The evangelist's message
- The target audience
- Supernatural help from the Holy Spirit
- First steps for converts.

The evangelist's message

There are several verses in Acts 8 that give a clear indication of the nature of the evangelist's message. Consider the following:

Those who had been scattered preached **the word** wherever they went (v.4).

Philip went down to a city of Samaria and proclaimed the **Christ** there (v.5)

… Samaria …accepted **the word of God** (v.14)

… they …testified and proclaimed **the word of the Lord** (v.25)

Then Philip began with that very passage of **Scripture** and told him the good news about **Jesus** (v.35).

These verses describe the message as *the word*. It is also called proclaiming *Christ* or talking about *Jesus*. To help us understand this better it will be useful to consider the way the word 'word' is used in Acts.

There are about 75 references in Acts to the word 'word'[28]. By far the majority of them are used to refer to God's word (as distinct from that of man). For example, consider the following expressions:

> ***The Word of God*** - *Acts 4:31, 6:2, 6:7, 8:14, 11:1, 12:24, 13:5, 13:7, 13:44, 18:11, 19:20*

> ***The Word of the Lord*** - *Acts 8:25, 13:48, 13:49, 15:35, 15:36, 16:32, 19:10.*

> ***The Word*** - *Acts 4:4, 6:4, 8:4 etc*

Now although we believe that *the Bible* is the word of God[29], we should not assume that these references to the word in Acts refer to the Bible as such, but rather to *the message of the gospel.* The word is:

− the word of *salvation - Acts 13:26*
− the word of *his grace - Acts 14:3*
− the word of *the gospel - Acts 15:7*

---

[28] In the NIV this is often translated as 'message'.
[29] N.B. The Early Church took the same position - see Acts 1:16, 4:24, 28:25.

These three expressions summarise very well what Luke means when he uses phrases like *the word of God* and *the word of the Lord*. He means:

the message of good news (the gospel) which tells us that God in his mercy (his grace) has provided in Jesus Christ a way for sinners to be saved (salvation).

This is clearly what Luke intends us to understand in Acts 8 when he says that Samaria had accepted *the word of God* preached to them by Philip (vv.12-14). This is what it means to preach Jesus Christ. This is the message of the evangelist.

The target audience

Now that we have identified the message of the evangelist it is clear what the target audience must be – *all people everywhere who do not yet know Christ as Saviour*. This may mean preaching to great crowds, but it will also involve speaking to individuals.

Philip's ministry in Acts 8 demonstrates this very well. The first part of the chapter (vv.1-13) deals with his ministry to crowds in Samaria. The final part (vv. 26-40) shows us the importance of the individual. We will consider each of these briefly.

Ministry to crowds

Acts 8:5-13 speaks of Philip's powerful ministry to crowds of people in Samaria (v.6). Among them were those who were possessed by evil spirits and others who were incurably sick (v.7). Until Philip arrived on the scene they had followed a sorcerer named Simon (v.9). *All the people*, both high and low, had given Simon their attention (v.10), but

> When they believed Philip as he preached the good news of the kingdom of God, and the name of Jesus Christ, they were baptized, both men and women (v.12).

People who had been deluded by the lies of Satan were now set free by the power and truth of the gospel.

This whole passage shows us the immense potential of the ministry of the evangelist. An entire city turned to Christ as a result of Philip's anointed ministry which brought deliverance to the diseased and demon-possessed and joy to the whole community. And the situation is no different today. There are still multitudes who are deluded by Satan, ignorant of the truth, and who need the deliverance that only the gospel can bring. There is still plenty of scope for evangelists to preach to vast crowds and we thank God for those who are doing it and seeing thousands turn to Christ!

Ministry to the individual

But evangelists do not only preach to crowds. They also preach to individuals[30]. It must have been difficult for Philip to leave the great work that God was doing in Samaria, but when told to head off into the desert (v.26) he obeyed. There he met a eunuch, a high official of the queen of Ethiopia, who had gone to Jerusalem to worship and who was now returning, sitting in his chariot reading part of Isaiah's prophecy.

Prompted by the Spirit, Philip approached the chariot and was able to tell him the good news about Jesus (v.35). This led to the man's conversion and baptism in water. It probably also led to the establishment of the Christian church in Ethiopia for the existence of which there is historical evidence dating back to the first century.

---

[30] In fact, even when preached to a crowd, the gospel message is for each individual within it.

64

From this we learn that it is as important for the evangelist to speak to an individual about Christ as it is to preach to great crowds. There are people in the most unlikely places who are seeking the truth but who will not find it *unless someone explains it* (v.31). The evangelist's role is to explain from the Scriptures the truth about Christ to anyone and everyone to whom the Spirit leads them. But that leads us naturally to the next important aspect of the evangelist's ministry – the need for supernatural help from the Holy Spirit.

Supernatural help from the Holy Spirit

It is very clear from Acts 8 that Philip received supernatural help from God in fulfilling his ministry. He received supernatural guidance as to where he should go (v.26) and what he should do (v.29)[31]. Moreover, the miraculous signs he performed (vv.6-7), which included the casting out of evil spirits and the healing of paralytics and cripples, arrested the attention of the crowds and persuaded them of the truth of the message he proclaimed. Preaching the good news of the kingdom of God (v.12) meant not just talking about it but manifesting it!

Of course, those who argue that supernatural gifts are not for the church today will not expect to see present day evangelists performing such miracles. But to reason like this is to rob evangelists of some of the mightiest weapons available to them, and indeed to deny the clear teaching of Scripture. In commanding us to go into all the world and preach the good news to all creation, Jesus

---

[31] And if the precise meaning of v.39 is unclear, *the Spirit of the Lord suddenly took Philip away* must at the very least mean that he was suddenly and spontaneously led to go elsewhere. The most obvious way to understand this verse, however, is that the Spirit supernaturally removed Philip to another location. If we are inclined to doubt this interpretation, it may be because we limit our understanding to our own experience rather than viewing the Scriptures in the light of the all-powerful nature of God.

clearly promised that miraculous signs would accompany the preaching of those who would believe (Mark 16:15-18).

And Paul tells us that to fully proclaim the gospel of Christ means doing so *by the power of signs and miracles, through the power of the Spirit* (Romans 15:18-19). And, as we have already seen, Philip is the only person clearly named as an evangelist in the New Testament. We have also seen that Acts 8 is the only description we have of his ministry. This must surely mean, then, that what we see of Philip's ministry there in Acts 8 must serve as a model for evangelists today. It's the only biblical model we have! And it's a model that includes the supernatural help of the Spirit of God as we proclaim the glorious gospel of Christ!

First steps for converts

Further lessons to be learned from Acts 8 about the ministry of the evangelist are with regard to what it teaches about first steps for converts. Preaching on the day of Pentecost, Peter said:

> Repent, and be baptized every one of you, in the name of Jesus Christ... and you will receive the gift of the Holy Spirit (Acts 2:38).

This represents the normal pattern of events in the Book of Acts with regard to the first steps in the Christian life:

1)   Initial repentance and faith in Christ
2)   Baptism in water
3)   Receiving the gift of the Holy Spirit[32].

---

[32] Cornelius (Acts 10:44ff) received the Spirit *before* baptism in water, but this was exceptional. Note, too, that in Acts, the expression *receiving the Spirit* is used, not to refer to the Spirit's work in regeneration, but to being empowered by the Spirit for service. For further discussion of this, see

Modern evangelism often leaves out steps 2 and 3, yet it is clear from Acts that they were considered highly important. This is particularly noticeable in Acts 8 which we have been considering with regard to the role of an evangelist. With regard to **baptism in water**, it is noteworthy that

> When they believed … they were baptized (v. 12).

This reflects the truth about baptism as we find it elsewhere in Scripture. People were not baptized before they believed, but they were baptized as soon as they believed. The same is true of the eunuch (vv.36ff.), a passage which also gives a wonderful picture of how baptism was performed in New Testament times – by immersion! Acts 8 seems to suggest, therefore, that it may be the responsibility of evangelists to see that those who come to Christ under their ministry are baptized in water[33]. This is completely in keeping with the command of Jesus (Matthew 28:19-20).

With regard to the question of **receiving the Holy Spirit**, Philip's experience with the Samaritans teaches us five important lessons:

First, it is clear that the expression *receive the Holy Spirit* (v.15) refers to the Holy Spirit *coming upon* them (v.16). This shows that Luke is not referring to the Spirit's work in regeneration,

---

Petts, D., *The Holy Spirit – an Introduction,* Mattersey, Mattersey Hall, 1998, pp. 63ff.

[33] The question arises as to whether Philip should have baptized Simon (v.13) bearing in mind that his conversion may not have been genuine (cf. vv. 21-23). However, neither Peter nor John appears to have told Philip that he was wrong to have baptized him. Perhaps this is because the responsibility for believing lies with the person being baptized, rather than with the one who is baptizing.

but to the receiving of *power for service* which Jesus said his disciples would receive when the Holy Spirit came upon them (Acts 1:8).

Secondly, the passage shows that it is possible to have become a Christian and to have been baptized in water and yet not to have *received the Spirit* in the sense referred to above.

Thirdly, *receiving the Spirit* in this way should happen as soon as possible after a person has become a Christian. As soon as the apostles in Jerusalem heard that the Samaritans had accepted the word of God (v.14) they sent Peter and John to pray for them so that they might receive the Holy Spirit.

Fourthly, it seems that although Philip was greatly used by the Spirit in healings and other miracles, he was not gifted to lay hands on people to receive the Spirit. Peter and John clearly were, as was also Ananias (Acts 9:17), but perhaps Philip was not. This suggests that praying for people to receive the Spirit may not be part of every evangelist's ministry, although it may be for some.

Finally, and closely connected with the last point, it is clear that evangelists need other ministries to complement their own. This is true, of course, of all of us. Whatever gift or ministry we may have, we are not self-sufficient. As members of the body of Christ we have different gifts and we all need each other (1 Corinthians 12:14-21). We are not to be independent. We are interdependent. However, this is perhaps a particularly important lesson for evangelists to learn, especially those whose ministry attracts a great following and who set up large organisations. This in itself is not wrong, provided that those involved recognise their need of other ministries and their dependence on other members of the body of Christ.

But that leads us naturally to ask whether the evangelist's ministry is necessarily itinerant or whether it can or should be based on a local church.

An itinerant ministry?

At first sight it would certainly appear from Acts 8 that Philip's ministry involved a great deal of travel. In verse 5 he travels from Jerusalem to Samaria, moving on to the desert road in verse 26. Then he appears at Azotus after which he

> travelled about preaching the gospel in all the towns until he reached Caesarea (v.40).

All this certainly gives the impression that an evangelist has an itinerant ministry, but all that it really proves is that it *may* be, not that it *must* be. Philip's travels in Acts 8 may simply have taken place because that was God's plan for him at that particular stage of his life.

We know from Acts 21:8 that he lived at Caesarea. What we do not know is how long he had been living there. However, since it was to Caesarea that he travelled at the end of Acts 8 it may well be that he settled there and perhaps even married there. By the time of Paul's visit in Acts 21 Philip had four unmarried daughters who all exercised the gift of prophecy (v.9).

Now none of this means that he did not continue to travel after Acts 8, but it does suggest that he was based in Caesarea. In the light of all this it is at least possible that Philip exercised his ministry within the context of the local church. There certainly seems no reason why not. From Ephesians 4:11 we see that an evangelist has the responsibility of equipping God's people for works of service (v.12). Perhaps that is what Philip was doing in Caesarea.

To summarise, then, an evangelist's ministry may involve a great deal of travel, but there is no reason to suppose that it cannot function entirely within a local church. It may, of course, involve a combination of both. At all events the evangelist, like all other ministries, should be accountable to the leadership of a local church.

Conclusion

The word *evangelist* occurs only three times in the New Testament and Philip is the only person who is clearly named as one. Since most of his ministry is described in Acts 8, almost all that we can learn about this important gift is to be found in that chapter.

From it we learn that the good news about Jesus is the heart of the evangelist's message. This is the word of the Lord. It must be preached to crowds and to individuals and the evangelist should expect God to confirm his word with miracles, signs and wonders. The Holy Spirit will also direct the evangelist where to go and what to do.

The evangelist should not only bring people to repentance and faith in Christ, but should see that they are baptized in water and, if need be, seek the help of other ministries to ensure that the converts receive the empowering of the Holy Spirit as soon as possible. Whether he or she travels widely or is based mainly in a local church, a willingness to co-operate with other ministries is an important feature of the role of the evangelist.

Finally, although not all God's people are gifted as evangelists, all are expected the share the good news about Jesus. That is the main reason in Acts why the Holy Spirit is given, that we might be witnesses of the power of the risen Christ in Jerusalem and Judea and Samaria, even to the ends of the earth (Acts 1:8).

CHAPTER FIVE

Pastors

As we come now to consider this important gift, our greatest problem may be that we all think that we already know what pastors are! Most of us have first-hand experience of someone who has been our pastor, and our view of what the Bible teaches is moulded by our experience. However, once again we need to put away our preconceived ideas and carefully examine what the New Testament has to say.

In this chapter I am going to put forward a view which, although held by many, is by no means held by all. I am going to argue that the *pastors* referred to in Ephesians 4:11 are elsewhere in the New Testament called *elders* or *overseers* and that these three terms are in fact interchangeable.

Whatever our view on this may be, it is generally agreed that the only practical guidance given to us with regard to the role of pastors is that which is given to elders and overseers. So even if a distinction *is* made between these three terms – and I believe that in the New Testament there is none – it makes good sense anyway to deal with them all together in this chapter.

Finally, by way of introduction to the subject, in saying that *pastor, elder* and *overseer* all refer to the same leadership role in the New Testament, it is not my intention to criticise any particular form of church leadership structure today. I am simply suggesting that, *at the time the New Testament was written,* pastors, elders and overseers were the same thing. How this teaching is worked out in practice today is for local church leaderships to decide.

We will deal with the subject under the following headings:

- *Pastor* means *shepherd*
- Shepherds in the New Testament
- *Elders* and *overseers*
- The pastoral team in the New Testament
- Pastors today

Pastor means *shepherd*

The English word *pastor* is actually a Latin word which means *shepherd*. The word used in the Greek New Testament is *poimen*, which in Ephesians 4:11 is translated *pastors,* but which everywhere else in the New Testament is translated *shepherd.* In the New Testament it is used in three ways. It may refer to:

- people who look after sheep – e.g. in the Christmas story (Luke 2: 8, 15, 18, 20).
- people who look after God's people[34]. This is, of course, its meaning in Ephesians 4:11.
- Jesus, the good shepherd (John 10:11, 14, cf. Hebrews 13:20, 1 Peter 2:25, 5:4).

In fact Ephesians 4:11 is the only occasion in the New Testament that *poimen* is used to refer to a leadership role in the church[35]. It simply tells us that:

> ... he (Christ) ... gave some to be... pastors (shepherds) ... to prepare God's people for works of service...

---

[34] The idea that God's people are sheep and he is their shepherd is well rooted in the Old Testament. Psalm 23 is an obvious example of this. The rulers of Israel were also seen as shepherds of the people (e.g. Ezekiel 34).
[35] With the exception of Jesus himself, of course, who is the head of the church.

So the question naturally arises as to who these pastors or shepherds were. No individual is named as a pastor anywhere in the New Testament. So there is no one person (or group of people) whose ministry we can look at as a model for today – unless, of course, we find elsewhere in the New Testament *different* words used to describe the role of these shepherds. And that as we shall see certainly appears to be the case.

Shepherds in the New Testament

So who were the pastors (shepherds) in the New Testament? To help us identify them it will be useful to compare the leadership roles listed in Ephesians 4:11 with those mentioned in Acts. In Ephesians we have apostles, prophets, evangelists, *pastors* and teachers. In Acts we have apostles, prophets, an evangelist, and some teachers, but there is no mention of the noun *pastor (shepherd)*. Does this mean that there were no pastors in Acts? By no means. If Acts does not use the noun *shepherd*, it certainly uses the verb *to shepherd*. And the people who are responsible for shepherding the flock in Acts are the *elders* or *overseers* of the church.

All this becomes very clear when we look at Acts 20. In verse 17 Paul calls for the *elders* of the church at Ephesus and in the following verses encourages them in their work for God. In verse 28 he says:

> *Guard* yourselves and all the flock of which the Holy Spirit has made you *overseers*. Be *shepherds*[36] of the church of God, which he bought with his own blood (my italics).

---

[36] The Greek word here is the verb *poimaino* from which comes the noun *poimen*. Both mean 'shepherd'.

So the *elders* are *overseers* who are to *guard (watch over)* the flock and to *shepherd* the church. It is clear from this that the elders of the church at Ephesus were its shepherds or pastors. It seems reasonable to assume, therefore, that when Paul writes to the Ephesians and refers to *pastors* in Ephesians 4:11, he is talking of the same kind of people – possibly the very *same* people – as he spoke to in Acts 21 who there are called *elders* and *overseers*.

Another New Testament passage that seems to say the same thing is 1 Peter 5:1-4. The *elders* (v.1) are told to be *shepherds* and *overseers* (v.2) of God's *flock* so that when the *Chief Shepherd* (v.4) appears they will receive a crown of glory[37].

These two passages strongly suggest that in New Testament times *pastors* were sometimes referred to as *elders* or *overseers*. See also Titus 1:5-7 where *elder* and *overseer* are clearly interchangeable terms.

However, it is sometimes argued that this is incorrect on the grounds that both pastors and elders are to shepherd the flock, but that the 'pastor' is a 'gift-person' (Eph. 4:11) whereas the 'elder', it is argued, is not. The difficulty with this view, however, is that in the case of the elder God would be giving a person a job to do without giving them the gift to do it! In my view this is unthinkable. Furthermore, the **only** people described as 'pastoring' in the NT are the elders, so why make a distinction between them?

The answer to this question is probably that people want to make a distinction between pastors and elders because of their experience or church tradition. In many churches people who are called elders are clearly not pastors! But we should not interpret the New Testament in the light of our own experience. We must let it speak for itself. In my view a true elder is a person who fits the

---

[37] It is sometimes suggested that the elders being the pastors was a temporary state of affairs (until some more gifted men could take over the church). However, Peter indicates that they are to shepherd the flock until the Lord returns!

scriptural qualifications and who is gifted by Christ to shepherd God's flock. All other so-called 'elders' today are not true elders[38] in the sense that the New Testament uses the word to refer to a church leader. This will become very clear later, when we consider the scriptural qualifications for eldership.

Elders and overseers

In the last section we argued that the terms *elder* and *overseer* are used in the New Testament as alternative terms for *pastor*. It will now be helpful to look at each of these terms a little more closely.

Elder

The Greek word for *elder* is *presbuteros*. This is the comparative of the adjective *presbus*, which means *old*, so *presbuteros* means *older* or *an older person* or *elder*[39]. Now since in both the Jewish and Greek cultures, which formed the background of the New Testament church, older people were respected for their greater experience and maturity, they were often looked to as leaders in their community. It was natural, therefore, that the Christian church should also refer to its leaders as *elders*.

However, this does not mean that all older people were elders in the church leadership sense, for not all older people are gifted with leadership qualities. When we read the New Testament, therefore, it is important to distinguish when *presbuteros* is being used simply to mean *an older person* from its use to refer to an *elder* of the church. This is usually quite easily done by looking at the context in which it is used.

Finally, before leaving this brief examination of the meaning of *presbuteros*, we need to stress that the word does not mean *old* but *older*. In the parable of the prodigal son, for example, the older

---

[38] They may of course be godly people without being gifted for leadership.

[39] N.B. In English *elder* is simply an alternative form for *older*.

brother was not an old man. He was simply older than his brother, so the word *presbuteros* is used. Of course, in this case it's clear that the word is not being used in the sense of a church elder, but it does illustrate the important point that elders don't have to be old people. They do, however, need to be more mature in Christ than the people they seek to lead.

Overseer

The other NT word that is sometimes used instead of *pastor* is *overseer*. Here the Greek word is *episkopos*. In the NIV this is correctly translated *overseer* but in the old Authorised Version (AV or KJV) it is sometimes translated *bishop* (e.g. 1 Timothy 3:1). However, the fact that we get our English word *bishop* from *episkopos* (note the similarity of the letters I have underlined), does not mean that the overseers in the New Testament were anything like the bishops in some church systems today. The word simply means someone who over-sees or watches over. A good modern translation would be *supervisor* which literally means the same thing. As we have already seen, these people were responsible for watching over and shepherding God's flock (Acts 20:28, 1 Peter 5:1-4) and were, therefore, the pastors of the church.

The pastoral team in the NT

I have headed this section *The pastoral **team** in the NT* because in the New Testament elders are usually referred to in the plural. This, I believe, is an important principle of local church leadership, and so we will discuss first the issue of plurality and the question of possible degrees of authority within the leadership of the church. We will then consider what the New Testament teaches about the team-members, their role, the qualifications they need, and the way in which they should be appointed.

Plurality

It is noteworthy that the New Testament generally talks of a plurality of pastors (elders) in each local church. We will consider first the NT evidence for this and then some common sense reasons for plurality.

NT evidence for plurality

This is easily seen from the following verses:

> Paul and Barnabas appointed elders for them in each church (Acts 14:23).

Four different churches are referred to here – Derbe, Lystra, Iconium, and Pisidian Antioch. Note that the apostles appointed *elders* (plural) in *each* church (singular). And in the church at Jerusalem:

> ...the apostles and elders, with the whole church, decided... (Acts 15:22).

Again, the elders are in the plural and the church is in the singular. This was also the case at Ephesus, for in Acts 20:17 we read that

> From Miletus Paul sent to Ephesus for the elders of the church.

Indeed, the letter of James, written to *the twelve tribes scattered among the nations* (James 1:1) appears to assume a plurality of leaders in every church, for in James 5:14 anyone who is sick is told to call for the elders (plural) of the church (singular).

Common sense reasons for plurality

Many churches have traditionally been accustomed to a 'one-man-ministry', but in recent years the value of team leadership has come to be increasingly appreciated. Some of the reasons for this are listed below.

Practical reasons for plurality in local church leadership	
1. Variety	No one person, however gifted, has everything that a church needs
2. Safety	Plurality of leadership ensures a balanced ministry and prevents a one-sided emphasis
3. Personality	Because of our different personalities, some people relate better to one person than another
4. Efficiency	The more on the job, the more can be accomplished, if organised properly
5. Responsibility	The burden of responsibility is too great for one person. It is better shared
6. Continuity	Under the 'one-man' system, when the 'minister' leaves there is sometimes a gap, which can lead to the break-up of the church. Under a plural system, there is continuity of ministry even during temporary absences of one or more of the leadership
7. Glory	With a 'one-man-ministry' it is easier for man (or woman) to get the glory for the success of the church. With plural leadership GOD is more likely to be glorified.

But, if there is to be plurality of leadership in the church today, and if there was normally more than one leader in each church in the New Testament, the question naturally arises as to whether there was one person who would take ultimate responsibility, and if so, whether there were different levels of authority within the leadership team of each church.

Different levels of authority?

As we approach this subject it is important to realise first that the role of elder was so significant in the New Testament that Paul instructed Timothy to receive no accusation against one unless it was levelled by at least two or three witnesses (1 Timothy 5:19). Furthermore, it is clear from 1 Timothy 5:17 that all elders were to be honoured but that those who worked extra hard[40] at preaching and teaching deserved 'double honour'[41]. All this suggests the importance of the role of elder in the New Testament. But were there different levels of authority among them?

In this connection, the following points need to be considered:

1. Apostles (who are also elders – see 1 Peter 5:1) had authority over the churches they had founded. Once appointed, elders would have shared responsibility for the affairs of the church, but respect would always have been due to the apostle who had founded it. The 'senior pastors' in some churches today may

---

[40] The Greek verb here literally means *work until weary*. There is no suggestion that some elders teach and others do not (as some translations [e.g. NIV] imply), for all elders must be able to teach (1 Timothy 3:2). The suggestion is that some work harder at it than others and are therefore worthy of extra respect – and pay!

[41] The word 'honour' here can also mean 'pay' as the following verse suggests. The fact that adequate remuneration should be given to those who labour in the gospel is well attested in the NT (see Luke 10:7, 1 Timothy 5:18, 1 Corinthians 9:3-14).

have apostolic gifting even though they are not always recognised as apostles.

2. James may have had a leading role in the church in Jerusalem. (See Acts 15:13ff. where James seems to have taken a leading role[42] and Acts 21:18 where he is mentioned by name along with 'all the elders'). This may suggest that he held a 'first among equals' position among the elders. However, if so, this may have been because he was viewed as an apostle. (See Galatians 1:19 and the section on *James, the Lord's brother* in Chapter 2 of this book).

3. As we have already mentioned, elders who directed the affairs of the church well and worked extra hard at teaching and preaching were worthy of double honour or pay (1 Timothy 5:17). This principle could easily be applied to those who are full-time pastors today.

4. Those who held the office longer may well have commanded more respect than those who had just been appointed. The significance of the word *presbuteros* (older, more mature) could possibly be taken to imply that those with greater experience in pastoral ministry would be rather more respected than those who had just started.

5. There was no one set model for church leadership in the early church. We see in Acts that its government developed dynamically, being adapted according to the church's needs. This means that there was great flexibility, not a rigid pattern.

---

[42] Though the argument here is by no means conclusive. James may have spoken up simply because he was led by the Spirit to do so.

6. The *angels of the churches* in Revelation 2-3 *may* indicate an overall leader in at least some churches. However, although the word *aggelos* (usually translated *angel*) does mean *messenger*, we cannot be sure that the 'angels' referred to in these chapters were church leaders. They may well have been angelic beings as this is the meaning of the word *aggelos* everywhere else in the New Testament.

7. In practice it is generally recognised today that one person needs to be ultimately responsible for vision and leadership. In my view there is no clear evidence for this in the New Testament, but it is not out of harmony with (5) above. However, in my view it is not wise to call that one person *pastor* and the rest *elders,* as all elders have pastoral responsibility. Appropriate terms should be chosen to suit the local situation in line with the overall biblical principles.

In my view, the seven points listed above show that, within the biblical principle of team leadership, there is ample scope for a variety of systems, including that of seeing one person as the overall leader of the church. What is important, however, is that elders should conform to the New Testament criteria. To clarify that further we will now consider their role in more detail. In so doing, of course, we will by definition be examining the role of pastors.

Role

The New Testament clearly shows us that it was the role of elders to take care of the church (1 Timothy 3:5). This was expressed in three main ways:

- As *shepherds*, looking after the flock
- As *teachers*, instructing God's people
- As *overseers*, supervising the affairs of the church.

Looking after the flock

We have already examined Acts 20:28 and 1 Peter 5:2 where the elders are told to be shepherds of God's flock (the church). Clearly it is a shepherd's job to look after the sheep and this is done in three main ways:

- Feeding
- Protecting
- Healing.

First, it is interesting to note that *poimaino* means *to feed* as well as *to shepherd.* The most important responsibility of the shepherd is to see that the flock are well fed. This will include not only feeding them personally, but leading them to pastures where they will feed themselves (cf. Psalm 23). If we apply this to elders as the shepherds of God's flock, the obvious way in which they must feed the sheep is by teaching them God's word which is the Christian's necessary food. (See Job 23:12, 1 Corinthians 3:2, Hebrews 5:12-14). It will also involve, very importantly, showing them how they can feed on God's word for themselves.

Secondly, it is the shepherd's responsibility to protect the sheep from such predators as wolves. Paul warns the Ephesian elders of this in Acts 20:28-30 when he says:

> Guard yourselves and all the flock... I know that, after I leave, savage wolves will come... men will arise and distort the truth.

Clearly, the 'wolves' here are those who teach false doctrine because they are said to *distort the truth.* Protecting the flock, then, means ensuring that God's people are not led astray by wrong teaching.

Finally, it is noteworthy that part of the shepherd's role in taking care of the flock involves the healing of sheep that are sick. The Greek verb that is used for *take care of God's church* in 1 Timothy 3:5 is *epimeleomai* which often has a medical connotation. Although this is not its main meaning in the context of the passage, it is clear that the word covers a broad range of caring. Shepherds are involved in caring in every aspect of the lives of their sheep. Accordingly in James 5:14 the sick Christian is encouraged to call for the elders of the church whose prayer of faith will make the sick person well.

Instructing God's people

Closely connected with the elders' role as shepherds is their work as teachers. 1 Timothy 3:2-3 tells us that an overseer must be able to teach and 1 Timothy 5:17 states that the elders who rule well and who work extra hard in teaching and preaching are worthy of double honour[43]. And in Titus 1:9 Paul teaches that elders must be able to *encourage others by sound doctrine and refute those who oppose it*. This is clearly connected with their role as shepherds in feeding and protecting the flock, which we considered in the last section.

Supervising and directing the affairs of the church

Finally, elders are not only described as shepherds and teachers, but also as overseers (Acts 20:17 cf. v.28, Titus 1: 6-7, 1 Peter 5:1-2). *Overseer* is not a greatly used word in English today, but the word *supervisor* which means essentially the same thing[44] is well known to us. This means that they *manage* (1 Timothy 3:5) and *direct the affairs of* the church (1 Timothy 5:17). However,

---

[43] See my comment as to the correct understanding of this verse under the heading **Different levels of authority.**

[44] The word *supervise* is derived from two Latin words, *super* and *video* which mean *over* and *I see.*

despite the authority and responsibility given to them they are not to *lord it over* those that God has entrusted to their care (1 Peter 5:3).

As we now conclude this section on the role of elders, one last comment is appropriate. Since, as we have seen, elders are *shepherds* who look after the flock, *teachers* who instruct God's people in his truth, and *overseers* who supervise and direct the affairs of the church, **what do pastors do if elders and pastors aren't the same thing?**

This point is further underlined as we turn now to consider the qualifications required of a person to be an elder, a member of the pastoral team.

Qualifications

The qualifications needed to fulfil the role of elder are to be found in 1 Timothy 3:1-7, Titus 1:5-9. From these two passages we learn that an elder should be above reproach, not married to more than one person, self-controlled, sensible, well-behaved, dignified and hospitable. They must also be capable teachers of the word, able to silence heresy, temperate in the use of wine, not quarrelsome, but gentle and considerate, not lovers of money, and not new converts. Elders must also have a good reputation with outsiders and must rule their own households well, keeping their children in order.

This last point shows us that elders are not necessarily old. They could be young enough to have children who were not yet grown up. As we have already pointed out, the Greek word *presbuteros* means *older*, not old. It simply indicates that elders must be spiritually mature.

This leads us now to the important question of how elders should be appointed.

Appointment

The elders in the church at Jerusalem simply emerged. We do not know how they were appointed. In Acts 14:23, however, Paul and Barnabas appointed elders in all the churches they had planted, so we might say that elders were ordained by apostles. Later elders appear to have been ordained by other elders. Paul tells Titus, to whom church tradition refers as an *episkopos (overseer)*, to *appoint elders in every town* (Titus 1:5). This suggests that the pastoral team should initially be appointed by the apostles who plant the church, but that thereafter new members are added to the team by those who are already members of that team.

However, the New Testament recognises that only God can make a person an elder or overseer or shepherd (Acts 20:28, Ephesians 4:7-11). The suggestion seems to be that God gives a ministry that we observe emerging. When the ministry is 'tested' then we recognise what God has given by laying hands[45] on the person concerned[46].

Pastors today

To make a general application of the NT principles we have been looking at to the role of pastors in the church today is by no means easy. Situations vary so much from one local church to another. However, if the principles are recognised as correct, then prayerful consideration of how they might be applied in any particular local church situation is bound to be beneficial. It will be helpful, therefore, to summarise here the principles we have been considering in this chapter and to make brief comment as to how this might affect local churches today.

---

[45] The Greek word for *ordain* implies the laying on of hands.

[46] The idea of being 'tested' comes from 1 Timothy 3:10 which applies to deacons, but note the word *also*. Deacons must be tested *as well as* overseers.

Terminology

The terms *pastor, elder* and *overseer* in the New Testament all apply to those who are to shepherd God's flock. Therefore, if we are looking for NT guidelines for pastoral work we must look at the role of elders/overseers. Furthermore, it is questionable whether a distinction should be made between pastors and elders/overseers in modern church life. To do so only leads to confusion when comparing the modern church with the New Testament.

Plurality

There appears to have been always more than one leader in any local church. Where a church today is led by one person only, that person should prayerfully consider who might be gifted to share the work. However, since only God can gift a person for this work, people who are not suitably qualified should not be appointed just for the sake of plurality. Nevertheless, the leader should constantly be on the lookout for ministries emerging in the church and meanwhile should bring in on a temporary basis those with gifts that the leader may lack.

Levels of authority

Many churches today function quite successfully with a system where one person is the overall leader (often called the *pastor* or *senior minister*) supported by a team of people with complementary gifts and ministries. Earlier in this chapter I suggested seven ways in which it might be possible to see a biblical rationale for such a system. However, in my view, a system which makes room for elders who do not have pastoral gifting is clearly to be avoided.

Role and qualifications

Since elders in the New Testament were to shepherd, instruct, and direct the affairs of the church, people who are not gifted to do these things should not be appointed as elders. The qualities of character, experience and ability listed in 1 Timothy 3 and Titus 1 are as important for church leaders today as they were in the New Testament.

Appointment

In the case of a new church being planted, those with apostolic gifting who planted it should appoint the pastoral team. In the case of established churches, where a pastoral *team* already exists, the existing members should appoint new team-members. Difficulties arise, however, where no such team exists[47]. It is not always wise for the outgoing pastor to appoint their successor, although this might be appropriate particularly where the pastor has apostolic gifting. Another possibility is that apostolic input could be sought from outside the local church.

But whatever the method of appointment, the question arises as to the role of the local church members. Some churches still have a 'democratic' method of appointing pastors while others have reacted strongly against this claiming that such methods are unscriptural. My own view is that, although the appointment should be made in keeping with the principles outlined in the last paragraph, it is always wise to consult the church membership in such important matters. It is the privilege of *all* God's children to be led by his Spirit (Romans 8:14). Jesus said that God's *sheep* (not just the *shepherds*) hear his voice (John 10:3-5, 14-16). But whatever the method of appointment, what matters above everything else is that those who are appointed conform to the

---

[47] We have already noted that this is not a biblical position for an established church to be in. However, it is a common situation today.

requirements of character, experience and gifting already mentioned.

Conclusion

In this chapter we have sought to identify who the *pastors* of the New Testament churches were, and we have concluded that they are those who elsewhere are referred to as *elders* or *overseers*. Their responsibility was to shepherd, teach, supervise and direct the affairs of the local church. There were generally several such leaders in each church, although there may have been different levels of authority within the pastoral team.

There is certainly room for a system of one person being a 'first among equals'. However, to call that person 'pastor' and the others 'elders' is not in line with the New Testament and may detract from the pastoral role that elders are to fulfil.

The pastoral team should initially be appointed by the apostle(s) who plant the church. Thereafter the existing members of the team may appoint new members to it provided that they conform to the NT guidelines with regard to character, experience and gifting.

Finally, in Acts we see the leadership system of each church developing as the church grew. And it varied somewhat from one church to another. Church leaders today need to identify the *principles* of leadership seen in the New Testament church and seek to be led by the Holy Spirit as to how to apply them in each local situation today. Those principles, I believe, have been outlined in this chapter.

CHAPTER SIX

Teachers

In this chapter we come to the last of the five gifts listed in Ephesians 4:11, that of *teacher*. Before considering the role of teachers in the church today, we will examine the meaning of the word *teacher* and how it is used in the New Testament. This will include consideration of whether the gift is separate from that of pastor or whether *pastors and teachers* should be viewed as one gift as some have suggested. We will deal with the subject under the following headings:

– The meaning of the word *teacher*
– The importance of teaching
– Teachers in the New Testament
– Teachers in the church today.

The meaning of the word *teacher*

Of course *teacher* is a word we are all familiar with from our school days, but there is obviously a difference between the role of those who employed by secular society to teach in our schools and that of those gifted by Christ to teach God's people[48].

However, the basic meaning of the word is the same. In Ephesians 4:11 the Greek word used for *teachers* is *didaskalos.*

---

[48] Of course, someone gifted as a teacher in the Ephesians 4:11 sense may use that gift in the context of a school. (In the early years of my ministry I personally combined pastoral work with teaching in a school). Clearly, however, school-teachers who are not Christians do not possess an Ephesians 4:11 gift.

This is part of the same word group as the verb *didasko* which does mean *to teach* but also means *to train*. A good teacher imparts theoretical knowledge, but also shows their students *how to do things*. For example, in Classical Greek the word *didaskalos* is used of those who wrote plays because they taught the actors their parts. A *teacher*, therefore, is simply *someone who teaches and trains others*. That is clearly its meaning in Ephesians 4:11, as teachers, along with the other gifts listed, are to help *equip God's people for works of service*.

The importance of teaching

The ministry of teachers may appear to some people less spectacular than that of the apostle, prophet, or evangelist, but their teaching is vitally important not only because it springs from the gift of God that makes them teachers, but also because of the high priority given to sound doctrine in the New Testament. The scriptures were written that we might *know the truth*, and that the truth might set us free (John 8:32).

There are at least 50 references to *teaching* in the New Testament, and the emphasis which the early church placed upon it is seen from the many references to Jesus and the apostles *teaching* as well as preaching the word (e.g. Matthew 4:23).

When the 3,000 converts on the Day of Pentecost had repented, been baptised, and received the gift of the Holy Spirit, the apostles knew that their first need was to be *taught*, and so these new converts *devoted themselves to the apostles' teaching* (Acts 2:42).

In fact, so important was teaching considered to be that maintaining one's spiritual experience was dependent on continuing in sound teaching:

> Anyone who... does not continue in the teaching of Christ, does not have God. Whoever continues in the teaching has both the Father and the Son (2 John 9).

90

This indicates that the effects of doctrine with regard to the person of Christ are so far-reaching that they determine a person's eternal destiny. But just as false teaching will lead a person into error, so sound teaching will lead into truth. We need to know *what* we believe and *why* we believe it so that we can *by sound doctrine convince those who contradict us* (Titus 1:9). It is by knowing the truth that people are set free (John 8:32). Timothy was still young when he was told:

> Devote yourself to... teaching. Watch your life and doctrine closely; persevere in them; because if you do you will save both yourself and your hearers (1 Tim. 4:13, 16).

Teachers in the New Testament

In this section we will consider teachers and teaching in the New Testament with a view to deciding what should be the role of teachers in the church today. We will deal with the topic under the following headings:

- *Pastors and teachers* – one gift or two?
- The role of teachers in the New Testament
- Necessary qualifications
- Apollos as a model
- Jesus, the supreme example.

Pastors and teachers – one gift or two?

In the last chapter we saw that one of the responsibilities of the pastor/elder is to teach the flock. Some have suggested that in Eph.4:11 *pastors and teachers* should be taken together on the grounds that they are both covered by the same definite article in the Greek. This is undoubtedly the most natural way to understand the Greek construction Paul uses but the argument is too technical to go into here[49].

The problem is easily resolved, however, by looking at examples of teachers in the New Testament. From what we have seen already, pastors clearly need to be teachers. They are responsible for feeding the flock and this may account for their inclusion together with teachers in Ephesians 4:11.

However a teacher need not necessarily be a pastor, for pastors need to be based locally, whereas a teacher might have an itinerant ministry. Apollos, for example, seems to have travelled continually (Acts 18:24-28, 1 Corinthians 16:12, Titus 3:13) at least for part of his ministry.

The role of teachers in the NT

Accepting that a teacher's ministry may not necessarily be based in one local church, however, does not mean that the itinerant teacher's ministry is essentially different from the teaching role of the pastor. Whether itinerant, or locally based as a pastor, the teacher's role will be the same. It will involve:

– Giving both theoretical and practical instruction from God's word (cf. most of Paul's epistles)
– Teaching others what to teach (2 Timothy 2:2, Ephesians 4:11-12)
– Correcting false doctrine and teaching others how to avoid it (Titus 1:9).

From this it is clear that the teacher's work is essentially to *be a help to those who have believed* (Acts 18:27). The teacher waters

---

[49] For further discussion of the problems that arise over the question whether or not one article, in any given instance, is intended to apply to separate nouns, see Moule, C.F.D., *An Idiom-Book Of New Testament Greek,* Cambridge, CUP, pp 109-110.

what someone else has planted and often builds on a foundation laid by someone else (1 Corinthians 3:6-10). We will say more about all this later when we consider the role of teachers today.

Necessary qualifications

Of course, those who teach in the secular education system today are required to be suitably trained and qualified. Hopefully, too, they have a measure of natural talent, which helps them to do the job! However, most of us can probably remember being taught in school by someone who, though academically qualified, had no real aptitude for teaching. They were not naturally gifted. What is needed, of course, is *gift* and *training*. These are the true qualifications.

And what is true of the teacher in the secular field has its counterpart in the life of the church. Teachers need first to be gifted by Christ (Ephesians 4:11). This is the primary qualification. But gifting in itself is not enough. Before anyone can teach they need to *learn*. Teachers must always be ready to learn *the way of God more adequately* (Acts 18:26). Clearly the better grasp you have of the Scriptures the better you will be able to teach others.

In my view, this may have been one of Paul's main reasons for not allowing the women of his day to teach (1 Timothy 2:12). In the culture of the day women were not as well taught as men and it would have been inappropriate for them to teach. But Paul was not a misogynist! His encouragement to Timothy that *a woman should **learn*** (1 Timothy 2:11), albeit in quietness and submission as suited the contemporary culture, was actually a *liberating* word for women[50].

In this connection it is noteworthy that in Acts 18:26 it was *Priscilla* and Aquila who *explained* to the great teacher Apollos *the*

---

[50] It is noteworthy that Paul allowed women to prophesy provided that they were modestly dressed (1 Corinthians 11:5).

way of God more adequately. This undoubtedly means that they taught him things he had not yet learned for he *knew only the baptism of John* (v.25). And it is perhaps significant that Priscilla's name is mentioned before her husband's! But that leads us naturally to the subject of Apollos.

Apollos as a model

As we have already noted, Apollos differs a little from the pastor/teachers whose ministry found its main outlet in one local church and which we considered in the last chapter. This is because he appears to be an example of a teacher who travelled a great deal (Acts 18:24-28, 1 Corinthians 16:12, Titus 3:13). He was a teacher rather than a pastor/teacher. That is why I have chosen him as a model.

Apollos was a Jew who was born in Alexandria in Egypt, the second most important city in the Roman Empire. It was also the home of a famous university. Acts 18:24 describes Apollos as *a learned man* and it is at least possible that he received his education there. He is also described as one who had a *thorough knowledge of the Scriptures*. This was undoubtedly because of his Jewish upbringing. This strong educational background, together with a natural gift of oratory, probably made Apollos the great public speaker that he was (Acts 18:25, 28).

Having heard, or at least heard of, the preaching of John the Baptist, Apollos became convinced of its truth and used his great ability to speak boldly and fervently in the Jewish synagogue the way of the Lord as best he knew it (Acts 18:25-26). However, his knowledge at that point was incomplete because *he knew only the baptism of John* (v.25).

This probably means that he did not yet know about Jesus, but believed John's message that the coming of the Messiah was imminent[51]. When Priscilla and Aquila heard him, they invited him into their home and *explained to him the way of God more adequately* (v.26). Later Apollos travelled to Corinth and was a great help to the Christians there because he was able to refute the Jews in public debate by proving from the Scriptures that Jesus was the Christ (v.28). From this short description of Apollos' ministry, several lessons may be learned.

First, teachers must always be ready to learn *the way of God more adequately* (v.26). Apollos became a better teacher because he was willing to become a student.

Closely connected with this we see, secondly, the teacher's need for humility. Paul warns us in 1 Corinthians 8:1 that *knowledge puffs up* – it can be a source of pride. Great scholar that he was, Apollos was willing to learn from others.

Thirdly, the teacher's work is mainly for the purpose of helping believers (v.27, cf. also 1 Corinthians 3:5-6). However, every Christian should seek to spread the good news about Jesus and teachers are no exception. Apollos' teaching ministry also had a powerful evangelistic edge (vv.25, 28).

Fourthly, the example of Apollos suggests that natural talent may well form a part of a person's gifting from God. His ministry was very much in keeping with his natural abilities. Although this is not always the case, it is often so. Paul could say in Galatians 1:15 that God had set him apart from birth (literally *from his mother's womb*) in order that he might preach, and Jeremiah was told that before he formed him in the womb God had set him apart as a prophet to the nations (Jeremiah 1:5). These verses may well suggest that God causes us to be born with the natural propensities that will partly enable us to fulfil the role that he has for us in life.

---

[51] The NIV rendering *taught accurately about **Jesus*** is confusing here. It contradicts the very next statement, that Apollos *knew only the baptism of John*. The majority of manuscripts read *taught accurately about **the Lord*** and in my view this is by far the preferred reading.

This understanding may well be the key to identifying our gifting in the Lord's service.

Finally, it is clear that Apollos taught with great enthusiasm (note the words *fervour, boldly, vigorously,* in verses 25, 26 and 28). There is no suggestion here that his teaching was ever 'dry'! No wonder Paul could say of Apollos that he *watered* (1 Corinthians 3:6)! This suggests that, over and above the natural abilities that formed part of this outstanding teacher's ministry, there was that necessary outflow of the rivers of living water which only comes from the Holy Spirit himself.

But if Apollos was a great teacher, there was one who was greater still, and he is our supreme example.

Jesus, the supreme example

Jesus was undoubtedly the greatest teacher the world has ever known. Nicodemus recognised that he was *a **teacher** come from God* because of the miracles which he performed (John 3:2). Others were

> amazed at his teaching because he taught as one who has authority and not as their teachers of the law (Matthew 7:28-29).

His hearers were left with *hearts burning within them* when Jesus opened up the Scriptures to them (Luke 24: 32). Everything he did was motivated by love and his teaching was no exception. Mark 6:33-34 tells us that

> he had compassion on the crowd because they were like sheep without a shepherd, **so he began teaching them many things.**

This passage not only illustrates the overlapping roles of pastors and teachers, but also challenges those who are gifted by Christ to teach his church as to their motive in doing so. If we are teachers we must teach because we love the people, not because we want to prove how much we know!

That leads us to another aspect of Jesus' teaching, its great simplicity. A great teacher is not a person who makes simple things appear difficult, but someone who takes difficult concepts and makes them understandable! Jesus taught the most profound truths, yet everyone (who wanted to) was able to understand. His teaching was clear, simple, and illustrated with familiar examples from everyday life.

But can we really expect to imitate him? Surely he was totally unique? He *was* the Word! He *was* the truth (John 1:1, 14:6). How can we ever aspire to teach as he did? Perhaps we can not, but we can certainly learn from him. In the mystery of the incarnation Jesus was God, but he was also man. As man, like us, he **grew in wisdom** (Luke 2:52). He did not know everything, yet everything he said was true! This was because he relied completely on God. On one occasion he said

> My teaching is not my own. It comes from him who sent me (John 7:16)

and a little later

> ...the Father who sent me commanded me what to say and how to say it... So whatever I say is just what the Father told me to say (John 12:49-50)

and

> These words you hear are not my own; they belong to the Father who sent me (14:24).

Perhaps these words make us feel that such a level of teaching is *beyond* our reach, yet understood another way they show that it is, in principle at least, *within* it! If *Jesus* needed to depend entirely on God for what he taught, it is abundantly obvious that we must do so too. If we are gifted like Apollos, our background and education will be of value in God's service, but there is no substitute for waiting on God to hear what he has to say through his Word. In the measure that we do that, the one who is the truth will teach his people through us. As Donald Gee once said:

> 'Through every teacher given by Him, the Spirit of Truth is taking the things of Christ and revealing them to us'[52].

Teachers today

The importance of teachers and teaching in the church today cannot be too greatly stressed. It is easy to become enthusiastic about the church-planting, miracle-working ministry of the apostle or the insightful predictions of the prophet. We are thrilled to see thousands make decisions for Christ as the evangelist preaches the gospel and God confirms it with signs and wonders. But God's people tend to be less excited about the teacher's systematic exposition of God's word.

Yet if the churches planted by the apostles are to be strong in the faith, and if the converts won through the evangelist's preaching are to grow and become established in the truth, the ministry of the teacher must be recognised and used to its full potential. It is the responsibility of the pastor/teachers who lead God's flock to ensure that the sheep are fed.

As we have already seen teachers are given to the church, along with the other gifts listed in Ephesians 4:11, that God's people might be equipped for works of service. This will involve both theoretical and practical instruction. The phrase *works of service*

---

[52] Gee, Donald, *The Ministry Gifts of Christ,* Springfield MO., GPH, 1930, p. 110.

(v.12) certainly implies a practical dimension. But the following verses show clearly that becoming mature and *attaining to the whole measure of the fulness of Christ* (v.13) means not being *tossed back and forth by the waves, and blown here and there by every wind of teaching* (v.14). The doctrinal element is, therefore, also strongly present in this passage.

The teacher's ministry today, then, must contain elements of both theory and practice, doctrine and right living, a combination which we see beautifully harmonised in the NT epistles. There would be no point to sound doctrine if people did not live right as a result of it! And it is impossible to live right until God's word enlightens our understanding. It is *the truth* that *sets free!* This is well illustrated in Romans 6 which makes clear that until I understand that I am dead to sin I cannot truly live free from sin. What we *believe* as Christians affects how we *behave*.

Because of this, teachers need to make sure that the content of their messages is both doctrinal and practical. Although it is by no means the only way of teaching, the systematic exposition of the Scriptures will, of course, ensure this as the Scriptures themselves contain both elements. It will also, incidentally, prevent the teacher from constantly stressing his favourite themes, and thereby avoiding passages and issues that are difficult or less popular!

This brings us to the important issue of who should be responsible for teaching in the church today. In the last chapter we saw that it is the task of the pastoral team (or eldership). In addition, there may be people like Apollos who exercise a wider teaching ministry across the churches. Such people must of course be suitably gifted, but must also be willing to learn and to go on learning. They should also be people who are rightly motivated, having a love for the people not just a zeal for the truth!

Even those who are relatively young in the faith may possess these qualities, even when they have learned relatively little themselves. Surely part of the teacher's role in helping to equip

God's people for works of service is to watch out for such people and bring them on to maturity in their gifting, by teaching them not only what to teach but also how to do it. This is presumably what Paul has in mind when he says to Timothy:

> The things **you** have heard **me** say... entrust to **reliable men** who will also be qualified to teach **others** (2 Timothy 2:2).

It is not difficult to see that there are four 'generations' of teachers in this verse. *Paul* taught *Timothy* to teach *reliable people* to teach *others*. This is completely in harmony with what Jesus commanded when he gave the great commission[53]. It also suggests that there may be different levels at which teaching may be done. In the local church the more experienced teachers might well give guidance to less experienced teachers as to what they should teach, for example, to some young converts or to a Sunday-School class or cell-group[54].

At a wider level, the teaching and training given by Bible College lecturers (who should never be mere academics[55], but those truly gifted with an Ephesians 4:11 ministry) can also be seen as a modern outworking of the same principle.

As far as teaching methods are concerned, space forbids detailed comment here. Perhaps it is enough to say that no teacher could ever do better than to follow the example of Jesus. Having heard from the Father what God wanted him to say, he said it with

---

[53] The apostles were to make disciples of all nations and to teach them to observe everything Jesus had commanded them (Matthew 28:12-20).

[54] We should probably not consider all those who teach at some of these levels as Ephesians 4:11 gifts. Just as all God's people should evangelise, though not all are evangelists, and just as not all who prophesy are 'prophets', so not all who teach are 'teachers'.

[55] Although an academic background may well, of course, be highly beneficial. Paul and Apollos both came into this category. Today there are many opportunities for on-going learning. These include the excellent Distance Learning courses and part-time postgraduate programmes offered at Mattersey Hall and similar colleges.

clarity, with simplicity, with directness, and with a wealth of illustration so that ordinary people heard him gladly.

Conclusion

Teaching is vitally important because it is the truth that sets us free. The role of the teacher in today's church is, therefore, as important as it ever was. This involves giving theoretical and practical instruction from God's word, teaching others what to teach, and correcting false doctrine and teaching others how to avoid it.

The people responsible for this are the members of the pastoral team, but those who have a wider ministry may also be invited to supplement their teaching. Apollos provides a good model for this, but there is no better example to follow than that of the Lord Jesus Christ.

Teachers should want to teach because they care about *people* not just about the truth. They should always be willing to go on learning, from God himself through his word, but also from others. The willingness to do so will lessen the danger of which Paul warned the Corinthians – knowledge puffs up! The teacher's true motivation is the love that builds up.

****

This chapter completes our study of the gifts listed in Ephesians 4:11. In Part Two we will turn our attention to the list of gifts mentioned in 1 Corinthians 12:8-10.

PART TWO

Gifts from the Spirit
1 Corinthians 12:8-10

CHAPTER SEVEN

Gifts from the Spirit

In **Part One** we considered the gifts mentioned in Ephesians 4:11. We saw that these are *people* – apostles, prophets, evangelists, pastors and teachers – given by *Christ* to his church. In **Part Two** we now turn our attention to the gifts of 1 Corinthians 12:8-10. These, as we have already noticed, are gifts from the Spirit given to individual members of the body of Christ[56]. In the following chapters we will consider each of these gifts in some detail, but in this introductory chapter we will seek to answer three main questions:

- – Are all these gifts supernatural?
- – Is the baptism in the Holy Spirit the gateway to these gifts?
- – What are the main purposes of these gifts?

Finally, we will briefly examine various ways in which these gifts have been classified into groups.

Are these gifts supernatural?

Early Pentecostal writers like Howard Carter and Harold Horton[57] insisted very strongly that all the gifts listed in 1 Corinthians 12:8-10 are entirely supernatural. This emphasis is still widely accepted among Pentecostal and charismatic Christians today, although some writers argue that only some of these gifts are

---

[56] See the table on p. 17, which illustrates this.
[57] See, for example, Horton, H., *The Gifts of the Spirit,* Nottingham, Assemblies of God, Ninth Edition 1968, passim. (First published in 1934).

miraculous[58]. However, in my view, there are good reasons to believe that Paul intends us to understand that all the gifts listed in these verses are supernatural in character. I will base my argument on two factors:

- The contents of the list
- The context in which the list is set.

The contents of the list

Few people would doubt that *most* of the gifts in the list are miraculous. Tongues, interpretation, and prophecy are clearly supernatural, as also are healings and the working of miracles. The gift of faith is almost certainly the *faith that can move mountains* of which Paul speaks in the next chapter (1 Corinthians 13:2). And although, as we shall see later[59], there is some disagreement over the precise nature of 'the ability to distinguish between spirits', however one understands this gift there is clearly a supernatural dimension to it.

That leaves the 'message of wisdom' and the 'message of knowledge'. Of course, the fact that seven out of the nine gifts mentioned here are supernatural by no means *proves* that the other two are! But since the Bible nowhere clearly defines these two gifts, it seems reasonable to me to assume that they are also miraculous gifts unless it can be proven otherwise from the immediate context[60]. However, far from indicating that these gifts are non-

---

[58] Wayne Grudem, for example, argues that a word of wisdom and a word of knowledge are probably not miraculous gifts. See:
Grudem, W., *Systematic Theology,* Leicester, IVP, 1994, pp.1080-1082.
[59] See Chapter 13.
[60] *Pace* Grudem who argues that for pastoral reasons Paul would almost certainly have included some non-miraculous gifts in this list. I find this argument most unconvincing. Grudem, W., *Systematic Theology,* Leicester, IVP, 1994, pp.1080-1082.

miraculous, the context reveals that these gifts are almost certainly supernatural in character.

The context in which the list is set

One of the most basic principles of interpreting the Bible rightly is that the meaning of a passage will only be correctly understood if we pay careful attention to its immediate context. And as we examine the verses that surround the list of gifts we are now considering, we see three possible indications that the gifts Paul mentions here may well be supernatural in character. These are:

- The use of *pneumatika* in v.1
- The reference to idol worship in v.2
- The reference to baptism in the Holy Spirit in v.13.

The use of *pneumatika* in v.1

In the Introduction to this book we explained the basic meaning of the word *charisma*. We said that *charis* means 'grace' and that *anything* that God gives us because of his grace is, therefore, a *charisma*. This means that our *natural* talents as well as any *supernatural* gifts God may have given us may all be correctly described as *charismata*.

Now with regard to the gifts in 1 Corinthians 12:8-10, it is interesting that, although Paul does use the word *charismata* in v.4, this is not the word he first uses to describe them. In v.1 he calls them *pneumatika*. The basic meaning of this word is 'spiritual' and so most versions translate it 'spiritual gifts' here. This is indeed the best way to translate it, provided that we remember that not all God's gifts are described in this way. In fact, although other lists of gifts are called *charismata*, **none of the other lists of gifts are referred to as *pneumatika*.**

This may well suggest that the gifts in the list we are now considering may have been unique in Paul's thinking. All God's gifts to us are *charismata*, but only *these* gifts are described as *pneumatika*. It is at least possible that Paul reserves the term *pneumatika* for those gifts which are supernatural in character. This idea is strongly backed up by his reference to idol worship in v. 2, which we must now examine.

The reference to idol worship in v.2

As we read the opening verses of 1 Corinthians 12 it is clear that Paul was very anxious that his readers should be able to distinguish the genuine from the counterfeit, the divine from the demonic. He did not want them to be ignorant about these things (v.1) and reminded them that before they had become Christians they had been idol-worshippers (v.2). This meant that, before their conversion to Christ, they had been involved with the demonic. In 1 Corinthians 10:19-20 we read:

> Do I mean then that a sacrifice offered to an idol is anything, or that an idol is anything? No, but the sacrifices of pagans are offered to demons, not to God, and I do not want you to be participants with demons.

This shows us that there is clearly a connection between idol worship and demons. Although the Corinthians themselves had been delivered from Satan's power there was always the possibility that unbelievers might come into their meetings[61] and, in the free atmosphere that prevailed in the Corinthian church, might actually seek to exercise some spiritual gift.

---

[61] That this was to be expected is clear from 1 Corinthians 14:23-25.

It was vital, therefore, that the Corinthians should be able to distinguish the true from the false – as indeed it is still vital today – and so Paul warned them that

> No-one who is speaking by the Spirit of God says 'Jesus be cursed' and no-one can say 'Jesus is Lord' except by the Holy Spirit (v. 3).

We will say more about this in Chapter 13, but for now it is sufficient to note that the list of gifts we are considering follows immediately after Paul's teaching on how to distinguish between manifestations which come from demons and those that come from the Holy Spirit. There is, therefore, a strong probability that the gifts he mentions in this context are those that are supernatural in character.

The reference to baptism in the Holy Spirit in v.13

I have written at length elsewhere on the subject of the baptism in the Holy Spirit[62]. Here it will be sufficient to point out that in Acts 1:5 Jesus, just before he ascended into heaven, promised his disciples that they would be baptised in the Holy Spirit a few days later. He went on to say in v.8 that this would be the power of the Holy Spirit coming upon them which would enable them to be his witnesses to the ends of the earth. In Acts 2, on the day of Pentecost, they received this power when they were all filled with the Holy Spirit and began to speak in other tongues as the Holy Spirit enabled them (v.4).

---

[62] See, for example: Petts, D., *The Holy Spirit – an Introduction,* Mattersey, Mattersey Hall, 1998, pp. 63-88. Also my article in:
Warrington, K. (ed.), *Pentecostal Perspectives,* Carlisle, Paternoster, 1998, pp. 98-119.

The same gift was promised to all those who would repent and be baptised (Acts 2:38) and Luke records how those who later became Christians were baptised in the Spirit and spoke in tongues as the first disciples had at Pentecost (Acts 10:46, 19:6). In the Book of Acts, therefore, the baptism in the Holy Spirit was closely associated with spiritual gifts like tongues and prophecy, and in the next section we will discuss whether it is right to view it as the gateway to the gifts. Here, however, my purpose is to draw attention to Paul's reference to the baptism in the Holy Spirit in v.13 of 1 Corinthians 12. In the NIV this reads as follows:

> For we were all baptised *by* one Spirit *into* one body.

But, as I have pointed out elsewhere[63], in the context of the chapter this is better translated:

> For we have all been baptised *in* one Spirit *for* one body...

Since, therefore, this verse probably refers to the baptism in the Holy Spirit, which in Acts was accompanied by supernatural phenomena, it seems reasonable to assume that the gifts of which Paul has just been speaking are also miraculous in character. In my opinion, therefore, early Pentecostal writers were right in their view that the gifts listed in these verses are supernatural gifts. Both the contents of the list and the context in which the list is set lead

---

[63] *The Holy Spirit – an Introduction,* pp. 68-70.
See also Donald Johns' article, 'New Directions in Hermeneutics' in McGee, Gary (ed.), *Initial Evidence,* Peabody, Hendrickson, pp. 160-161, where Johns agrees with my view.
John Rea is also of the same opinion. See: Rea, J. *The Holy Spirit in the Bible*, London, Marshall Pickering, 1992, pp. 254-259.

strongly to that conclusion. But that leads us to the another interesting question.

Is the baptism in the Holy Spirit the gateway to these gifts?

Before attempting to answer this question it is important to establish a basic principle. *We must decide what to believe on the basis of what we understand the Bible teaches, not on the basis of our experience.* Once we have done that, we may evaluate our experience in the light of Scripture, rather than trying to read our experience into God's word. In this section, therefore, we will approach the question from a biblical perspective before attempting to explain how this may, or may not, work out in practice today.

A biblical perspective

In my view the baptism in the Holy Spirit is correctly understood to be the gateway to these gifts because of:

- The sequence of events in Acts
- The meaning of 1 Corinthians 12:13.

The sequence of events in Acts

It is significant that in Acts the baptism or infilling[64] of the Spirit always came *before* the manifestation of spiritual gifts. The first disciples did not begin to speak in tongues until they were first filled with the Spirit at Pentecost (Acts 2:4). The same is true of

---

[64] It is important to realise that Luke uses a variety of expressions which appear to mean much the same thing. These interchangeable terms include being baptised in the Spirit, being filled with the Spirit, having the Spirit come upon you, receiving the gift of the Spirit etc. For a table demonstrating the interchangeability of these terms, see *The Holy Spirit – an Introduction,* p. 125, cf. ibid p. 65.

Cornelius and his household (Acts 10:44-46). And in Acts 19:1-6 the Ephesians spoke in tongues and prophesied after the Holy Spirit came upon them. Indeed, the fact that people were usually baptised in the Spirit on the day they were saved suggests that the manifestation of spiritual gifts before being baptised in the Spirit would have been unlikely.

The meaning of 1 Corinthians 12:13

I have already suggested that, understood correctly in its context, 1 Corinthians 12:13 means that we have been baptised in the Spirit for the benefit of the church. The Corinthians had been baptised in the Spirit, but were using gifts like tongues for their own edification instead of seeking to edify the church (cf. 14:1-12). Paul had to teach them that spiritual gifts were not given for their own selfish benefit, but for the good of all (12:7). He seems to be saying much the same thing in 12:13, which might be paraphrased as follows:

> You have been baptised in the Spirit for the good of the whole church, so that by the spiritual gifts which result from that baptism, you might edify, not just yourself, but the whole body of believers.

If this understanding is correct, then clearly the baptism in the Spirit is rightly understood to be the gateway to spiritual gifts. Indeed, we might well ask how anyone could expect to manifest the gifts that come from the Spirit without first being filled with the Spirit himself[65].

---

[65] However, some argue that we cannot insist that the baptism in the Spirit must precede the manifestation of spiritual gifts on the grounds that the disciples worked miracles before their baptism in the Spirit at Pentecost. However, it is clear that they did so in a special authority delegated to them by Jesus at that time. After Jesus went away they needed the Spirit if they were to continue to work miracles (cf. John 14).

But we must now ask how all this works out in practice.

Practical application

The idea that the baptism in the Spirit is rightly understood from a biblical perspective to be the gateway to supernatural gifts raises certain practical questions with regard to how this teaching should be applied today. What, for example, can we say of Christians who exercise spiritual gifts but who either would not claim to have been baptised in the Spirit or who do not believe in the baptism in the Spirit as we do? How do we explain this and what should be our attitude to such people?

In my view we should certainly not say that their gifts are not genuine! Personally I distinguish between what I see in the Bible, and therefore teach, and what God in his mercy may do today even if it is not completely in line with my understanding of the biblical pattern. It seems to me that God is far more willing to give than we are to receive. He is longing to lavish his gifts upon his people if only we would desire them more! This means that he is pleased when any of his children seek after any spiritual gift, whether or not they have come to understand or believe in the baptism in the Holy Spirit. This may well explain why some have been greatly used in healing even though they do not have a 'Pentecostal' understanding (or experience) of the baptism in the Spirit. In my view we should thank God for the way he is using them, but still encourage them to receive the baptism in the Spirit with its accompanying blessing of speaking in tongues, for how else will they be able to pray with their spirit (1 Corinthians 14:14ff)?

But instead of looking at the experience of others we would do better to consider our own. If we have been baptised in the Spirit we should press on to the gifts by eagerly desiring them and praying for them. We will say more on this in Chapter 15. And if we have not yet received the baptism in the Spirit, we should ask God to fill us today. Our heavenly Father does give the Holy Spirit to those who ask him (Luke 11:13) and Jesus said that if we are thirsty we will drink (John 7:37-39). As we reach out in faith he will not disappoint us[66].

The main purposes of these gifts

There are probably two main purposes for spiritual gifts listed in these verses, edification and evangelism. We will deal with each of these in turn.

Edification

It's clear from 1 Corinthians that it's possible for a Christian to use a spiritual gift for the wrong purpose. This was precisely what was wrong with the church at Corinth. They were using their gifts for their own personal edification instead of for the edification of others[67]. That's why Paul stresses the importance of using gifts for the good of others. Their major purpose is for the edification of the church. The manifestation of the Spirit is given *for the common good* (1 Corinthians 12:7). We've been baptised in the Spirit *for the benefit of the body* (1 Corinthians 12:13) and the value of a gift is determined by the measure in which it edifies the church, for

> He who prophesies is greater than he who speaks in tongues, unless he interprets, so that the church may be edified (1 Corinthians 14:5).

And Paul longed to see the Romans so that he might impart some spiritual gift *to make them strong* (Romans 1:11). We'll be

---

[66] For practical help on how to receive the baptism in the Holy Spirit, see *The Holy Spirit – an Introduction*, Chapter 7.
[67] Cf. 1 Corinthians 14 where Paul seeks to correct this tendency.

saying more about this in Chapter 15, but for the time being it's enough to note that if we are eager to be used in spiritual gifts, our chief motive should be that we want to be a blessing to others, either by edifying our fellow-Christians or by evangelising those who are not.

Evangelism

In 1 Corinthians Paul confines his discussion to the purpose of supernatural gifts in the church, for that was the immediate problem at Corinth. Elsewhere, however, it is clear that he recognised their great value in evangelism. In Romans 15 he speaks of what Christ has accomplished through him in leading the Gentiles to obey God, by what he has said and done

> by the power of signs and miracles through the power of the Spirit... So from Jerusalem all the way round to Illyricum I have fully proclaimed the gospel of Christ[68],

thereby suggesting that the gospel is not 'fully proclaimed' unless it is attested by signs from heaven.

And when Jesus commanded his disciples to go into all the world and preach the gospel to all creation, he promised them that miraculous signs would accompany the preaching of the word (Mark 16:17-18). Mark 16:20 tells us that this in fact took place and the Book of Acts continues the story with a catalogue of miracles that confirmed the message of the early disciples. God himself testified to it

> by signs, wonders and various miracles and gifts of the Holy Spirit distributed according to his will (Hebrews 2:4).

---

[68]Romans 15:18-19

How we need to pray and believe, like the disciples in Acts 4:29-31, that God will stretch out his hand to heal and that signs and wonders may be done in the name of Jesus so that God's servants might speak his word with boldness! Spiritual gifts make evangelism effective.

Classifying the gifts

We have seen that the nine gifts listed in 1 Corinthians 12:8-10 should probably be understood to stand apart from other *charismata* because they are also described as *pneumatika*. This may well suggest that Paul intends us to understand that these particular gifts are all supernatural, as the immediate context seems to indicate. In saying this we have already put them in a distinct category of their own, but the question arises as to whether further classification is possible.

Harold Horton, for example, divides the nine gifts into three groups of three[69] as the table below reveals:

Gifts of: Revelation	Power	Inspiration
A word of wisdom	Faith	Tongues
A word of knowledge	Miracles	Interpretation
Discerning of spirits	Healings	Prophecy

Of course, whether this classification is right or not will depend on the definition of each particular gift. If, for example, a word (NIV 'message') of wisdom[70] and a word of knowledge are not, as Horton believes, fragments of divine wisdom and knowledge imparted to God's people, then the whole classification breaks down. And even if Horton's understanding of these gifts is correct,

---

[69] Horton, H. op. cit. pp. 33-34.
[70] The slight difference in terminology is due to Horton's use of the Authorised Version.

115

there is still no good reason to believe that Paul intended us to classify them in this way. The order in which Paul lists them certainly does not seem to support Horton's classification. To do so it would require the discerning of spirits (AV) to come third in the list instead of seventh[71].

Despite these difficulties, however, it seems fairly clear that the second and third groups in Harold Horton's classification are broadly correct. Prophecy, tongues and interpretation, are undoubtedly inspirational gifts and faith, healings, and working miracles may reasonably be described as gifts of power. It is with regard to the first group, however, that Horton's analysis is open to question. The reason for this is simply that it is by no means certain that Horton's definitions of these gifts are correct.

We will face these problems as we come to each of the gifts in question, but for the sake of convenience I will leave discussion of these gifts to last. We will begin with the 'inspirational' gifts, *tongues, interpretation*, and *prophecy*. Then we will consider the gifts of power, *healings, miracles* and *faith*. Finally we will turn to the more controversial gifts, *discerning of spirits, a word of wisdom* and *a word of knowledge*.

---

[71] For alternative systems of classification, compare:
Lim, D., *Spiritual Gifts, a Fresh Look,* Springfield MO, GPH, 1991, p. 65
Fee, G. D., *The First Epistle to the Corinthians,* Grand Rapids, Mich., 1987, pp. 590-591.

Both these writers group the gifts according to the order in which Paul lists them, classifying the first two gifts together, then the next five, then the final two. Their analysis takes into account Paul's use of *heteros* and *allos* throughout the list. However, Fee sees the middle group as a random list whereas Lim sees them as 'ministry to church and world'. Although there may be merit in dividing the list in this way, this analysis sheds no additional light on the precise nature of the gifts themselves. Further, since it is highly likely that Paul never intended his readers to divide these gifts into categories, it is questionable whether there is any point in our attempting to do so today!

CHAPTER EIGHT

Tongues and Interpretation

W e will deal with these two gifts together, starting with the gift of tongues, simply because the use of tongues is clearly necessary before the gift of interpretation of tongues can be exercised[72].

As we examine the gift of tongues we'll first consider what it is and then outline a variety of biblical reasons for which the gift is given. We will notice that there is a clear distinction between its use in private and its use in a meeting of the church. And as we look at what the Bible has to say on the matter, we will clear up certain popularly held misunderstandings with regard to this gift.

In the second part of the chapter, when we consider the gift of interpretation, we'll discuss the form the gift should take, how it should be used in church, and how the gift may be received.

Tongues

What is 'speaking in tongues'?

The first thing to say in answer to this question is that 'speaking in tongues' is an unfortunate translation of the Greek text in which the NT was written. In 1611, when the Authorised Version (otherwise known as the King James Version) was produced, the word 'tongue' was regularly used in English to mean 'language'. This is clear from the title page of that version which refers to the

---

[72] In this connection, please note that the gift is not 'interpretation', but 'interpretation of *tongues*'. However, for the sake of brevity, we will at times refer to it simply as 'interpretation'.

'Old and New Testaments translated out of the original *tongues*'. Quite simply, 'tongues' meant 'languages', and so when the AV translators came to Acts 2:4, they recorded that the disciples 'began to speak with other *tongues*, as the Spirit gave them utterance'. By 'tongues' they meant 'languages'.

This is, of course, also perfectly clear from the context in Acts 2. On the day of Pentecost, the disciples were speaking languages they had never learned by the supernatural power of the Holy Spirit (Acts 2:1-11) and this is what amazed the crowd (vv.7-8, cf. v.11) and led ultimately to the conversion of some 3000 people (v.41).

On this basis, therefore, we may define the gift of tongues as:

The supernatural ability, imparted by the Holy Spirit, to speak a language one has never learned.

This definition is in harmony with the view that we expressed in Chapter Seven, that all the gifts mentioned in 1 Corinthians 12:8-10 are supernatural, and that includes the gift of tongues. It is important to notice, however, that it is not the *language* that is supernatural, but the ability to speak it! Speaking in tongues is not the ability to speak 'supernatural languages' (whatever they may be!). 'Tongues' are *natural* languages *supernaturally* spoken as is clear from Acts 2:6-11.

And what was true of the 'tongues' on the day of Pentecost is true of the other references to tongues in the New Testament. The Greek words used in Acts 10:46; 19:6; 1 Corinthians 12:10; 13:1 and in a variety of verses in 1 Corinthians 14 are precisely the same as those used in Acts 2:4ff., and simply mean 'to speak in (other) languages'. There is no contextual or linguistic justification whatsoever for modern translators (e.g. New English Bible and others) to insert the words 'of ecstasy'. Speaking with tongues may sometimes be ecstatic, but it certainly does not have to be, and this

118

misleading phrase is to be found nowhere in the Greek of the New Testament[73].

Perhaps the misconception has arisen partly because of the continued use of the seventeenth century English expression 'tongues' to which we have already referred. Today we tend to talk of the 'French *language*', the 'German *language*' rather than the French or German '*tongue*'. Accordingly, to be consistent with modern usage, 1 Corinthians 12:10, for example, should in my view be translated 'to another various kinds of languages; to another the interpretation of languages'.

There is nothing essentially different about the language with which I speak to God in 'tongues' from the language with which I address him in English (apart from the fact that they are of course different languages!). What is different is the manner in which they are spoken. One is spoken supernaturally, for the meaning of the words I speak is unknown to me, and I use those words only as the Holy Spirit inspires me to speak them. The other is spoken naturally, for it is my mother tongue, (although I still need the help of the Holy Spirit even when I pray in English).

Quite simply, if, when I speak in tongues the Holy Spirit inspires me to speak Swahili (a language I have never learned), it is

---

[73] From this it should be clear that I reject the view promoted in some circles that a distinction is to be made between *glossolalia* (speaking in tongues) and *zenolalia* (speaking in foreign languages). There is no NT evidence to support such a view, and the fact that tongues are not always *recognised* as languages (as they were at Pentecost) by no means implies that they *are* not always real languages. In Acts 10:46 Cornelius and his household spoke in tongues as the disciples had at Pentecost (cf. Acts 11:17), even though there was no-one present to identify the languages they spoke.

For over 75 documented accounts of tongues being recognised as foreign languages in the 20th century, see Harris, R.W., *Spoken by the Spirit,* Springfield MO, GPH, 1973. See also my personal testimony with regard to tongues and interpretation later in this chapter.

still *Swahili* that I am speaking – not supernatural Swahili, or heavenly Swahili, if there are such things! – but ordinary Swahili as it is spoken in Africa. What is supernatural is the fact that I, who have never learned it, can speak it!

Of course, we may be tempted to the view that speaking with tongues is not a 'real' language when we listen to some people speaking with tongues! We need to be very careful here, however. The structure and form of different languages around the world varies enormously, and by no means all languages resemble the few European languages with which most English-speaking people are familiar. We must be careful not to judge the genuineness of a manifestation of the gift of tongues with our human intellect, but with our spirit, for the things of the Spirit are spiritually discerned (1 Corinthians 2:14). But that leads us to the question of 1 Corinthians 13:1.

> If I speak in the tongues of men and of angels, but have not love,
> I am only a resounding gong or a clanging cymbal.

Here at first sight Paul seems to indicate that a language spoken in tongues might be either human or angelic. However, before we jump to the conclusion that there are many 'angelic' languages in heaven, we need to remind ourselves that the reason given for the existence of many languages on *earth* is human sin (Genesis 11:1ff.). Since there is no sin in heaven, there seems to be no good reason to assume that there is more than one language spoken in heaven. Furthermore, it is quite likely that in this passage Paul is exaggerating to make his point, for he goes on to say

> If... I can fathom all mysteries and all knowledge... but have not
> love, I am nothing (v.2).

Clearly Paul does not mean that he could possibly have *all knowledge* – only God knows everything – but he uses hyperbole to stress that, *even if he had,* without love he would be nothing. Similarly, therefore, in v.1 he may simply mean that *even if he could* already speak the heavenly language[74] without love he would be nothing.

There is every indication from the Scriptures, therefore, that when we speak in tongues we are speaking by the power of the Holy Spirit an actual human language[75]. If I am right in saying this, then there is an obvious answer to the frequently asked question, *Can the devil understand tongues?* The answer is clearly yes. Indeed, even if we allow that tongues can at times be the language of heaven, since Satan is a fallen angel, there is no good reason to suppose that he cannot understand it. But what does it matter? Our prayers in English are no less effective because he can understand them! Indeed the Bible nowhere states, or even implies, that the devil cannot understand tongues. What it does clearly state is that *we* cannot understand them. But that raises the obvious question:

> *What is the purpose of speaking a language we cannot understand?*

What's the purpose?

Perhaps before we seek to answer such a question we ought to remind ourselves that it is God himself who has chosen to make this gift available to his people. Even if we ourselves could see no

---

[74] It is quite likely that the Corinthians mistakenly thought that when they spoke in tongues this is what they were doing.

[75] This could presumably be a language once spoken, but now extinct, or a language yet to be spoken somewhere on earth. It is interesting to conjecture that, since God knows the end from the beginning, the Christians of the New Testament could, in principle at least, have spoken a modern language such as English!

purpose for it, it should be sufficient that God sees fit to give it. However, the Scriptures are by no means silent as to the purposes for which this gift is given, and some writers have been able to list as many as seventeen reasons why a Christian should speak with tongues! Here, however, I will mention just four biblical reasons for the gift of tongues:

- A sign to unbelievers
- Prayer with the spirit
- Personal edification
- Edifying the church.

A sign to unbelievers

In Mark 16 speaking with tongues was one of the signs which the Lord Jesus promised would accompany the preaching of the gospel, confirming the word of his messengers. On the day of Pentecost this was wonderfully fulfilled when 3,000 people were added to the church, having been first attracted under the sound of the gospel by the miraculous sign of speaking in tongues.

Paul seems to recognise this use of speaking in tongues in 1 Corinthians 14:22 where he says that tongues are a sign for unbelievers. However, in verse 23 he foresees the problem that if unbelievers come into a believers' meeting and everyone is speaking with tongues, they will quickly conclude that the Christians are out of their minds! Accordingly, he encourages the Corinthians to prophesy (vv 24-25). Putting it very simply, tongues can be a sign to unbelievers, but it can also put them off.

For this reason, in my view, speaking with tongues should not normally accompany the preaching of the gospel. It is not enough to say that the tongues will be interpreted, for interpretation is for the edification of the *church* (1 Cor. 14:5) not for unbelievers. When tongues were used as a sign to the unbeliever on the day of Pentecost, the tongues needed no interpretation, for they were the very languages that were spoken and understood by the unbelievers present. On this basis we could say that if tongues is to be a sign to convict rather than to confuse the unbeliever, it will be a language which he or she will personally recognise, as on the day of Pentecost. Such a sign required no interpretation though it did need to be followed by the preaching of the gospel (Acts 2:14-36).

Prayer 'with the spirit'

In 1 Corinthians 14:14-15 Paul tells us that when he prays in tongues his spirit (as distinct from his mind) is praying. The Corinthians were probably abusing the gift of tongues and Paul needed to emphasise *to them* the importance of prayer with the mind. To many Christians today, however, he would almost certainly have emphasised prayer with the spirit (i.e. in tongues). It is important that we should pray with our spirit as well as with our mind[76]. Both are important (v. 15).

Furthermore, in these verses tongues are described not only as praying with the spirit but as singing with the spirit (14-15), blessing with the spirit (v 16), and giving of thanks (16-17). This is in complete harmony with verses like Acts 2:11 where speaking with tongues is described as 'declaring the wonders of God', and Acts 10:46 which speaks of tongues as 'praising God'.

How grateful we should be that God has provided this wonderful way in which we may praise him with our spirit. As we praise him in a language we do not understand we are set free from the limitations imposed upon us by our finite minds. In the dimension of the spirit we touch the Infinite. Whatever we may like to believe on this matter, the clear implication of these verses is

---

[76] The value of speaking words we do not understand may not be immediately obvious, but in doing so we are set free from the limitations of our vocabulary and of our finite minds. When we just don't know how we should pray in English, it's a wonderful blessing to pray in tongues.

that by speaking with tongues we pray in a manner quite distinct from praying with our minds in English. We pray with our spirit. If asked, "But is there no other way of praying with the spirit than by praying in tongues?" we are compelled to reply that we see no other clearly mentioned in the Bible, and we wonder why the enquirer is so anxious to avoid speaking with tongues!

This does not mean that all prayer *in* the Spirit is speaking with tongues, but tongues is clearly a form of prayer, and all true prayer should be in the Holy Spirit (Ephesians 6:18). If, as is clear from this verse, we are to pray with '*all prayer... in the Spirit*', it would seem that true prayer in the Spirit is at least partly comprised of prayer with the spirit (i.e. in tongues). Bearing this in mind we could well see a reference to speaking with tongues in Jude 20 where we are told to edify (build up) ourselves by praying in the Holy Spirit.

Personal edification

In 1 Corinthians 14:4 we are told that 'He who speaks in a tongue edifies himself'. In the context Paul was in fact encouraging the Corinthians to seek the gift of prophecy on the grounds that 'he who prophesies edifies the church' whereas the speaker in tongues only edifies himself – unless of course his utterance is interpreted (v. 5). Nevertheless, although in the context of the church prophecy is preferable to tongues, it is clear from verses 18-19 that tongues is of great value in one's private devotions. The fact that Paul spoke in tongues more than them all (v.18) and yet did not do so in the church (v. 19) is sufficient evidence that he edified himself by speaking in tongues in private.

Tongues, then, is prayer with the spirit and a valuable means of building ourselves up spiritually. This then raises the question as to whether speaking in tongues is something which all Christians should be able to do. At first sight 1 Corinthians 12:30 seems to give the answer no. However, here tongues is linked with interpretation and it is clear that in asking the questions 'Do all speak in tongues? Do all interpret?' Paul is referring to the use of tongues which, when interpreted, will edify the church. There is no suggestion that all should not speak in tongues privately as a means of prayer 'with the spirit'. Indeed, in 1 Corinthians 14:5 Paul expresses the desire that everyone should speak in tongues!

In my view, since speaking in tongues is the only way revealed in the Bible by which a person may pray with their spirit as distinct from with their mind, it can hardly be God's intention that some Christians should have it and not others! And as we look in the Book of Acts we discover that speaking in tongues was the common experience of new converts when they were baptised in the Holy Spirit[77].

Edifying the church

It seems clear from 1 Corinthians 14:14-15 and 18-19 that as far as Paul was concerned it was the private use of speaking with tongues that was by far the most valuable. Hearing the gift in use would have been of no benefit whatsoever to those who could not understand the meaning of the words spoken (1 Corinthians 14:6-11). But this by no means meant that there was no place for the use of the gift in public. When accompanied by the gift of interpretation of tongues an utterance in tongues would be as beneficial to the church as the gift of prophecy (1 Corinthians 14:1-5).

However, even when interpreted so that the church might be edified, speaking with tongues in public was to be limited to two or three utterances (1 Corinthians 14:27). If no one present possessed the gift of interpretation, speaking in tongues aloud was forbidden.

---

[77] For defence of the view that speaking in tongues is the initial evidence of the baptism in the Holy Spirit, see:
Petts, D., *The Holy Spirit- an Introduction,* Mattersey Hall, 1998, pp.70-78 (cf. p. 125)

However, the private use of the gift, 'to himself and to God', seems to have been permissible for the purpose of personal edification even in a public meeting, provided that the speaker did so quietly (1 Corinthians 14:28).

Paul also encouraged those who spoke in tongues to pray for the gift of interpretation (1 Corinthians 14:13). In so doing they would be able not only to edify themselves by speaking in tongues, but also to edify the church by their interpretation.

Interpretation of Tongues

In the last section we defined speaking in tongues as:

> *The supernatural ability, imparted by the Holy Spirit, to speak a language one has never learned.*

From this it follows that the gift of interpretation of tongues is:

> *The supernatural ability, imparted by the Holy Spirit, to interpret a language that neither the speaker nor the interpreter has ever learned.*

We will consider this gift in the following way:

- The form of the gift
- Receiving the gift
- Using the gift.

The form of the gift

Paul tells us in 1 Corinthians 14:5 that the purpose of the gift of interpretation is 'that the church may be edified'. But what form will that edification take? It has for a long time been assumed by many that the interpretation of tongues is equal to prophecy on the grounds that both prophecy and interpretation edify the church (cf. 1 Corinthians 14:4-5). Accordingly it is believed that interpretation must take the form of a prophecy with the result that in many churches the interpretation of tongues always sounds exactly like a prophecy.

On the other hand, others have argued that, if tongues is a form of prayer or praise (e.g. 1 Corinthians 14:14ff.), then interpretation should not sound like a prophecy but should reflect the nature of the tongue, whether prayer or praise[78]. This view is strongly backed up by Paul's statement in1 Corinthians 14:2 that

> Anyone who speaks in a tongue does not speak to men but to God.

From this it certainly appears that the interpretation of tongues should take the form of praise or prayer rather than prophecy. Indeed, the fact that both prophecy and interpretation edify the church (vv.4-5) by no means implies that they must take the same form. What Paul clearly states in 1 Corinthians 14:5 is not that tongues with interpretation is *equal* to prophecy, but that the *value* of tongues with interpretation is equal to that of prophecy, for both edify the church. But that is not to say that all interpretation must take the form of prophecy, for the gift may be used to edify the church in quite a different way.

That there has been some disagreement on this matter over a period of many years is evident in that as early as 1934 Horton felt it necessary to deal with the subject at some length[79]. It is not my intention, however, to take sides in this matter. I agree that a correct

---

[78] It is interesting to note that in traditional Pentecostal circles the 'prophetic' form of interpretation is normal, whereas in the 'charismatic' meetings of the neo-pentecostals the gift is frequently exercised as praise. There are of course exceptions to this.

[79] See Horton, op. cit., pp.174-176.

understanding of the nature of the gift of interpretation will depend upon a correct understanding of the nature of the gift of tongues. However, despite 1 Corinthians 14:2, it is by no means clear that tongues is always addressed to God.

It is certainly true that verses such as Acts 2:11, 10:46, 1 Corinthians 14:16, and especially 1 Corinthians 14:2 seem to give the impression that speaking with tongues is essentially 'to God'. But all that these verses actually show is that speaking with tongues *may* take the form of praising, magnifying or blessing God. They do not demonstrate that it *must* do so.

Even 1 Corinthians 14:2, when taken in its context, does not conclusively demonstrate that tongues is *essentially* 'to God'. The *reason* that speaking in tongues is said to be 'not to man' is given in the self-same verse. It is because *no one understands* it[80]. Paul is not making a blanket statement here to cover all utterances in tongues. He is saying that tongues *without interpretation* must be to God, because without interpretation nobody can understand it. But this by no means implies that with interpretation tongues cannot be the vehicle of a message from God to man.

Indeed, in the same verse Paul goes on to say that the speaker in tongues is speaking 'mysteries' with his spirit. What is important about this is the fact that when this word is used elsewhere in Paul's writings it signifies a secret made known by God *to man* (my italics) through his Spirit (e.g. Ephesians 3:4-5).

Furthermore, 1 Corinthians 14:28 could well be taken to imply that if in the absence of an interpreter the speaker in tongues must speak quietly to himself and to *God*, then in the *presence* of an

---

[80] The NIV translation is unfortunate here. It puts a full-stop after 'God' and begins the next sentence, 'Indeed...' However, the Greek conjunction *gar* usually means 'for' rather than 'indeed'. What the verse is actually saying, then, is that speaking in tongues is not to man but to God *because* no one but God understands it. (Situations like the day of Pentecost would clearly be an exception to this).

interpreter, his audible utterance might well be to *man* when interpreted. It is also noteworthy that in v. 21 Paul refers to God using another tongue to speak *'to this people'*.

Finally, it is interesting that prophecy is described in verse 3 as being 'to *men*', yet can on occasion be 'to the *Lord*' (cf. Numbers 11:24ff, 1 Chronicles 25:3). It could well be argued, therefore, that, conversely, tongues which without interpretation is of necessity 'to God' (v. 2), may also be sometimes 'to men' especially when it is interpreted.

In short, speaking with tongues is the ability to speak supernaturally a language we have never learned. The direction of that speaking (whether to God or to man) is not an essential part of the nature of the gift. As outlined above, the Scriptures indicate that tongues may be in either direction. The interpretation of those tongues may, therefore, be either God-ward or man-ward. It would be quite wrong to suggest that the interpretation of tongues should *never* sound like a prophecy (to man). It would be equally wrong to teach that it should never sound like praise (to God). There is certainly no scriptural warrant whatsoever for the practice, current in some circles, of saying that an utterance in tongues requires no interpretation on the grounds that it is 'only praise'. As far as Paul was concerned *all* public utterances in tongues required interpreting that the church might be edified – and how wonderfully edifying an inspired utterance of praise can be!

Receiving the gift

In the final chapter we shall be dealing with the subject of how to receive the gifts of the Spirit in general, but perhaps at this stage a word of encouragement to those who are seeking the gift of interpretation would be appropriate.

1 Corinthians 14:13 encourages all those who speak in tongues publicly to pray for the gift of interpretation. And, since God would hardly instruct us to pray for something that he did not intend us to receive, we may surely take this verse as an encouragement to our faith.

The Bible does not tell us exactly how the gift will be received, from which we may conclude that there is a variety of ways in which the interpreter is given the interpretation. It may come audibly or visually or as an impression in one's spirit. In my personal experience the gift came as a result of much prayer after an utterance in tongues in a particular church had not been interpreted. Knowing this to be unscriptural, I asked God to give me the gift of interpretation so that such an occurrence would not happen again. On the next similar occasion, feeling a burden in my heart that something needed to be said, I spoke out in faith, believing that God would not let me be ashamed.

For months I wondered if the gift I had received was genuine, or whether it was 'just me'. Then, one day, at the close of a meeting in which I had interpreted, another brother came up to me and told me that he had received word for word the interpretation which I had given. I had exercised the gift in faith for months, but finally I had God's confirmation that it was real. Similar confirmation has come dozens of times since[81] and is a common evidence of the genuine moving of the Spirit upon thousands of Pentecostal congregations the world over.

This does not mean, however, that interpreters always receive the same interpretation word for word. God speaks through the mind and personality of the interpreter, and although the substance of the interpretation should always be the same, the manner in which the burden of the Lord is expressed may well vary from

---

[81] See especially the final section of this chapter, **A remarkable confirmation.**

interpreter to interpreter. But that leads us to the question of how the gift should be used in the local church.

Using the gift

Paul gives us basic instructions for the use of this gift in 1 Corinthians 14:27. This verse tells us that

1. Two, or at the most three, people should speak in tongues
2. They should do so one at a time
3. Someone must interpret.

Although at first sight these instructions appear very simple to understand, a number of differences have arisen as to how they should be applied today. First, with regard to (1) above, the question is sometimes asked whether the restriction to three utterances applies to the duration of the meeting, however long or short. Since we have no detailed knowledge as to how long the meetings in Corinth would have lasted, it is difficult to answer the question with any certainty. Perhaps the most important thing is to understand the *spirit* of what Paul is saying. The meeting is to be balanced and all that happens should be for the edifying of the church.

In line with this overall understanding of what Paul is teaching in the chapter as a whole, I have personally always applied Paul's teaching in this respect to the normal meetings of the church. However, if we are spending a day, or a night, in prayer, and the meeting is therefore far longer than usual, I would certainly not expect utterances in tongues to be limited to three. My advice to those who have difficulty with this is to suggest that they divide the day (or night) into several sessions and apply the 'two or at the most three' teaching to any one session.

The next question that often arises is closely connected with this. Since the biblical instruction is that tongues should be restricted to at the most three utterances, what should interpreters do if there is a fourth utterance in tongues? Before answering the question directly one important observation needs to be made. If leaders teach the church the biblical guidelines, this situation will hardly ever arise! However, if it does, my personal view is, contrary to long Pentecostal tradition, that the fourth utterance *should* be interpreted.

I say this on the basic principle of what Paul is teaching in 1 Corinthians 14. Everything must be done for the edifying of the church (cf. vv. 4, 5, 12, 17, 26). What is more edifying? For a fourth utterance in tongues to be interpreted, or for it to remain uninterpreted? Clearly it is better for it to be interpreted. Accordingly I would interpret a fourth utterance in tongues, but lovingly point out (either privately or publicly, depending on the circumstances) that in future there should only be three.

As I have already pointed out, the practice of leaving a fourth utterance uninterpreted on the grounds that it is 'just praise' rather than a 'message' really won't do. Paul mentions no such distinction. In fact he never refers to tongues as a message. If I have understood Paul correctly, all public tongues (unless it is private and relatively quiet) needs to be interpreted on the grounds that all who hear it will be unedified unless there is an interpretation.

The third question arising from these verses is what Paul means when he says 'Let someone interpret' (NIV). Although this is a valid translation of the Greek text, the verse literally reads, 'Let *one* interpret'. The word that Paul uses here is the numeral 'one' (as in one, two, three, etc.) and it is therefore more specific than 'someone'. Because of this, some teach that only one person should interpret in any one meeting. In other words, if there are, say, three utterances in tongues, then whoever interprets the first utterance must interpret all three. This way only 'one' person will have interpreted.

However, this is not the only way to interpret the verse. Apart from the possibility, suggested by the NIV translation, that Paul simply meant that someone should interpret, it is also possible to suggest that Paul meant that only *one* person should interpret *each* utterance. The Corinthian church was far from orderly in its worship and it is quite likely that several people were competing to give the interpretation to any utterance in tongues. The purpose of Paul's instruction was to stop this, making it clear that for any one utterance in tongues only one interpretation must be given.

Although we cannot be certain that this was Paul's intention, we can't be sure of any of the other ways of understanding the verse either. In my view, the suggestion outlined in the last paragraph is quite likely to be correct, but since we can't be sure, it must be left to the leadership of each local church to decide how best to understand the verse and to teach the people accordingly. In the final analysis, it will not matter whether one or two or three people are involved in interpreting[82], as long as everything is done in a fitting and orderly way (v.40).

A final question with regard to the gift of interpretation concerns the matter of speaking in tongues in private. As we have already seen, Paul seems to value the private use of tongues very highly (vv.18-19) and it seems natural to ask whether, if we have the gift of interpretation, we should interpret our own private use of tongues. The answer to this is almost certainly that we should not. The gift of interpretation is given in order that *the church* may be edified (v.5) and there is always the need for gifts like interpretation and prophecy to be 'weighed carefully' by others (v.29). In the light

---

[82] A case can also be made for as many as possible interpreting on the grounds that Paul encourages 'everyone' to participate in the meeting (v.26). Perhaps the restriction to one interpreter per utterance in tongues is given to avoid misunderstanding of 'everyone' in v.26.

of this it is a wise procedure to limit the use of the gift of interpretation to those utterances in tongues that take place when God's people are gathered together.

A remarkable confirmation

Finally, before leaving the subject of tongues and interpretation, the following testimony from my own experience should prove encouraging, both as a testimony to God's faithfulness and as an evidence of the genuineness of these gifts.

In November 1977 I was serving as Acting Principal of Mattersey Hall prior to becoming Principal in 1978. One Saturday evening we took a bus-load of about 45 students to Bethshan Tabernacle in Manchester. There were several hundred people in the meeting during which the students sang and testified and I preached. As soon as I had finished preaching, a woman near to the back of the meeting began to speak in tongues. As I was still at the microphone, it seemed appropriate for me to interpret so that everyone present would hear and be edified. As usual I spoke out in faith what I felt the Lord had put on my heart. When I had finished, we sang a hymn and the pastor closed the meeting in prayer.

As soon as the meeting was over, one of our students, Guetawende Roamba from Burkina Faso rushed up to me. He was clearly very excited, and when I asked him what was the matter, he told me that the woman who had spoken in tongues had been speaking his native language. Now in Burkina Faso they speak French, and because I also speak French fairly fluently, I knew that she had not been speaking French. So I wondered what language it might be.

'What language?' I asked. 'Moré', he replied. Frankly, at that time I had never heard of it – and we found out later that the Irish lady who had spoken in tongues had never heard of it either! But I was excited that I had been present when speaking in tongues had been recognised as a real language. At the same time I was not a little concerned because I was the one who had given the interpretation! I had been interpreting tongues since I was a student at Oxford in 1960, but it had always been (as it always must be) 'by faith', and I had no certain evidence that the gift was genuine. I had simply trusted the promise of Jesus that God gives good gifts to those who ask him (Matthew 7:11). Of course I had no need to fear, but it's easy to imagine how embarrassed I would have been if I had 'got it wrong' in the presence of one of my Bible College students!

I hardly dared ask the question, but I knew I had to. 'And what about the interpretation, Gueta? Was it accurate?' Of course, you know the answer because I wouldn't be telling this story if the interpretation had been wrong! What an amazing thing! The Holy Spirit inspired an Irish woman to speak an African language which she had never heard, or even heard of, and then gave the interpretation to an English man who had never heard of it either! God is faithful. His word is true. And his Spirit is still at work distributing his gifts as he himself determines. The atheists – and for that matter those Christians who say that the gifts are not for today – have no answer to experiences like these!

CHAPTER NINE

The Gift of Prophecy

We noticed in Chapter Seven that Harold Horton classifies the gift of prophecy as one of the 'gifts of inspiration' along with tongues and interpretation. For that reason we shall deal with it here. However, we will also consider in this chapter whether the gift might also contain an element of revelation as well as inspiration.

We have, of course, already considered the ministry of *prophets* in Chapter Three and there we saw that there is a difference between the Ephesians 4:11 gift of prophet and the simple gift of prophecy mentioned in 1 Corinthians 12:10. We noticed in fact that in the New Testament there appear to be three different levels of prophecy:

1. As from the outpouring of the Spirit on the day of Pentecost there is a sense in which *all* God's people prophesy (Acts 2:17-18). Quite simply, we are given God's Spirit that we might speak for him.
2. *Some*, but not all, of God's people exercise the gift of prophecy, the major purpose of which is edifying the church (1 Corinthians 12:10, cf. Romans 12:6).
3. *Some*, but not all, of those with the gift of prophecy (referred to in 2 above) are also Ephesians 4:11 prophets, which we discussed in Chapter Three.

In this chapter we'll concentrate on the gift referred to in (2) and will discuss its nature, value, and use.

The Nature of the Gift

In 1 Corinthians 14:1 Paul tells us that we should eagerly desire spiritual gifts, especially the gift of prophecy. In verses 3-4 he goes on to say:

> Everyone who prophesies speaks to men for their strengthening, encouragement and comfort... he who prophesies edifies the church.

Although this should not be taken as Paul's *definition* of the gift of prophecy, it does give us clear insight into his understanding of the basic nature of the gift. It involves speaking to people in order to strengthen them, encourage them, comfort them and build them up. Since this is a gift given by the Holy Spirit (1 Corinthians 12:10), the clear indication is that the message spoken will have come from him. To that extent we need to understand that this gift is supernatural, as we argued in Chapter Seven. On this basis we could say that the gift of prophecy is:

> *Speaking to people on behalf of God by the inspiration of the Holy Spirit for the strengthening, encouragement, comfort and edification of the church.*

This means that a simple prophecy need not contain any element of prediction or of revelation, but that it should nevertheless be understood to be quite different from preaching. We will consider each of these ideas in turn:

– Prophecy and prediction
– Prophecy and revelation
– Prophecy and preaching.

Prophecy and prediction

For many Christians the word 'prophecy' has come to mean nothing more than 'prediction' or 'foretelling the future'. This is probably due to the fact that the Scriptures of the Old Testament so eloquently predict in so many places the coming of the Lord Jesus Christ[83].

But, as we have already seen in Chapter Three, prophecy is not essentially predictive even in the Old Testament. Some of the prophets *were* foretellers, but their primary function was as people who spoke on behalf of God[84]. A true Old Testament prophet, then, was not necessarily someone who foretold the future – though he or she *might* do so by the inspiration of the Holy Spirit – but someone who was a spokesperson for God. And as we saw in Chapter Three, the same is true of the ministry of the Christian prophet in the New Testament. He or she brings revelation from God to his people, which *may* at times include a predictive element.

And the same appears to be true of the New Testament gift of prophecy. It is interesting that in 1 Corinthians 14:1-5 Paul makes no mention of prediction as part of the function of this gift. However, there is no good reason to suppose that a person exercising the simple gift of prophecy should not, under the inspiration of God the Holy Spirit, at times speak words which

---

[83] The Hebrew Bible consisted of three main divisions, the Law, the *Prophets* and the Writings; but in New Testament thought it was not *the Prophets* alone who had prophesied, for *all* the sections of the Old Testament were seen as pointing forward to the coming of the One upon whom all the Scriptures are focused (Luke 16:16; 24:25, 27, 44; Romans 1:2; 3:21 etc.).

[84] The Hebrew word '*nabi*' which is usually translated 'prophet' and the Greek word '*prophetes*' both mean fundamentally 'someone who speaks on behalf of another'. This point is clearly illustrated in Exodus 7:1-2 where Aaron is described as Moses' 'prophet' because he was going to speak on his behalf.

prove to be predictive. But that raises the question as to whether, when the simple gift of prophecy includes a measure of prediction or revelation, there are other gifts involved as well, like a word of wisdom or a word of knowledge. We will discuss this in the next section as we consider the question of prophecy and revelation.

Prophecy and revelation

We said earlier that the simple gift of prophecy need not contain any element of revelation because its essential purpose is for the strengthening, encouragement and comfort of the church (1 Corinthians 14:3). Before discussing this further, however, we need to distinguish two different ways in which the word 'revelation' may be used in connection with prophecy:

1. There is a sense in which the gift is *always* a form of revelation in that the person speaking is *revealing* by the Spirit what God wants to say to the church or to an individual at any given time.

2. This understanding of the word 'revelation' needs to be distinguished, however, from a quite different use of the word which signifies supernatural insight into events, past, present, or future, of which one would be otherwise unaware except by 'revelation' from the Holy Spirit.

As we now come to consider certain verses where Paul appears to link the gift of prophecy with revelation, it will be important to ask which of the two meanings of 'revelation' is intended in the verse in question. Indeed, if revelation in the second sense is found to be closely connected with the gift of prophecy, it may affect our understanding of the nature of gifts like a word of wisdom and a word of knowledge which were understood by Horton (and by many people since) to be the gifts which convey this type of revelation. We will consider this matter further in Chapter Fourteen. The verses we will briefly consider here are 1 Corinthians 13:2, 9, 14:6, 25, 30.

In 1 Corinthians 13:2 Paul clearly connects the gift of prophecy with the ability to 'fathom all mysteries and all knowledge'. It is interesting to note that the word Paul uses for 'mysteries' here is the same as the one used in Ephesians 3:3-6 where he speaks of the 'mystery of Christ' which had been made known to him 'by revelation' and which

> ...was not made known to men in other generations as it has now been *revealed* by the Spirit... (v.5).

Paul, therefore, appears to understand a mystery to be something that is hidden until it is *revealed* by the Spirit. If this is the sense in which he is using it in 1 Corinthians 13:2, it is clear that the gift of prophecy is at least in some way linked with supernatural revelation[85].

Further examples are to be found in 1 Corinthians 14 where revelation is connected with prophecy in vv. 6, 24-25, and 29-30. However, in v. 6 the link between prophecy and revelation is far from conclusive as the verse could well be understood to distinguish between them rather than to connect them. And the passage in vv. 29-32 may reasonably be interpreted to mean that revelation is connected with the Ephesians 4:11 gift of *prophet* rather than the simple gift of prophecy[86].

---

[85] A similar idea seems to be conveyed in vv. 9-10 where Paul talks of our prophesying 'in part' until perfection comes and the imperfect disappears. Compared with that final day when we shall see 'face to face' (v.12) we see at present only 'a poor reflection'. Our knowledge is far from complete, even with the revelation gained by prophetic insight.

[86] This is by no means certain, however. In the overall context of 1 Corinthians 14, it is quite possible that Paul is using the word 'prophet' to

But that leaves vv. 24-25 where Paul says that if an unbeliever comes in while people are prophesying, 'he will be convinced by all that he is a sinner and will be judged by all, and *the secrets of his heart will be laid bare...'*. This surely seems to suggest that an element of supernatural revelation is to be expected when the simple gift of prophecy is exercised.

The answer to the question we raised earlier, therefore, seems to be that at least some NT passages seem to indicate that supernatural revelation may well form part of the simple gift of prophecy. If this understanding is correct, then the idea that, if a prophecy contains a supernatural revelation, another gift such as a word of wisdom or a word of knowledge must be working along with it, is clearly mistaken. It would seem that the gift of prophecy *in itself* has the potential for revelation of a supernatural character. Indeed, we can be by no means certain that the gifts of a word of wisdom and a word of knowledge are 'gifts of revelation', as we shall see in Chapter Fourteen.

It may well be wise, therefore, to retain an element of revelation in our understanding of the gift of prophecy itself[87]. In doing so, however, we are not insisting that all prophecy will contain revelation of a supernatural kind. It may well simply speak for the strengthening, encouragement and comfort of the church. But that raises the important question as to how, if at all, it differs from preaching.

mean someone with the gift of prophecy, rather than an Ephesians 4:11 prophet.

[87] And even if the gifts of a word of wisdom and knowledge are revelation gifts (as Horton suggests), there is no reason to suppose that prophecy itself may not also be classed as a revelation gift. It is important that we avoid the temptation to classify the gifts too rigidly. Some gifts may well 'overlap' others in the way they function.

Prophecy and preaching

Because of the simple description of prophecy given in 1 Corinthians 14:3 some have understandably but mistakenly assumed that prophecy is to be equated with preaching or teaching. On this basis one leading Bible teacher claimed to possess the gift of prophecy because by his teaching ministry he was 'speaking on behalf of God'. And indeed he was, but he was not prophesying!

The ministry of the prophet is quite clearly distinguished from that of the teacher in such verses as Ephesians 4:11 and 1 Corinthians 12:29. The Old Testament prophets may well have preached as well as prophesied. A prophet may well be a capable preacher, and conversely the preacher's sermon may very well contain an element of the prophetic. But the two separate gifts must not be confused, though in practice they may sometimes be blended.

True preaching expresses the mind of God by the exposition of Holy Scripture. True prophecy expresses the mind of God *independent* of Holy Scripture, yet always in accordance with it. Good preaching will be no less inspired by the Holy Spirit than prophecy, but the content of its message comes from God through the Scriptures. The message given by prophecy comes from God direct and is therefore likely to be more specific.

This is by no means to say that if we have prophecy we have no need of teaching! Each of the gifts is given for a purpose and the church is in need of every one of them. There is no substitute whatsoever for the proclamation of sound doctrine by the anointed exposition of Holy Scripture, but those who are privileged to exercise such a ministry are not thereby exempted from the scriptural exhortation to 'be eager to prophesy' (1 Corinthians 14:39).

Prophecy, then, is speaking on behalf of God by the direct and immediate inspiration of the Holy Spirit, independent of Scripture, but always in accordance with it. God is not the author of confusion. The Holy Spirit will inspire nothing today that is contradictory to what he has already inspired in Scripture.

Now that we have clarified the relationship between prophecy and prediction, revelation, and preaching, we are hopefully in a better position to offer a more adequate description of the gift. From what we have seen, the gift of prophecy is:

> *speaking on behalf of God by the supernatural inspiration of the Holy Spirit for the strengthening, encouragement and comfort of the church. It may at times contain elements of revelation or even prediction, but must be distinguished from the ministry of the teacher whose message comes from God by way of the Scriptures.*

This description of the gift indicates something of its importance to which we shall now turn our attention in more detail.

The Value of the Gift

It is clear from such verses as 1 Corinthians 12:31 that some gifts of the Spirit are of greater value than others. Although we are not told specifically what the 'greater gifts' are it would seem that the criterion for the value of any particular gift is the measure in which it edifies the church (1 Corinthians 14:5). The motive for exercising any of the gifts should always be love (1 Corinthians 13), and if we love our fellow-Christians we will want them to be edified.

Accordingly, the gift of prophecy must be valued very highly because the person who prophesies edifies the church (1 Corinthians 14:4). For this reason, we are commanded to 'eagerly desire spiritual gifts, especially the gift of prophecy' (1 Corinthians 14:1, cf. 14:39). A comparison of this verse with 1 Corinthians

12:31 would seem to indicate that prophecy is undoubtedly one of the 'greater gifts' referred to.

However, while recognising the potential value of the gift for the edification of the church, Paul makes it clear that the operation of the gift is by no means infallible. This is because, although the gift comes from God himself, it is exercised by fallible human beings! Prophetic utterances are to be 'weighed carefully' or 'judged' (1 Corinthians 14:29). The gift must not be despised, but it must be proved and only that which is good adhered to (1 Thessalonians 5:20-21). This clearly indicates that prophetic utterance must not be considered infallible.

But this raises the question as to *how* prophecy is to be judged. There must be a standard by which to judge it! That standard is the teaching of Scripture. Passages like 2 Peter 1:19-21 and 2 Timothy 3:16 strongly support the view that the Bible is God's infallible word, inspired by the Holy Spirit. As such it stands above judgment and is itself the standard by which all later prophecy is to be measured. Since God does not contradict himself, any manifestation of the gift of prophecy which is not in accord with Holy Scripture is, therefore, not inspired by the Spirit who inspired the Scriptures[88]. This fact seems to be totally ignored by those who teach that they no longer need the Bible on the grounds that they are instructed through the gifts of the Spirit.

But if a prophetic word is not in line with the Scriptures, where has it come from? The answer to this is that a prophecy may come from any one of three possible sources. Genuine prophecy is, of course, inspired by the Holy Spirit. Scriptural examples can be found in such passages as 2 Samuel 23:2, Jeremiah 1:9 and Acts 19:6 and 21:11. It is possible, however, for a man to prophesy from his own spirit as in Jeremiah 23:16 and Ezekiel 13:2-3. Worse still,

---

[88] We must, of course, be sure that our *interpretation* of Scripture is correct when we make such judgments.

144

prophecy may be inspired by an evil spirit as Paul indicates by his teaching in 1 Corinthians 12:1-3. Finally, perhaps we should mention that a prophecy inspired largely by the Holy Spirit may contain an element of the human spirit from time to time.

Prophecy, then, is certainly one of the greater gifts because of its value in edifying the church. It is not, however, infallible and must be judged in accordance with its conformity to Holy Scripture. When touching an area outside the scope of Scripture, as in the case of more specific revelation concerning the mind of God for an individual, or for an assembly of God's people, its inspiration must be judged (1 Corinthians 14:29). Having then briefly assessed the value of the gift according to the scriptures, we will now turn our attention to its use.

The Use of the Gift

As we have already seen, prophecy is one of the 'greater gifts'. God encourages us to desire it eagerly and it is certainly his intention that it should be in evidence in his church. The exercise of the gift of prophecy is preferable to the use of the gift of tongues (unless accompanied by the gift of interpretation) as far as Christian believers are concerned (1 Corinthians 14:5). It is also more beneficial to the unbeliever if he should happen to come into the meeting (1 Corinthians 14:23-25). Consequently Paul gives clear instructions for its use which are to be found largely in 1 Corinthians 14.

First, those who do not yet possess the gift are encouraged to desire it eagerly. The chapter both begins and ends with this exhortation (vv. 1 and 39). In Chapter Fifteen we will say more about how the gifts of the Spirit may be received, but it is important to notice here that if God commands us to desire something eagerly it seems quite likely that he want us to have it! He is the author of neither confusion nor frustration. He *satisfies* the longing soul, and to withhold from us indefinitely that which he commands us to desire would seem contrary to his divine nature.

Once we have received the gift we are to exercise it in faith (Romans 12:6). That the gift is subject to our control is clear from such verses as 1 Corinthians 14:32 and from the fact that specific instructions are given for its use. If the use of the gift were only dependent upon the Holy Spirit himself such instructions would be both inappropriate and unnecessary.

Because of our responsibility for the control of the gift God has given us, Paul teaches that we are able to:

– regulate the number of prophetic utterances in any one meeting (14:29)
– cease prophesying if something is revealed to someone else (14:30)
– prophesy rather than speak in tongues if unbelievers are present (14:23-25).

Our ability to control the gift also implies that we are responsible for the terminology in which we express the message that God has given us. Since we are not infallible, we would be wise to phrase our prophecies in the third person rather than the first, to talk of God as *he* and not *I*. In other words it would be better to say, 'The Lord will...' than to say, 'I will do this, says the Lord'. We may believe that God has given us something to say, but we are not God, and we should not talk as if we were! 'I will do this, O My children, says the Lord' and similar expressions, were appropriate for those prophesying on the infallible level of Holy Scripture, but appear quite inappropriate in the mouths of some exercising the gift of prophecy today! 'The Lord will...' would be far more suitable phraseology.

Perhaps, too, we should mention that prophecy need not be expressed in sixteenth century English! This is, fortunately, less common than it was, but I am amazed that some Christians still prophesy (and pray) in this way, no doubt because of their love of the language of the Authorised (King James) Version of the Bible. But the language of the Spirit is not five hundred years old! It is not the Holy Spirit who inspires us to use this terminology, but the traditions in which we are accustomed to hear the gift exercised. This is not to say that such utterances are *not* inspired, but rather that they would lose nothing in inspiration if they were expressed in modern English!

It's also important to remember that the level of inspiration of a prophecy is not determined by its length! A few words spoken under the inspiration of the Spirit can have a powerful effect. Some years ago, in one of the ministers' business sessions of our Assemblies of God General Council, the chairman decided that we should interrupt the business in order to spend some time in prayer together. At that particular time I was facing certain difficulties which were causing me some anxiety and about which nobody present knew anything. As we moved into small groups for prayer, one of our pastors, Fred Durrant, came up to me.

'David', he said, 'I have a word from the Lord for you'.
'Yes', I replied, eager to hear what it might be.
'It's very simple', said Fred. 'The Lord just wants me to tell you this: David, it's all right!'

David, it's all right! Just a few words! But at that moment I felt every bit of anxiety drain out of me from the top of my head to the tips of my toes! And it *was* all right! The things that had concerned me turned out to amount to nothing. Fred's prophecy was short, but it was very powerful. We should certainly not hold back from bringing a word from the Lord because we think it isn't long enough! In fact, some prophetic words seem to decrease in inspiration the longer they go on!

147

Finally, those who exercise the gift of prophecy should remember the purpose for which it is given. It is for the 'strengthening, encouragement and comfort of the church' (1 Corinthians 14:3-4). Paul's words here certainly do not suggest rebuke. The gift is not intended for that purpose. Neither does he mention guidance. Of course, some Christians have received wonderful guidance from God through the gift of prophecy, but we must always remember that as sons of God it is our privilege to be led personally by the Spirit of God (Romans 8:14). Guidance received through prophecy should simply serve as confirmation of something that God has already spoken to us about in our hearts (Acts 13:1-3). See also Paul's attitude to prophecy in this connection in Acts 21:1-15 to which we referred in Chapter Three.

In conclusion, then, prophecy is certainly a wonderful gift. It is an amazing privilege to speak on God's behalf to his people under the inspiration of the Holy Spirit. Yet it is a gift that God tells us we should eagerly desire. The purpose for which God has filled us with his Spirit is that we might prophesy (Acts 2:16ff). There is a sense, as we have seen, in which we can all do that. We may not all be Ephesians 4:11 prophets, but we can all in some measure speak for God, and we can – and should – eagerly desire to strengthen and encourage the church through the gift of prophecy. Jesus said that John the Baptist was the greatest of all the prophets (Matthew 11:11) *yet he who is least in the kingdom... is greater than he!* One of the greatest privileges of being part of God's kingdom is that we can prophesy!

CHAPTER TEN

Gifts of Healing

The Bible has a great deal to say about God's power and willingness to heal the sick and the 'gifts of healing' referred to in 1 Corinthians12:9 are just one aspect of this. For this reason this chapter will not only look at the *gifts* of healing, but will also seek to cover some major aspects of a more general nature with regard to what the Bible teaches about healing in general. We will consider the subject under the following headings:

- Different kinds of healing
- Our healing God
- Healing for Christians – James 5
- Gifts of healing
- Why some are not healed yet
- The ultimate healing.

Different Kinds of Healing

The basic meaning of the verb 'to heal' is that of restoring a sick or wounded person to health. In a great many cases we know that healing takes place naturally. The chemical processes that God has built into our bodies do their work and restore, for example, a cut finger to its original condition. Sometimes a little first aid or medical attention will hasten the cure or alleviate suffering while the natural processes are taking place. At the very least such treatment may prevent additional complications that might otherwise arise.

Of course, there are occasions when, humanly speaking, the condition is so serious that without medical treatment the natural processes alone will be insufficient to restore the person to health. On these occasions most people are content to entrust themselves to the skill and care of the medical profession, and Christians are grateful to God for the restoration to health that both natural and medical healing can bring[89].

Sadly, however, there are those conditions for which there is as yet no known medical cure, and it is in these circumstances that people sometimes seek healing elsewhere. Opinions vary as to the wisdom of getting involved with some forms of what is often called *alternative medicine*. Some may be quite harmless, but there are some forms of healing that in the long run do far more harm than good! A visit to the local faith-healer or spiritualist medium, for example, may prove physically beneficial, but what so many people do not realise is that these healings are brought about by satanic power. We will say more about this in Chapter Thirteen when we discuss the question of the reality of a satanic counterfeit of spiritual gifts[90].

In my view, therefore, for the Christian there is only one wise 'alternative' to natural or medical healing. That is the healing which is provided supernaturally by God himself. There is absolutely no

---

[89] Although there is a strong emphasis on supernatural healing in the New Testament, it also gives broad support to the work of the medical profession. Jesus himself said that the sick need a doctor (Mark 2:17) and Paul refers to 'our dear friend Luke, the doctor' (Colossians 4:14). He also recommends Timothy to take a little wine for the sake of his frequent stomach problems (1 Timothy 5:23). This is clearly medicinal. Other relevant passages are Luke 10:29-37 and possibly Revelation 3:18.

[90] See also the sub-section headed **The reference to idol-worship** in Chapter Seven.

need whatsoever to seek healing from any other source than from God himself. *Divine* healing[91] is available to God's children.

Our Healing God

As evidence for the fact that the healing of our sicknesses is the privilege of the people of God we may point first to God's promise in Exodus 15:26. Israel had been brought out of Egypt by a supernatural act of divine deliverance. The Egyptians had perished beneath the waters of the Red Sea. As a further demonstration of his mighty power the Lord had made sweet the bitter waters of Marah (Exodus 15:23-25). God was showing his people that he was able to meet all their needs. Then came the reassuring promise:

> If you listen carefully to the voice of the Lord your God, and do what is right in his eyes... I will not bring on you any of the diseases I brought on the Egyptians; for I am the Lord who heals you (v.26).

Some, of course, did not meet the conditions of the promise, and were therefore unable to receive God's provision of healing. But this in no way invalidates the promise. It rather confirms it. It was God's will for his people to be healthy. Sickness was a curse, and it resulted from disobedience (Deuteronomy 28:59-61).

God's willingness to heal is also confirmed in the ministry of our Lord Jesus Christ who

> went around doing good and healing all who were under the devil's power (Acts 10:38).

---

[91] As noted above, we do not deny the efficacy of natural or medical healing. Indeed, we would see the hand of God at work in such healing. But when we use the term *divine* healing we mean the removal of disease or infirmity by the supernatural and unaided power of God.

The Gospels provide many examples of this (Matthew 4:23-24, 8:16, 9:35, Mark 6:56, Luke 6:17-19, for example).

And when Jesus sent his disciples out to preach he commanded them to *cure every kind of disease and sickness* (Matthew 10:1, 7-8). This commission to heal was not limited to the time of his earthly ministry. In his final words to his disciples before his ascension Jesus commanded his disciples to go into all the world and preach the gospel. Those who believed would cast out demons, speak with new tongues and heal the sick in his name (Mark 16:15-20).

The fact that they did so is well illustrated in the book of Acts. In Acts 3:7-9 a lame man was healed in the name of Jesus, resulting in the salvation of thousands of people (Acts 4:4). In Acts 4:30 the early church prayed that God would stretch out his hand to heal in the name of Jesus. In Acts 5:14-16 multitudes were healed in the streets of Jerusalem. Miracles were performed in the ministry of Stephen (Acts 6:8) and the sick were healed as Philip preached the gospel to the Samaritans (Acts 8:6-8). Peter was used to heal the sick and to raise the dead in Acts 9:33-42. At Paul's command a cripple leapt to his feet and walked (Acts 14:8-10), diseases departed (Acts 19:12) and the dead were raised (Acts 20:9-12). And it does not seem that the power to heal was ever withdrawn, for in the very last chapter of Acts the sick are still being healed (Acts 28:8-9).

All the healing miracles mentioned in the last paragraph are wonderful examples of the gifts of healing at work, and it is noteworthy that most, and possibly all, of them were performed on people who were not yet Christians. In James 5:14-16, however, explicit instructions are given to Christians who need healing. We will consider this next.

Healing for Christians – James 5

The healing which takes place in James 5 after the anointing with oil and prayer of the elders is an example of divine healing, but it should probably not be seen as a case of the gifts of healing at work. I say this because spiritual gifts are distributed to individual Christians as the Holy Spirit determines (1 Corinthians 12:11), and *not all* have the gifts of healing (1 Corinthians 12:30). But it would seem that *all* elders are expected to pray the prayer of faith that the sick might be healed in the name of the Lord (James 5:14-15).

Despite this, however, we will consider James 5 briefly here because it is an important example of divine healing and is probably the main way taught in the New Testament for Christians to receive healing from God. In James 5:13-16 we read:

> 13 Is any one of you in trouble? He should pray. Is anyone happy? Let him sing songs of praise. 14 Is any one of you sick? He should call the elders of the church to pray over him and anoint him with oil in the name of the Lord. 15 And the prayer offered in faith will make the sick person well; the Lord will raise him up. If he has sinned he will be forgiven. 16 Therefore confess your sins to each other and pray for each other so that you may be healed. The prayer of a righteous man is powerful and effective.

This is probably the clearest promise of healing for Christians to be found anywhere in the New Testament. It is important, therefore, that we understand what James is saying. We will work through the key points in the passage systematically.

First, we should note that the passage applies to *any one of you* (v.14). Since James's letter was written to Christians we can confidently say that his teaching here applies to all Christians without exception.

Secondly, it is interesting that the sick person is told to *call* the elders of the church (v.14). This may well suggest that the person

James has in mind is at home in bed, rather than in the church meeting. This idea is backed up by the fact that the elders are to pray *over* him (v.14) and by the promise that the Lord will *raise him up* (v.15), which may suggest that the sick person is lying down.

Thirdly, notice that the *elders* are to be called for. As we saw in Chapter Five, in New Testament times the elders were the pastoral team of church leaders. The sick person is told to call for *the elders* not *an elder*. The idea seems to be that they should *all* be there. As church leaders their presence represents the church as a whole and the sick person is reminded that they are not alone, but that they are part of a family, God's people. Furthermore, together the elders should be in a better position to hear what God may be saying in this situation and accordingly to pray in faith.

Then we are told that the elders are to *anoint* the sick person *with oil* (v.14). The word 'anoint' is strongly connected both with healing and with the Holy Spirit in the New Testament (cf. Luke 4:18ff., Acts 10:38) and the oil here is almost certainly intended to by symbolic of the Holy Spirit himself[92]. This symbol is a reminder to the sick person, and to the elders, of the Holy Spirit's healing power. The healing is not dependent on human skill or ability, but on the supernatural power of almighty God. This symbol of the Holy Spirit's presence may also serve as a reminder of that final healing that will take place when the Spirit of him who raised Jesus from the dead, and who lives in us, will one day raise our mortal bodies from the dead[93] (Romans 8:11).

The next thing to notice is that the elders are told to do this anointing *in the name of the Lord* (v.14). In this connection it is

---

[92] There is no suggestion that the oil is intended to be medicinal. Although olive oil is medically beneficial in some circumstances, it is hardly likely that James thought that it could cure *all* diseases!

[93] See also my comments below on *The Lord will raise him up.*

important to realise that this is not to be thought of as a magic formula! Saying 'In the name of Jesus' after our prayers is no way of guaranteeing their answer! In Bible times to do something in someone's name meant that you did it with their approval and authority. Even Jesus himself said that he could do only what he saw the Father doing (John 5:19). He had come in his Father's name (John 5:43) and that meant with his Father's authority. That authority sprang from the fact that he only did what his Father told him to do. In my view, healing the sick in Jesus' name (here in James 5 and also in Mark 16: 17-18) means more than using his name in our prayers. It means first hearing what he is saying in each particular situation.

That leads us to the next main point, that *the prayer offered in faith will make the sick person well* (v.15). Since faith comes by hearing, and hearing by the word of God (Romans 10:17) it seems quite likely that the elders will only pray in real faith if they have first heard from God on the matter. It's one thing to have faith that God *can* heal. It's quite another to pray in full assurance that he *will* heal immediately. For that kind of faith we need a word from the Lord. Notice, too, that according to James it is the elders who are to have faith, not the sick person. It is interesting that in the ministry of Jesus, wherever faith is mentioned in connection with healing, it is always the person bringing the request who is required to have faith, not necessarily the sick person.

And so the prayer offered in faith will make the sick person well and *the Lord will raise him up* (v.15). What exactly does James mean by this? Clearly the first thing we are to expect is an immediate miracle of healing. This is obviously the primary intention behind what James is saying. The sick person will make an immediate recovery. We can thank God for the many times this has happened in answer to believing prayer, but we must also honestly recognise that this is not what always happens. In my view, when there is no immediate sign of improvement after prayer, the sick person should be encouraged to go on believing and to expect either a gradual or even a delayed healing.

But that raises yet another possibility. How long might the healing be delayed? Indeed, what if the healing is to be delayed until the final resurrection? Although this suggestion may appear at first sight to be lacking in faith, we need to remember another passage in James at the end of Chapter 4:

> 13 Now listen, you who say, "Today or tomorrow we will go to this or that city, spend a year there, carry on business and make money". 14 Why, you do not even know what will happen tomorrow. What is your life? You are a mist that appears for a little while and then vanishes. 15 Instead you ought to say, "If it is the Lord's will, we will live..." (James 4:13-15).

This passage makes it perfectly clear that we do not know if it is God's will for us to be alive tomorrow! The promise of healing in James 5, therefore, must be balanced by these verses. However, even if an immediate healing is not the Lord's will, we still have the certain promise that *the Lord will raise us up*, for the word that is used here is the one that is used for the resurrection of our body (1 Corinthians 15:35ff). But we will say more about this in the last section of this chapter, headed *The Ultimate Healing.*

Finally, still in James 5, we need to note the statement *If he has sinned, he will be forgiven* (v.15). This seems to imply that the person's sickness may have been caused by his or her personal sin. But the word 'if' also implies that it need not be! We discuss this further under the heading *Why some are not healed yet* but for now it is enough to note the possibility that sickness *might* be caused by personal sin. If so, the remedy is clear. We are to confess our sins in order that we might be healed (v.16). Thank God, if we confess our sins, he is faithful and just, and will forgive us our sins and purify us from all unrighteousness (1 John 1:9).

But we must now turn from James 5 to the specific subject of the gifts of healing and, as we shall see, if the instructions in James 5 are addressed to Christians, the gifts of healing are probably intended to be largely for those who are not.

Gifts of Healing

I have already mentioned that the passage in James 5 should not be considered as an example of the gifts of healing. Another reason for saying this is that in James 5:15 it is very clear that it is the *Lord* who heals, whereas with the gifts of healing it seems as though there is a sense in which it is the *believer* who does the healing!

Of course we need to tread very carefully here. In the final analysis it is God and God alone who heals, and those who are healed by the power of God should be grateful to God alone and not to the person who was instrumental in their healing. This is of very great importance. But when this basic truth is held in perspective we discover that there is a sense in which the Bible says that it is the Christian who heals.

For example, Jesus did not tell his disciples to *pray* for the sick, but to *heal* them (Matthew 10:1, 8; Luke 10:9). When Peter addressed the cripple at the Beautiful Gate of the Temple (Acts 3), his words were 'What I have I give you!' *He* had something and *he* gave it, and as a result the cripple was gloriously healed! Of course it was the Lord who healed him, because what Peter gave him had first been given to Peter by the Lord himself. Peter simply passed it on. It was undoubtedly in this sense that Jesus told his disciples to 'heal the sick' in the verse already referred to. They had freely received; they were to *give* freely (Matthew 10:8).

So today the Holy Spirit may give gifts of healing to a Christian who in turn may give healing to the sick. This does not mean, of course, that a person possessing the gifts of healing can heal everybody. He is not said to have *the gift* of healing, but *gifts* of healing. The word is in the plural both in 1 Corinthians 12:9 and in 12:30.

It seems likely too that this is because God gives a separate gift for each individual case of sickness. So Peter received from the Spirit the gift of the cripple's healing which he in turn passed on to the cripple. That this was not just an isolated incident and that Peter was in fact given '*gifts* of healing' is indicated by the fact that he was subsequently used to heal a variety of other people (Acts 5:15-16; 9:32-35).

If this analysis of the use of the plural word 'gifts' is correct[94] it would seem to imply that just as each separate gift of the Spirit is given as the Spirit wills so is each separate gift of healing. A person possessing the gifts of healing, therefore, is able to heal only as and when he receives from the Spirit the gift of a particular individual's healing.

Now since provision is made in James 5 for Christians who are sick, it seems reasonable to assume that the main purpose for the gifts of healing is in connection with the unconverted. The healing of the sick was frequently used in New Testament times to draw people within the sound of the gospel (Matthew 4:23-25; Mark 3:7-8; John 6:2; Acts 3 and 4; 5:12-16; 8:6). It was also a demonstration of the authenticity of the gospel (Mark 16:15-18; Acts 4:29-30) and undoubtedly had the effect of turning people to the gospel (Acts 3 and 4:4; 8:6-7; 9:34-35).

So the purpose of the gifts of healing is not just the alleviation of physical suffering but the meeting of a deeper need, the forgiveness of sins. The helpless paralytic needed to hear more than 'Rise up and walk'. That he was able to do so at Christ's

---

[94] An alternative explanation is that the word 'gifts' is in the plural because some people seem more successful in the healing of certain particular diseases. However, there seems no biblical basis for this view.

command merely confirmed the Saviour's authority to utter those far more important words 'Your sins are forgiven' (Luke 5:18-26).

Sadly, human beings seem always to be more conscious of the needs of their bodies than of their souls. But if the gifts of healing can bring people under the sound of the message that Christ died for our *sins*, and provided that the so-called 'gospel of healing' does not become a substitute for the true gospel of repentance, their value can hardly be overestimated.

As we have already seen, the Book of Acts provides abundant examples of the use of the gifts of healing in connection with the preaching of the gospel. It is in Mark 16:15-20, however, that we find our Lord's clear-cut promise that healing is to be one of the miracle-signs given in confirmation of the gospel message:

> 15 He said to them, "Go into all the world and preach the good news to all creation. 16 Whoever believes and is baptized will be saved, but whoever does not believe will be condemned. 17 And these signs will accompany those who believe: In my name they will drive out demons; they will speak in new tongues; 18 they will pick up snakes with their hands; and when they drink deadly poison it will not hurt them at all; they will place their hands on sick people and they will get well".
>
> 19 After the Lord Jesus had spoken to them, he was taken up into heaven and sat at the right hand of God. 20 Then the disciples went out and preached everywhere, and the Lord worked with them and confirmed his word by the signs that accompanied it.

It is in these verses, then, that we find the key to the use of gifts of healing today. Three things are noteworthy:

First, it should be noticed that the promise is given largely in the context of pioneer evangelism, and although this by no means implies that they cannot occur in other situations, it does suggest that this is the area in which we can most frequently expect them.

Second, the exercise of these gifts is conditional upon faith (v.17), particularly on the part of those who are laying hands on the sick. The point of the sign is to help an *unbeliever* to believe. So the responsibility for believing must, of necessity, lie largely with the *believing* preacher rather than with the sick *unbeliever*! Evangelists should *expect* miracles of healing to confirm the preaching of the gospel. How we thank God for the wonderful things that are happening around the world as God continues to confirm his word with accompanying signs!

Finally, the gift must be exercised in the name of Jesus (v.17). Not that his name need necessarily be audibly mentioned (cf. Acts 14:10), but with *his* authority[95], for *his* glory, for *his* kingdom and in obedience to *his* command his servants may still lay hands on the sick *and they will get well.*

Why some are not healed – yet!

Although, as we have seen, the Bible gives us great encouragement to have faith for healing, we know from our experience that not everybody is healed, and we naturally wonder why. There is no simple answer to this, but in this section I will offer some pointers which may shed some light on this difficult subject. However, before we consider why some are not healed, we need first to examine what the Bible tells us about where sickness comes from and why people get sick in the first place.

---

[95] See my comments in the last section on the meaning of doing things in Jesus' name.

Why we get sick in the first place

We will seek to answer this question by first asking why there is sickness in the world at all, and then by considering why we ourselves may be sick.

Why sickness is in the world at all

To answer this question we need to go back to the very beginning of the Bible. This tells us that when God made man and woman he made them perfect and put them in a perfect creation. Everything God made was 'very good' (Genesis 1:31). It is clear that Adam and Eve were not only morally, but also physically perfect. At first there was no sin, neither was there sickness in the Garden of Eden. But when Adam and Eve disobeyed God, we read in Genesis 3 how he placed a curse upon the earth. As a result, sickness and death entered the world.

Paul tells us more about this in Romans 8 where we read that the *creation was subjected to frustration* by the will of God in the knowledge that ultimately it would be *liberated from its bondage to decay* (Romans 8:20-21). Meanwhile, *the whole creation has been groaning as in the pains of childbirth right up to this present time* (v.22), and we Christians are waiting patiently for *the redemption of our bodies* (vv.23-25).

This means that as a result of that first sin in the world the following things happened:

- God cursed the whole physical creation
- As a result sickness and death entered the world
- This state of affairs continues to this present day
- All humankind (including Christians) suffer along with the rest of creation until the Lord returns

- Meanwhile we have the Holy Spirit as a 'firstfruits' (foretaste) of the age to come
- Then our bodies will be redeemed and the creation itself will be set free.

The biblical answer then to why there is sickness in the world is that both sickness and death entered the world because of the curse God placed upon it when Adam and Eve sinned.

Why *we* get sick

The first part of the answer to this question is to be found in what we have just said. We may be sick simply because **we are living in a fallen world** and on most occasions this is probably the only reason for our sickness. We catch a cold or get the 'flu' simply because we live in a world where colds and influenza exist and our bodies are not immune to these things[96].

But the Bible does reveal other possibilities. We may also be sick because of our **irresponsible behaviour**. Unwise eating habits or lack of healthy exercise can either make us ill or lower our resistance to disease. It is interesting that God's promise to keep the Israelites healthy was based on the condition that they kept all his commandments and these included instructions concerning their diet! They also included the command to rest on the Sabbath and, although the New Testament set Christians free from a legalistic observance of the seventh day of the week, the *principle* of taking regular rest is surely clearly established in the Scriptures. We do not glorify God by wearing ourselves out in his service!

Yet another possible cause of personal sickness is **personal sin**. The Old Testament teaches us that sometimes God punishes sinners by inflicting them with sickness. Israel is promised health if she will obey God's laws (Exodus 15: 26) and threatened with disease if she disobeys (Deuteronomy 28:58-60).   Cases are recorded where individuals were smitten with leprosy because of their sin (e.g. Miriam in Numbers 12:10, Gehazi in 2 Kings 5:25-27, and Uzziah in 2 Chronicles 26:16-21). On the other hand, in the Book of Job it is clear that personal sin is *not necessarily* the cause of personal sickness. Job was sick although he was a righteous man.

In the New Testament we see something very similar, for although there are cases where sickness is caused by personal sin there are also passages which make it clear that it need not be. Jesus says to the man at the Pool of Bethesda, 'Sin no more lest a worse thing come upon you' (John 5:14) and in Acts Herod is smitten with worms and dies because of his pride (12:21-23). Elymas is stricken with blindness for resisting the Gospel (13:11). The Corinthians are told that some of them are sick as a result of their behaviour at the Communion (1 Corinthians 11:30), and James 5:15 implies that sickness may be connected with sin.

Other NT passages, however, clearly show that sickness is not necessarily caused by personal sin. The passage in John 9:1ff. concerning the healing of the man blind from birth indicates that although the disciples thought that his sickness was the result of personal or parental sin (v.2) Jesus denied this assumption in the following verse.   Further, the passage in James 5:14ff., which implies that sickness *may be* connected with sin, also affords clear evidence that it *need not be*, for forgiveness is promised to the sick '*if* he has committed sins' (v.15).

So we should certainly not assume that if someone is ill they must have sinned in some way. However, if sin is the cause, then it should be confessed and forgiveness and healing asked for. Christ's sacrificial death atoned for sin. If we confess our sin God

---

[96]This includes the physical deterioration that everyone experiences with old age. Paul says that though outwardly we are 'wasting away', yet inwardly we are being renewed day by day (2 Corinthians 4:16).

will forgive us our sin (1 John 1:9). As we have seen, James 5:15-16 suggests that confession of sin makes way for healing.

Finally, the Bible reveals that some sickness is the result of **the activity of Satan** or of evil spirits. In Acts 10:38 Peter refers to Jesus as *healing all who were oppressed by the devil*, and although this should not be taken to mean that all sickness is of satanic origin, it certainly implies that some is. This is confirmed by such passages as Matthew 12:22 and Mark 9:17 and 25, where blindness, deafness and dumbness are said to have been caused by evil spirits.

Another interesting example is Luke 13:11 where Jesus attributes curvature of the spine to both a 'spirit of infirmity' (v.11) and to 'Satan' (v.16). Presumably the spirit is seen as an agent of Satan. There is no suggestion that the woman's condition had been caused by her sin; rather, as a 'daughter of Abraham' she had a right to be set free from her long-standing affliction without a moment's delay – without even waiting for the Sabbath day to pass (v.16). Sickness is seen as a bondage from Satan[97] from which Jesus had come to set people free (cf. Acts 10:38).

So sickness may be the result of:

– our own irresponsible behaviour
– personal sin
– satanic attack

---

[97] It is important to notice here that there is no suggestion that the woman was demon-possessed. A clear distinction is made between demon possession and sickness in Matthew 4:24. It is noteworthy that Jesus does not 'cast out' the demon in this situation. He simply places his hands on her and tells her that she is set free from her infirmity (v 12).

or it may simply come because we live in a fallen world. But we must now turn our attention to the question we raised at the beginning of this section, why some are not healed.

Why some are not healed

Having outlined some of the reasons that people get sick, we are now in a better position to consider why some are not healed despite the fact that the Bible encourages us to expect God to heal us. In this connection I am going to suggest five possible factors, any one of which might be the reason for a person not being healed:

– Refusal to bring one's life in line with God's word
– Failure to detect the satanic origin of a sickness
– Lack of faith
– When *physical* sickness is for our *spiritual* good
– The sovereignty of God

First, then, refusal to bring one's life in line with God's word may certainly be a reason for failure to be healed. This can range from the kind of things we mentioned when we talked earlier about irresponsible behaviour to a persistence in personal sin which may or may not have been the original cause of the sickness.

The examples we gave earlier were mainly cases where God sent sickness directly as a judgment on those who were sinning. However, it is probably more often the case that sickness results from sin *indirectly*. By this I mean that because of the way God has made the world there are certain consequences that result from certain actions. If we put our hand in the fire, we know it will be burned.

So if we are seeking healing, it is important to make sure that we are living according to God's word by only doing those things that we know he is pleased with, and by pursuing a sensible and healthy life-style. If we have been failing in this respect, thank God he will forgive us if we ask him to and if we are prepared to change our ways.

Another possible reason why people are not healed may be that the disease has a satanic origin and this has not been detected. We have already pointed out that *not all* sickness comes from Satan, as some have taught, for some sickness comes directly from God. However, where it is the result of demonic activity it should be rebuked in Jesus' name. It must surely be the responsibility of those ministering healing to recognise the source of the sickness, perhaps through the use of the gift of discerning of spirits (cf. Chapter Thirteen), rather than that of the person who is sick.

But where a demonic source is detected, the Christian has no need to fear. The New Testament teaches us that by his victorious death on the cross Jesus has conquered Satan and all his forces. Colossians 2:15 tells us that by the cross Jesus disarmed the powers and authorities (the demons). He made a public spectacle of them, triumphing over them by the cross. He is far above all of them and everything is under his feet (Ephesians 1:21-22). And we are complete in him who is the head of all power and authority (Colossians 2:10). He has given us authority to overcome *all* the power of the enemy and nothing will harm us (Luke 10:19). In his name we have authority to deal with sickness caused by demons.

The next reason why some are not healed is lack of faith. This need not necessarily be on the part of the sick but it may be the person praying who lacks faith. We have already seen that it is the responsibility of the one ministering healing to have faith (Mark 16:17-18, James 5:14-15), and where this is absent we cannot expect an answer to prayer (James 1:6-7). It is all too easy for evangelists (and elders) to put all the responsibility for believing on the sick person when these verses indicate that it is *their* faith that will produce the healing. However, there is also a responsibility on the sick to have faith, as Jesus so often said *"Your* faith has healed you" (Matthew 9:22, Mark 10:52, Luke 17:19 etc). Indeed Mark 6:5-6 tells us that even Jesus could not do any miracles in his home town because of their lack of faith. Of course, some people lack faith simply because they have not heard the truths of God's word about healing. The remedy for this is regular reading of the Scriptures and sound biblical teaching[98].

My next suggestion as to why some people are not healed is for many Christians more difficult to accept. However, there is evidence in the Bible that God sometimes withholds healing when he knows that *physical* sickness will be for our *spiritual* good. In the Old Testament the book of Job is an outstanding example of this principle[99] and in the New Testament the writer to the Hebrews tells us that God disciplines[100] us for our good that we may share in his holiness (Hebrews 12:10-11). It is also possible, though by no means certain, that Paul's thorn in the flesh was a sickness (2 Corinthians 12:1-10). Whether it was or not, it is certainly a case of God allowing a physical problem because it would result in spiritual benefit.

Finally, we need always to remember that God is sovereign. His ways are higher than our ways and his thoughts than our thoughts. We cannot tell the Creator of the universe what he should do. The reason that some are not healed may well remain a mystery until that day when we see him face to face. Then we will fully know. Till then, we know in part and see only a poor reflection (1 Corinthians 13:9-12).

---

[98] We will say more on the subject of faith in Chapter Twelve.
[99] See also Genesis 32:22-32 where Jacob limped as a result of a mighty experience with God.
[100] We cannot rule out the possibility that sickness is in mind here. According to v.11 the discipline is painful and in v.6 discipline is connected with punishment. The Greek word used here is also sometimes used for sickness (cf. Mark 3:10, 5:29, 34, Luke 7:21).

We simply do not know why Jesus did not heal all the people at the Pool of Bethesda (John 5:1-9), or why Paul was sick in Galatia (Galatians 4:13) or why he left Trophimus ill in Miletus (2 Timothy 4:20) or why Epaphroditus was so ill he nearly died for the sake of God's work (Philippians 2:25-30). But we do know that our God is a healing God and that one day his promise to heal all his people will surely be fulfilled. But that is the subject for the final section of this chapter.

The Ultimate Healing

In the last section, under the sub-heading **Why sickness is in the world at all,** by comparing Romans 8 with the opening chapters of Genesis, we saw that sickness and death entered the world because of Adam's sin. But God has not left us without a ransom for sin! Jesus has died for us! And in doing so he has provided the ultimate remedy for sickness! By Christ's atoning death on the cross he has reconciled to God all those who believe. By faith in the sacrifice offered at Calvary repentant sinners are brought into right relationship with God. Their sins are washed away. Sin, the root cause of sickness, is atoned for. By restoring us to fellowship with our Maker, Christ has, by his death, made provision for the healing of our bodies. It is in this sense that healing may be rightly said to be 'in the atonement'[101].

This does not mean, however, that Christ died for our sicknesses in exactly the same way as he died for our sins. Adam's sin was the cause of *death*. We have the forgiveness of sins *now* but the final victory over *death* will not be ours until Jesus comes again (1 Corinthians 15:50-57). Similarly, Adam's sin was the cause of *sickness* in the world. But although we have the forgiveness of sins

---

[101] For detailed discussion of this, see my PhD thesis, *Healing and the Atonement,* Nottingham University, 1993.

now the final victory over *sickness* will not be ours until Jesus comes again.

Every healing we have now is only a foretaste of the age to come. At present we bear the likeness of the earthly man (Adam) but then we will bear the likeness of the man from heaven (1 Corinthians 15:49). Our bodies will be changed, in a flash, in the twinkling of an eye. The trumpet will sound and the dead will be raised and we shall be changed. Our bodies will be immortal and imperishable! They will be like *his* glorious body.

What a day! Then there will be no more sickness. This is the ultimate healing!

> The dwelling of God is with men, and he will live with them. They will be his people and God himself will be with them and be their God. He will wipe every tear from their eyes. There will be no more death, or mourning, or crying, or pain, for the old order of things has passed away (Revelation 21:3-4).

But until that day, although we may suffer along with the rest of creation, while we wait for our 'adoption as sons, the redemption of our bodies', we already have the firstfruits of the Spirit (Romans 8:18-27). And it is that same Holy Spirit who gives gifts of healing to his people, just as he determines (1 Corinthians 12:9-11).

CHAPTER ELEVEN

Miracles

When we considered the gifts of healing in the last chapter we found it necessary to distinguish between what the Bible teaches about healing in general and the specific 'gifts of healing' mentioned by Paul in 1 Corinthians 12. We saw that not all miracles of healing are manifestations of the gifts of healing. Similarly, as we now come to examine the gift of the working of miracles[102], we will see that not all miracles are manifestations of this particular gift. Most of this chapter will deal with the subject of miracles in general, but discussion of the spiritual gift will, of course, be included within it.

We will deal with the subject by seeking to answer the following questions:

– What is a miracle?
– Who can expect to do them?
– Why are miracles important?
– When do miracles happen?

What is a miracle?

Usually we use the word 'miracle' to refer to something that is beyond our understanding and which cannot be explained naturally. It is *super*-natural, *above* and *beyond* the natural. In line with this, the Oxford English Dictionary defines a miracle as a 'marvellous event due to some supernatural agency'. According to this definition *all* the spiritual gifts we are considering come under the

---

[102] NIV 'miraculous powers'.

category of miracle because they are all quite clearly marvellous events due to the supernatural agency of God the Holy Spirit. Yet only one of them is specifically described as 'the working of miracles' or 'miraculous powers'. This means that in the New Testament the word *miracle* is used in two distinct, but closely related ways:

1. In a general sense, to refer to *any* supernatural event
2. In a specific sense to refer to the spiritual gift.

Used in the first way, the word would include:

- All miracles performed directly by God without human agency[103]
- All manifestations of spiritual (supernatural) gifts[104]
- Miracles performed by the power of Satan[105].

Used in the second way, it refers only to *that supernatural gift imparted to a Christian by the Holy Spirit enabling him or her to perform miraculous deeds.*

However, since we argued in Chapter Seven that *all* the gifts listed in 1 Corinthians 12:8-10 are miraculous, this particular gift must be more carefully defined in order to distinguish it from the others. It is clear, for example, that although the gifts of healing are

---

[103] Consider, for example, the destruction of Sodom and Gomorrah (Genesis 19), where no human being is involved in performing the miracle. Miracles like this are not an example of the use of spiritual gifts, as with spiritual gifts God always uses human beings. The gifts are given to *us*.

[104] See Chapter Seven for my discussion of the use of *pneumatika* in 1 Corinthians 12:1.

[105] Matthew 7:21-23 is probably an example of this. Cf. Matthew 24:24, Mark 13:22, 2 Thessalonians 2:9.

miracles in the general sense of the term, they should not be included within the scope of the gift of the working of miracles. Paul says that the gifts of healing are given to one person and the working of miracles to another (vv.9-10, cf. vv.28-29).

So by 'the working of miracles' he presumably has in mind those miraculous manifestations of the Spirit which are not included among the other gifts. This means that, largely speaking, our understanding of what Paul means by the gift of 'the working of miracles' should probably be limited to supernatural events like turning water into wine, the feeding of the five thousand, and possibly raising the dead.

However, an examination of the rest of the New Testament seems to indicate that the word 'miracle' was generally used in the wider sense of the word and would have embraced the other gifts of the Spirit within its definition. For this reason we must bear in mind that what we learn about 'miracles' from the rest of the New Testament will relate not only to the gift of the working of miracles in particular, but to the gifts of the Spirit in general.

Who can expect to do them?

In seeking to find out who we might expect to do miracles today, we need first to look at who performed them in New Testament times. As we consider this, our thoughts are immediately drawn to **the Lord Jesus Christ** himself. Even his opponents acknowledged that he did many miracles (John 11:47), while those who believed in him reasoned

> When Christ comes, will he do more miraculous signs than this man? (John 7:31).

His miracle-working power was well known, as Peter pointed out on the Day of Pentecost. Jesus of Nazareth was

...a man accredited by God to you by *miracles, wonders, and signs* which God did... through him *as you yourselves know* (Acts 2:22).

Indeed it seems amazing that even after Jesus had done many miraculous signs in their presence some people would still not believe in him (John 12:37). What is highly significant, however, is that although many rejected his teaching and his claims to deity, there is no record that they denied his miracles. The facts were too widely known!

But Jesus did not just do miracles himself. He empowered his disciples to do them too. When we considered the ministry of **apostles** in Part One, we saw that miraculous signs regularly accompanied their ministry. Acts 5:12 tells us that

> the apostles performed *many* miraculous signs and wonders among the people.

Even their enemies were forced to admit that it would have been pointless to deny their miracle-working power (Acts 4:16). Just as in the ministry of Jesus, the facts were too widely known. In fact, miracles were so common in their ministry that some miracles were referred to as *extra*ordinary (Acts 19:11) – not the *usual* kind! So Paul could claim to have led the Gentiles to obey God by what he had both said and *done*

> ...by the power of signs and miracles, through the power of the Spirit (Romans 15:19)

and in doing so had *fully proclaimed* the gospel of Christ[106].

And of course the miracle-working power of the Holy Spirit was not confined to the apostles. As we saw in Chapter Four, miracles are part of the **evangelist's** ministry too. Acts 8:6 and 13

---

[106] Cf. 2 Corinthians 12:12 where Paul refers to *signs, wonders and miracles* as the things that mark an apostle.

tells us of the miraculous signs Philip did and of the effect they had in bringing the people of Samaria to accept the word of God.

So apostles and evangelists should certainly expect to see miracles in their ministry, but the gift is by no means limited to them. Men such as Stephen did great wonders and miraculous signs among the people (Acts 6:8), a fact which quickly led to his martyrdom. Although Stephen was one of the Seven appointed, possibly as deacons, in Acts 6:5, nowhere is he described as an apostle or an evangelist. It must therefore surely be right to conclude that the gift of miraculous powers may be given, not only to apostles and evangelists, but also to **anyone to whom the Holy Spirit decides to give it** (1 Corinthians 12:8-11). The promise of supernatural confirmation of the message of the Gospel was not just given to those who were apostles and evangelists, but to all who would believe (Mark 16:17-18, John 14:12).

Finally, before bringing this section to a conclusion, it is important to mention that there have always been those who have performed the miraculous by a power that is not of God, even, sometimes, claiming to do so 'in the name of Jesus' (see Matt. 7:22, cf. Matt. 24:24, Mark 13:22, 2 Thess. 2:9). We will discuss this further in Chapter Thirteen, but for the time being it is sufficient to note that the fact that Satan *can* work miracles is no reason to attribute *all* miracles today to a satanic origin! Such thinking springs from those who mistakenly believe that genuine miracles ceased with the first apostles. And as we now come to consider why miracles are important, it will be clear that they are needed as much today as they were in the New Testament period.

Why are miracles important?

The New Testament uses three main words to refer to miracles – *miracles, wonders, and signs.* These are to be found together in three different places in the New Testament (Acts 2:22, 2 Corinthians 12:12, Hebrews 2:4).

In Acts 2:22 the apostle Peter, preaching on the day of Pentecost, declares

> Men of Israel, listen to this: Jesus of Nazareth was a man accredited by God to you by *miracles, wonders, and signs* which God did among you through him, as you yourselves know (my italics).

In 2 Corinthians 12:12 Paul tells us that *signs, wonders and miracles* are the things that mark an apostle, and in Hebrews 2:4 the writer says:

> God also testified to it (the gospel) by *signs, wonders,* and various *miracles,* and gifts of the Holy Spirit distributed according to his own will (my italics).

We will consider each of these three words in turn and in doing so will gain a clearer understanding of why miracles are important.

Miracles

The first of the three words for miracles used by Peter in Acts 2:22 is the word 'miracles' itself. To explain the full significance of this a short Greek lesson is necessary! The word he uses is *dunameis* which is the plural of *dunamis* which means power (cf. Acts 1:8), so *dunameis* literally means 'powers'. Paul uses the same word in 1 Corinthians 12:10 when he refers to the gift of the working of miracles. It is literally 'the working of powers' and NIV tries to capture the force of this by translating the phrase 'miraculous powers'.

My purpose in drawing attention to this is to emphasise that one purpose of this gift is to manifest the **power** of God. As a gift that often accompanies the preaching of the gospel, it demonstrates to those who do not yet know him how powerful God is. And in a context where demonic forces have already been at work, as with Simon the sorcerer in Acts 8, or the Ephesians in Acts 19, this mighty gift shows to those who have been blinded by Satan and are in bondage to his power how much more powerful is the true and living God!

In a world where billions still do not know the truth, how urgently we need this powerful gift to open their eyes and turn them from darkness to light, and from the power of Satan to God (Acts 26:19).

Wonders

The next word Peter uses is 'wonders' (Greek *terata*). In the New Testament this is always found in the plural and is always linked with the word 'signs' (which we will consider in the next section). On three occasions, as we have seen, it is also connected with the word 'miracles'.

The simple way to explain the meaning of this word is to say that a 'wonder' is something that makes you *wonder!* It is an extraordinary event that causes the onlooker to marvel. The New Testament often tells us of how people were *amazed* at the miracles performed by Jesus and his disciples. In this sense they were 'wonders'.

After the healing of the paralysed man, Mark 2:12 tells us that, when he got up, took up his mat and walked out in full view of them all,

> ...this amazed everyone, and they praised God, saying, 'We have never seen anything like this!'

After the calming of the storm in Mark 4:41, we read that

> They were terrified and asked each other, 'Who is this? Even the wind and the waves obey him!'

The miracle had caused them to *wonder*.

And the same is true of the miracles in the Book of Acts. The miracle of tongues on the day of Pentecost brought a crowd together *in bewilderment* (Acts 2:6) and in verses 11 and 12 we read

> 11 '...we hear them declaring the wonders of God in our own tongues!'. 12 *Amazed and perplexed* they asked one another, 'What does this mean?' (my italics)

Similarly, after the healing of the man crippled from birth, we are told in Acts 3:10 that

> ...they were *filled with wonder and amazement* at what had happened to him (my italics).

So miracles, by their very nature, are events which cause amazement. They are wonders. But they are not only wonders. They are also *signs*. As wonders they arrest our attention and cause us to think. But as signs they point us to the answer!

Signs

The third word Peter uses in connection with miracles in Acts 2:22 is 'signs' (Greek *semeia*). If the word *dunameis* (powers) shows that miracles are intended as a demonstration of God's power, and *terata* (wonders) indicates the amazement that miracles will cause, the word *semeia* (signs) reveals the most important purpose of a miracle. It is intended to **point** us to Christ and the truth of his gospel.

The Word of God himself (Christ the Incarnate Word) was accredited by miracles (Acts 2:22). God himself testified to the apostles' preaching with signs and wonders and miracles (Hebrews 2:4), and this is a confirmation which Jesus teaches all believers to expect (Mark 16:16-20).

It is significant that nowhere, except in the case of Christ himself, are miracles seen as confirming the man himself. It is God's word in man's mouth that is confirmed. Miracles are primarily signs demonstrating and vindicating the glorious message of the gospel.

As such they are intended to produce repentance, or to vindicate the righteousness of God's judgment when people refuse to repent (Matthew 11:20-23). They are also given to encourage faith as in John 20:30-31. By confirming the authenticity of the gospel message, by producing repentance and encouraging faith, they are obviously an invaluable aid in world evangelism. They should also bring glory to Jesus. It is God, not man, who should be glorified for his miracle-working power among us (Luke 19:37).

When do miracles happen?

So the three words used for miracles show that their purpose is to demonstrate God's power, to cause people to wonder, and to point them to Christ by confirming the truth of the gospel. But when can we expect them to happen? The answer to this question comes in three parts. Miracles will happen:

– when there is a need
– when we are ready
– when it is God's will.

We will consider each of these aspects in turn before concluding this chapter with a wonderful example of a modern miracle.

When there is a need

The Bible gives us many examples of how God in his mercy worked miracles to meet people's needs. Before considering some of these, however, it is important to point out that he does not work miracles to satisfy curiosity, and he does not do so when there is no real need.

Luke 23:8 tells us that Herod had wanted to see Jesus for a long time because 'he hoped to see him perform some miracle', but the next verse says that Jesus gave him no answer. Similarly, Matthew 12:38 speaks of the Pharisees who came to Jesus and said

> Teacher, we want to see a miraculous sign from you

but Jesus replied

> A wicked and adulterous generation asks for a miraculous sign, but none will be given it... (v.39).

These verses make it clear that God does not work miracles to satisfy the curiosity of those who have no intention of believing even if a miracle were performed.

Neither does God work miracles when there simply is no need. A good example of this is God's miraculous provision of food for the Israelites when they were travelling through the desert. Exodus 16 reveals how God provided 'manna' for his people. There was always enough for each day and on the day before the Sabbath there was enough for two days! And this provision lasted throughout the forty years they were in the desert

> ...*until* they came to a land that was settled; they ate manna *until* they came to the border of Canaan (v.35).

This is confirmed in Joshua 5:12

> The manna stopped the day after they ate... food from the land; there was no longer any manna for the Israelites, but that year they ate the produce of Canaan.

The lesson from this is very clear. God has many *natural* ways of providing for the needs of his people. It is when our needs are beyond our natural resources that we may expect God to provide *supernaturally*. God does not work miracles when there is no need for them.

So when *does* he work them? The Bible gives us many examples from which we can learn the kind of circumstances in which we might expect God to work a miracle for us. The following list is borrowed largely from the ideas of Harold Horton. Although I have simplified it considerably, and put his terminology into more modern English, the examples listed are largely his[107]. According to Horton, then, God works miracles for the following reasons:

- To deliver his people from their enemies (Exodus 14:16)
- To provide for those in need (Exodus 17:1-6)
- To exercise judgment (Exodus, Chapters 7-11)
- To confirm the preaching of the gospel (Acts 13:11-12)
- To deliver from danger (Matthew 8:23-27)
- To raise the dead (Acts 9:40)
- To display God's power and glory (John 11:38-43)

I have provided just one scripture reference for each of the above points, but many more could be given. However, these examples show us some of the purposes for which God worked miracles in Bible times, and it seems reasonable to assume that these are the kind of situations in which a miracle might happen today. However, that may depend on whether or not we are ready, and it will certainly depend on whether it is God's will.

---

[107]See Horton, H., *The Gifts of the Spirit,* Ninth Edition, Nottingham, AOG, 1968, pp.126-135.

When we are ready

As we will see in the next section, the working of miracles, like any other spiritual gift, is subject to the will of God. But in saying this we must be careful not to eliminate the element of human responsibility. Miracles are performed in accordance with the Spirit's will (1 Corinthians 12:11) and by the Spirit's power (Romans 15:19), but it is undoubtedly the responsibility of every Christian to

- exercise faith, and
- keep filled with the Spirit.

We need to exercise faith

Mark tells us that even Jesus himself could do no mighty work where there was unbelief (Mark 6:5-6) and Paul reminds the Galatians that God worked miracles among them, not because they observed the law, but because they *believed* what they heard (Galatians 3:5). And the promise of miraculous signs accompanying the preaching of the gospel is given to 'those who believe' (Mark 16:17). Miracles are performed as the Spirit will, but it seems that he 'will' respond to faith!

We need to keep filled with the Spirit

Jesus said that his disciples would receive power (Greek; *dunamis*) when the Holy Spirit came upon them (Acts 1:8). As we have already seen, the word used in connection with the gift of working miracles is *dunameis* (the plural of *dunamis*). We are clothed with power in order that acts of power (miracles) might be manifested in our lives.

But Paul also uses another word when he describes this gift – *energēmata*. This word literally means 'things worked *in* us' by

God[108]. So the gift of the working of miracles is 'things of power(s) worked in us' by the Holy Spirit. If miracles are to happen *through* us, the power of the Spirit must be at work *in* us. That's why Paul tells us in Ephesians 5:18 that we must keep on being filled with the Spirit[109].

One way we can do this is to fan into flame the gift of the Spirit that is in us (2 Timothy 1:6) by regularly praying with our spirit by speaking in tongues (1 Corinthians 14:14-15). Jackie Pullinger, British missionary to the drug addicts in Hong Kong, testifies how God began to do wonderful miracles among them, when she began to speak in tongues for fifteen minutes every day[110].

Whether we are apostles like Peter, or evangelists like Philip, or deacons like Stephen, or just simple believers claiming the promises of Mark 16, if we want to see miracles among us we must keep filled with the Spirit and move forward in faith. In doing so we must, of course, remember that all these gifts are given as the Holy Spirit determines.

When it is God's will

Having said that if we want to see miracles we must seek to keep filled with the Spirit and to act in faith, we need always to remember that God is sovereign. Indeed, there are times when he performs miracles without any human participation at all. The earthquake that delivered Paul and Silas from prison, for example, was not a manifestation of any of the gifts of the Spirit, but it was a

---

[108] Cf. 1 Corinthians 12:6 where the same word is used in the phrase 'different kinds of *working*' (my italics)

[109] See also my comments in Chapter Fifteen with regard to the mean of the word 'manifestation' (1 Corinthians 12:7) in connection with receiving spiritual gifts.

[110] See Pullinger, J., *Chasing the Dragon*, London, Hodder and Stoughton, 1980, Chapter 5.
Cf. her later book, *Crack in the Wall,* London, Hodder and Stoughton, 1993, pp.27-28.

miracle of deliverance performed by God alone for the benefit of his servants.

But even when there is human involvement in the performing of a miracle (as there must be when the gift of the working of miracles is exercised), it must be remembered that the Holy Spirit is still sovereign and that the gifts are distributed as he, the Spirit, determines (1 Corinthians 12:11, Hebrews 2:4). We cannot tell God what to do. He is God! But if we learn to hear the voice of the Spirit, *he* can tell *us* what to do, and it is then that we have the faith that enables us to believe for the miracle[111].

But when all is said and done, there are many things that remain a mystery. We don't know everything. We know in part and we prophesy in part (1 Corinthians 13:9). Until we see him 'face to face' there will be much that we do not understand. Who, for example, knows why Peter, and Paul and Silas, were miraculously set free from prison (Acts 12:6-10, 16:22-36), while Stephen was stoned to death (Acts 7) and James was put to death with the sword (Acts 12:2)? When the miracle we have been praying for does not happen, we can only put our trust in the infinite wisdom of our loving God. He is God. He knows best. And whatever may happen, we know that *in all things* he works for the good of those who love him (Romans 8:28).

But the fact that we do not always get the miracle we ask for does not mean that miracles do not happen today. They most certainly do, as the testimony in the final section of this chapter demonstrates.

A modern miracle

Nigerian pastor, Daniel Ekechukwu, was delivering a Christmas present to his father on November 30, 2001, when the

---

[111] See my comments on faith in the next chapter.

brakes of his 20-year-old car failed and he smashed into a stone pillar.

Daniel suffered a severe head injury and heavy internal bleeding. He was certified dead on arrival in hospital, but his wife, Nneka, was convinced he would recover. The Bible verse 'Women received their dead, raised to life again' kept ringing in her mind (Hebrews 11:35). So she refused to let them bury him, despite the fact that burials are usually done quickly in hot countries!

His body was left in the mortuary where, after injecting it with a chemical to prevent *rigor mortis*, the mortician spent a disturbing night being woken by 'church singing' from among 'the dead'. Three times he investigated the sounds, but they stopped each time. Finally, the frightened man asked a relative to take the body earlier than planned.

But that suited Nneka. She was sure that the atmosphere at the church where evangelist Reinhard Bonnke was speaking would be sufficient to raise her dead husband to life[112]. The next day the mortician, worried about how it would look with a body being taken away, dressed it up for a funeral, laid it in a coffin, and shut the lid.

After initially being refused entry to the church compound by security officials who suspected a terrorist ploy, Daniel's persistent wife finally gained access for the coffin, which was placed in a quiet room. Bonnke was preaching upstairs in the main auditorium. The corpse was laid out on a table where it was guarded by church staff, who found *rigor mortis* had stiffened the limbs.

After a while they noticed a slight twitching of the stomach. Then the corpse drew a breath, followed shortly afterwards by irregular breathing in 'short bursts'. Encouraged by this the pastors threw themselves into fervent prayer, stripped the body of the

---

[112] Miracles of healing are a regular feature of Bonnke's huge evangelistic meetings.

184

mortuary gloves, socks and shirt, and began to massage it from head to foot – it was 'as stiff as an iron rod'.

Finally, at 5.15pm on Sunday December 2, **nearly two days after he died** Daniel opened his eyes and sat up. He asked for water and was carried into the church sanctuary where hundreds saw him slowly recover. For a while he could not recognise anyone – not even his own son – but within hours he had regained full consciousness and coherence. What's more, there is now no trace of the serious injuries that caused his death[113].

---

[113] This entire section has been taken, almost verbatim, from *Joy Magazine*, March 2002, p.15, by kind permission of the Editor.

N.B. I have included this remarkable story in the chapter on the working of miracles, but it is possible that it would be better understood as the gift of faith in operation (see next chapter). However, the important thing is that the miracle happened, not what gift was in operation!

CHAPTER TWELVE

The Gift of Faith

One of the things that we noticed in the last chapter was that not all miracles come under the category of the gift of the working of miracles. In the *general* sense of the word, *all* the gifts of the Spirit are miracles, but the *gift* of the working of miracles is more *specific*. Similarly, a manifestation of divine healing need not necessarily be an example of the gifts of healing at work. A miracle of healing can be either an exhibition of divine healing in *general*, or a *specific* case of the *gifts* of healing in particular.

So too, as we come to consider the gift of faith, we shall discover that the word is used in both a general and in a specific sense. In the first part of this chapter we will examine a variety of ways in which the word 'faith' is used in general, and then narrow our discussion down to the *gift* of faith in particular. In the second part we'll consider what it means to live by faith.

Different kinds of faith

The word 'faith' is used in a variety of ways and it is important that we do not confuse them. In this section we will look at five different uses of the word, the last of which will be the gift of faith itself. We will consider:

- Natural faith
- Saving faith
- The fruit of faith
- The faith by which other gifts operate
- The gift of faith.

Approaching the subject in this way will help us to distinguish the gift of faith from the other types of faith and to identify its meaning.

Natural faith

The Oxford English Dictionary defines 'faith' as 'trust', and in turn 'trust' is defined as a 'firm belief in the honesty of a person'. An obvious example of this is when we lend people things. If we know the person well and feel that we can trust them, we simply expect that what we have lent them will be returned. We exercise faith in them.

I have called this kind of faith 'natural' faith because it is possessed to a greater or lesser degree by all human beings. It is by no means exclusively Christian. Yet it is in a very real sense a gift from God. People who lack this basic trust in their fellow men usually end up as nervous wrecks! This natural ability to trust, (which is partly a matter of individual personality, and partly the result of a loving and secure home background), is very important to us as human beings. It is a gift from God, for *all* good is of God, since 'there is none good, but One, that is God' (Matthew 19:17), and every good gift comes from him (James 1:17).

But it is not the gift of faith referred to in 1 Corinthians 12:9, for the gifts of the Spirit cannot be received by those who are not Christians. They are given only to those who are members of the body of Christ (1 Corinthians 12:12).

Saving faith

Having briefly discussed a form of faith that may be said to be the possession of all men, we now turn to a 'faith' that is the exclusive possession of Christians. *All* true Christians possess it (for without it they would not be Christians), and *only* Christians possess it. When the Philippian jailor asked the apostle, 'What must I do to be saved?' Paul replied, '*Believe* in the Lord Jesus Christ, and you will be saved' (Acts 16:31).

John's Gospel makes it very clear that we receive eternal life by exercising faith in Jesus Christ, the Son of God (John 1:12; 3:16-18, 36; 5:24; 6:47; 20:31 etc.), and one of the great themes of Paul's letters is that we are justified by *faith* (e.g. Romans 5:1; Galatians 2:16). In Ephesians 2:8 we are told that we are saved by grace through faith, and that not of ourselves, it is the *gift* of God.

Yet even though this saving faith is here described as a *gift* from God, it is clearly not be the gift of faith referred to in 1 Corinthians 12:9. The gift of saving faith is given to *all* Christians, for without it they would not be Christians at all; but the spiritual gift referred to as 'faith' is only received by *some* Christians, because Paul says

> To *one* there is given through the Spirit the message of wisdom, to *another* the message of knowledge... to *another* faith by the same Spirit (1 Corinthians 12:8-9).

Some Christians possess it. Others do not.

The fruit of faith

Another form of 'faith' possibly referred to in the Bible is the 'fruit' of faith (Galatians 5:22). In the NIV this is referred to as 'faithfulness', which is probably the best translation in the light of the context. However, the Greek word used here is *pistis* and this is exactly the same word as is used for the gift of faith in 1 Corinthians 12:9. Clearly, if the NIV translation is correct, then the fruit of 'faithfulness' is not likely to be confused with the gift of 'faith'.

But even if Paul intends us to understand the fruit of the Spirit to be 'faith' rather than 'faithfulness', this must not be confused with the *gift* of faith found in 1 Corinthians 12. The fruit of the Spirit is to be distinguished from the gifts of the Spirit. For one thing, with the one exception of the word *pistis* (faith or faithfulness) which occurs in both lists, the list of fruit given in Galatians 5:22-23 is completely different from the list of gifts given in 1 Corinthians 12:8-10. The gifts of the Spirit are supernatural manifestations of power. The fruit is a manifestation of Christ's character springing from his indwelling Spirit within the Christian. Christians are expected to exercise only *some* of the gifts but are required to show *all* of the fruit in their lives.

There is, therefore, clearly an essential difference between the fruit and the gifts of the Spirit[114] and it follows that there must be a difference between the fruit and the gift of faith. *Some* Christians will be *given* the supernatural *gift* of faith. The *fruit* of faith (or faithfulness) should *grow* in the life of *every* Christian.

Saving faith is imparted by the hearing of the word of God (Romans 10:17). By that incorruptible seed we are born again (1 Peter 1:23). But the seed of the Word, which created faith in our hearts in the first place, must be fostered and fed if it is to grow into fruit. As we will see later, the Christian life is a progression 'from faith to faith' (Romans 1:17). The fruit of faith should be constantly growing in every Christian's heart. This will happen as we learn to live daily 'on every word that comes from the mouth of God' (Matthew 4:4).

The faith by which other gifts operate

Finally, before turning to the gift of faith itself, it is important to recognise that the gift of faith is not the faith by which all the other gifts operate, as some have suggested. It is probably true that

---

[114] Though, as Paul makes clear in 1 Corinthians 13, the fruit and gifts are complementary. The supernatural gifts without the complementary *fruit* (not gift) of love are utterly worthless.

faith is necessary for all the spiritual gifts[115] mentioned in 1 Corinthians 12:8-10. But the faith that is needed cannot be the faith referred to in verse 9, because Paul clearly says, 'To *another* faith...' clearly implying that not all Christians will have this gift. Yet, since all Christians are encouraged to desire spiritual gifts eagerly (v.31), all *are* expected to have faith for whatever gift they may exercise.

So, for example, the fact that I need faith to exercise the gift of prophecy (Romans 12:6) does not mean that I must have the gift of faith to do so, because faith is a different gift from prophecy. In short:

— Spiritual gifts operate by faith
— *All* Christians are encouraged to desire spiritual gifts
— Therefore *all* Christians need faith to do so
— But *not all* Christians will be given the gift of faith
— Therefore the gift of faith is *not* the faith by which the other gifts operate.

We have now considered four uses of the word 'faith' that are *not* what Paul means by the 'faith' in 1 Corinthians 12:9. He does not mean natural faith, or saving faith, or the fruit of faith, or the faith by which the other gifts operate. So what *does* he mean? What *is* the gift of faith?

The gift of faith

The gift of faith is one of the nine spiritual gifts listed for us in 1 Corinthians 12. These are supernatural manifestations given by the Holy Spirit to the individual Christian as outward evidences of

---

[115] See, for example, Mark 16:17ff: *These signs will accompany those who* **believe...** *Romans 12:6 If a man's gift is prophesying, let him use it in proportion to his* **faith.**

his power and presence within, and the gift of faith must be interpreted in this light. Paul himself gives us a very strong indication of what he has in mind when he says in 1 Corinthians 13:2

> If I have the gift of prophecy and can fathom all mysteries and all knowledge, and if I have *a faith that can move mountains*, but have not love, I am nothing (my italics).

The point of this verse is that it does not matter what gift of the Spirit we may exercise, if we do not have love, we are nothing. It is clear that Paul is still talking about spiritual gifts here, because he refers to tongues in v.1, and to prophecy and knowledge in v.2 (cf. also 1 Corinthians 12:31). The faith that he mentions, therefore, must be the gift of faith that he has referred to earlier in 1 Corinthians 12:9, and this he describes as *faith that can move mountains*.

This is obviously a very special kind of faith, a faith that believes for the impossible. Indeed, in using this expression Paul is undoubtedly referring to Mark 11:22-23 where Jesus said

> Have faith in God... I tell you the truth, if anyone says to this mountain, 'Go, throw yourself into the sea,' and does not doubt in his heart, but believes that what he says will happen, it will be done for him.

Jesus said this in response to the disciples' surprise when they saw that the fig tee that Jesus had cursed had withered and died (vv.12-14, 20-21). This surely indicates that what Paul had in mind when he referred to faith as a spiritual gift was a supernatural faith that produces miraculous results.

But that raises the question as to how this gift differs from the working of miracles, the gift we discussed in the last chapter. A possible answer to this is that faith is passive while the working of miracles is active. Harold Horton, for example, says

> Miracles' power *does* things by the Spirit: Faith's power *receives* or *enjoys* things by the Spirit[116] (my italics).

Similarly, C. L. Parker argues that with a gift of faith you simply believe what the Holy Spirit says, whereas with a miracle you *act* to bring his power to bear upon the situation[117]. Applying this principle to the question of moving mountains, Aaron Linford claims that this may be either by the working of miracles or by the gift of faith:

> If Miracles, then the operation is *energised* by the worker of miracles; if Faith (as 1 Cor. 13:2 shows it may be) then the operation is *commanded* by the possessor of Faith[118] (my italics)

These writers offer a variety of biblical examples to illustrate this distinction between the active nature of the working of miracles and the passive nature of the gift of faith, but perhaps the clearest is the case of Jesus calming the storm. In this connection Horton states:

> If the disciples in the tempest-tossed boat had remained calmly assured in spite of the roaring and the turbulence of wind and wave, the Lord would have shown them a Miracle of Faith, taking them through the billows as though they did not exist. Since He could not get them to trust Him *in* the storm, He was compelled to remove it by... the Working of Miracles[119].

Although this distinction between the gift of faith and the working of miracles is nowhere clearly stated in the New Testament, it seems to me that this explanation is as good as any. I say this

---

[116] Horton, H. op.cit., p.138.

[117] Parker, C.L., *Covet Earnestly,* London AOG, 1961, p.61.

[118] Linford, A., *Spiritual Gifts,* London, Linford, undated, p. 45.

[119] Horton, H., op.cit., p. 138.

because it is clear from 1 Corinthians 13:2 that Paul intends us to understand that the gift of faith produces miraculous results, and yet it is different from the working of miracles (1 Corinthians 12:9-10). Horton may well be right then when he defines the gift of faith as:

Supernatural trust (passive) in God for the miraculous[120].

Having said that, we need to be careful not to be over dogmatic on this matter. The Bible itself gives us no clear definition. Perhaps all we can say with certainty is that the gift of faith produces supernatural results and that it is nevertheless different from the working of miracles.

With this in mind we are now in a position to suggest some basic purposes for the gift of faith by considering some biblical examples of the gift in operation. These might well include:

Faith for protection in time of danger
Shadrach, Meshach, and Abednego in the fiery furnace (Daniel 3)
Daniel in the den of lions (Daniel 6)
Paul before the shipwreck (Acts 27:25)

Faith for provision in time of need
Elijah in time of famine (1 Kings 17)

Faith to bring God's blessing on others
Isaac blessing Jacob (Hebrews 11:20-21)
Peter and John laying hands on the Samaritans (Acts 8:17)
Paul 'imparting' a spiritual gift (Romans 1:11)

Faith to remove obstacles in people's lives
Moving mountains (Mark 11:23, cf. 1 Cor.13:2)

---

[120] ibid., p.33.

Casting out demons (Mark 9:18-19)
Escape from prison (e.g. Peter in Acts 12)

Faith for victory
Moses (Exodus 17:11)
Joshua at Jericho (Joshua 6, cf. Hebrews 11:30)

Faith for the impossible
Abraham, for a child in old age (Gen. 21:5, Rom. 4.20)
Raising the dead[121] (1 Kings 17:17-23, 2 Kings 4:32-35, Luke 7:11-15, 8:49-56, John 11, Acts 9:36-42, 20:7-12).

Finally, before concluding this section, we need to mention Hebrews 11, which is possibly the greatest chapter in the Bible with regard to the subject of faith. This makes inspiring reading and provides us with many cases of faith in operation. This does not necessarily mean that every example given was a manifestation of the *gift* of faith. In some cases the writer may well be giving an example of faith in general rather than referring specifically to the spiritual gift. But we will return to Hebrews 11 in the next section of this chapter as we come to consider the more general topic of the *life* of faith.

Living by faith

As we saw in the last section, although only *some* Christians may be given the spiritual gift of faith, *all* are expected to grow in faith in their daily lives. The Bible calls this 'living by faith' and, although this expression is often used today to refer mainly to

---

[121] However, this may involve a combination of spiritual gifts. In the raising of Lazarus, for example, Jesus may well have exercised not only faith, but the working of miracles and the gifts of healing – Lazarus had died of a sickness but was raised to life whole!

people who are trusting God for their livelihood, the New Testament teaches us that faith is to be the lifestyle of *every* Christian. This is made clear from the three occasions when NT writers quote Habakkuk 2:4 where God tells the prophet that *the righteous will live by faith*. These are to be found in Galatians 3:11, Romans 1:17 and Hebrews 10:38. From these passages we learn that:

– Living by faith is for all Christians
– Christians will always need faith
– There is room for progress in the life of faith
– Living by faith means plenty of problems!

We will consider each of these in turn before concluding the chapter with some important lessons on how we can develop our faith and trust in the Lord.

Living by faith is for *all* Christians

We have already mentioned four different Bible passages all of which tell us that *the righteous will live by faith*. So if we ask the question, 'Who does God expect to live by faith?' the answer is very clear. The *righteous* will live by faith. But who are the righteous? The answer to this is given in Galatians 3:11 where we read:

> Clearly, no one is justified before God by the Law, because 'The righteous will live by faith'.

To understand what Paul is saying here we need to be aware of the reason for which he wrote his letter. Paul had probably planted the churches in Galatia during his first missionary journey (Acts 13 and 14) preaching that through Jesus

...everyone who believes is justified from everything you could not be justified from by the law of Moses (Acts 13:39) (my italics).

His message was clear. We are justified (made righteous) in God's sight, not by works, but by faith. Unfortunately, after his departure, some began to teach that in order to be truly righteous it was necessary to be circumcised. This was causing division and distress in the Galatian churches and so Paul wrote his letter. Its purpose was to re-emphasise that salvation is by faith and not by works.

To prove his point that we do not gain salvation by obeying the law of the Old Testament, in chapter 3 he quotes several times from the Old Testament itself to show that salvation is by faith and not by works. This is the purpose of the quote from Habakkuk 2:4 in Galatians 3:11. God has justified us (made us righteous) because we have put our trust in Christ as Saviour. We have eternal life because of our faith in him. So *the righteous* in this verse refers to those who are justified by faith, that is, *all Christians.* And therefore all Christians *live by faith.*

But this does not simply mean that we *have life* because of our faith. It says that we *live* by faith. Faith is, or should be, the Christian's lifestyle. This is made clear in Romans 1:17 where Paul tells us that it is by faith *from first to last.*

Christians will *always* need faith

Some people seem to think that we get saved by faith when we receive Christ into our lives and that after that we receive God's blessings by earning them! But as we made clear right at the start of this book, everything we have comes as a result of God's grace and is received by faith. As Paul tells us in Galatians 2:20

The life I live in the body, *I live by faith* in the Son of God, who loved me and gave himself for me (my italics).

Elsewhere the NT literally describes the Christian life as a walk[122]. This occurs so frequently as a metaphor that NIV often translates 'walk' as 'live'. So in 2 Corinthians 5:7 where Paul says literally

> We walk by faith and not by sight

NIV translates

> We *live* by faith and not by sight (my italics).

Whichever translation we adopt, however, it is clear that as Christians we need faith throughout the whole of our earthly life. As Paul says in Romans 1:17, it is by faith from first to last. The writer to the Hebrews expresses this truth very clearly when he says

> All these people were still living by faith when they died (Hebrews 11:13).

If I may illustrate this principle from my personal experience, at the end of Chapter Eight I told how in 1977 in a meeting in Manchester I interpreted an utterance in tongues which was subsequently identified by one of our African students as Moré. He also verified the accuracy of the interpretation. When I started interpreting tongues as a student in Oxford in 1960 I did so by faith. Seventeen years later in Manchester I was still interpreting by faith, and today some twenty-five years later still, I need as much faith to interpret tongues as I did when I first started over forty years ago. Until we get to heaven and see face to face, we live by faith and not by sight. Like the people in Hebrews 11:13 we will need to be still living by faith right up to the day we die. The Christian life really is *by faith from first to last.*

---

[122] Romans 6:4, 8:1, 2 Cor. 5:7, 10:3, Gal. 6:16, Eph. 2:10, 4:1, 5:15, Col.1:10, 1 Thes.4:12 etc.
N.B. The word *walk* is the literal translation of the Greek text in these verses, though NIV does not always translate it so.

Progress in the life of faith

We have already referred to Romans 1:17 which tells us that the Christian life is by faith from first to last. Another translation of this phrase, however, is *from faith to faith* and this suggests the idea of progression in the life of faith. Our Christian walk is step by step with Jesus, and the further we walk with him, the better we get to know him, and the better we know him the more we come to trust him.

No one climbing a ladder would attempt to start by putting their foot on the top rung first. We climb one rung at a time. A person taking up weightlifting does not begin with the heaviest weight first. That could result in a serious accident. He begins with the lighter weights until his muscles are developed. Then gradually he progresses through the weights until he can cope with the heaviest. And this progress is not achieved overnight! So it is with the life of faith. We progress from one degree of faith to another.

After we first receive Jesus as our Saviour our steps of faith may be relatively small, but they are nevertheless important. They prepare us for bigger steps in the future. Some years ago, after I had preached on this theme in a London church, a lady wrote to me to tell me what had happened. In the morning service I had challenged the people to ask God to give them something that would develop their faith. This lady, wondering what she might do, felt that the Lord was telling her to put the last coin she had with her in the offering. She needed it for her bus fare home as it was far too far for her to walk. But by faith she put it in the offering anyway, expecting the Lord to provide some other way home for her.

When the service ended she waited to see if anyone would offer her a lift, but nobody did. Then she wondered if someone might give her some money, but again nobody did. So she walked out of the church and started in the direction of home. Perhaps she would find the £1 coin she needed on the pavement. But again she was disappointed. Eventually, when she was about halfway home she found a bank with a cash dispenser and obtained some money that way. But surely, she thought, that wasn't the Lord's way of providing for her need.

Feeling rather let down in her first attempts to develop her faith, she returned to church for the evening service. When the time for the offering came, a most unusual thing happened. The man who was sitting next to her, who was a complete stranger, and who knew nothing of what had gone on, took out his offering to place in the offering bag. But with it he took out an extra £1 coin, which to the lady's total amazement he quite deliberately dropped into her handbag!

She had acted in faith. God had tested her faith. But he honoured her faith by giving her back what she had given to him. I have purposely chosen this illustration because of its simplicity. What the woman was believing for was minimal! But it was a starting point for her faith. It was a step from which she could climb to higher things.

This leads me to share briefly a little from my own experience of learning to trust God for progressively bigger things. On graduating from Oxford I got married to Eileen and we went to live in Colchester where I had been offered the pastorate of an Assemblies of God church there. The church was so small that they could not possibly pay me enough to live on, so I took a job as a schoolteacher to make ends meet.

After four years God spoke to me very clearly and told me to give up my teaching job, even though the church was still in no position to pay me an adequate wage. This was a massive leap of faith for us as we had two small children and we did not feel it would be right for Eileen to go out to work at that time. But God had spoken so clearly that we knew what I had to do. So I gave up my teaching job and we started trusting God for everything.

During that period, which lasted some eighteen months, it is our testimony that God met all our needs – though not all our *wants* – and we never went without a meal, and somehow all the bills got paid. However, our income was so much lower than it had been that we drastically reduced our standard of living. I'm sure God had a purpose in that and I'm happy to say that all our children have gone on with God and are serving him in positions of church leadership today, despite the fact that their parents were far from well off during their childhood.

Ten years later, when I was pastoring in Basingstoke and being paid a relatively good salary, a situation arose in the church which led me to tell the deacons to stop paying me and pay another member of our pastoral team instead. I would once again trust the Lord for my income. This time, however, Eileen and I agreed together to believe God that we would not need to reduce our standard of living as we had at Colchester. This was an even greater step of faith than before because we were in the habit of taking the family to Switzerland for our holiday most years. We also at that time changed our car each year for a new one or at least a newer model.

This situation lasted only one year, as at the end of that time I was appointed Principal of Mattersey Hall and began to be paid a regular salary again. But during that year when we were trusting the Lord for our income, we did indeed change our car for a newer model and take the family to Switzerland as usual. We proved that God could provide for far more than our basic needs.

The point of this story is not to suggest that God wants everyone to be rich! It is simply to illustrate a progression of faith. At Colchester we had not yet grown sufficiently in our faith to trust God for the kind of things we believed for ten years later at Basingstoke. We were – and still are – on a journey of faith. It is by faith from first to last, and we move from faith to faith.

But the Basingstoke episode was far from the end of the story. Within two years of going to Mattersey we were involved in a £600,000 building programme – by today's figures probably comparable to £2 million – with no money in the bank! But I'll reserve the rest of that story to the end of the chapter! The thing we need to consider right now is the fact that living by faith means plenty of problems!

Living by faith means plenty of problems

The fact that we can expect plenty of problems in the life of faith is made clear in Hebrews 10:32-38 where we read:

> 32 Remember those earlier days after you had received the light, when you stood your ground in a great contest *in the face of suffering.* 33 Sometimes you were *publicly exposed to insult and persecution...* 34 You... *joyfully accepted the confiscation of your property*, because you knew that you yourselves had better and lasting possessions.
>
> 35 So do not throw away your confidence; it will be richly rewarded. 36 You need to persevere, so that when you have done the will of God, you will receive what he has promised. 37 For in just a little while, 'He who is coming will come and will not delay. 38 But *my righteous one will live by faith'* (my italics).

Some people have difficulty with passages like this because they feel that if we have enough faith all our problems should be solved. But that is a very one-sided view of faith. It is true that sometimes faith is the means of *escape* from our problems, but it is also on occasions the means to *endure* them. Habakkuk, the man to whom God first said, *'My righteous one will live by his faith'* (Habakkuk 2:4) certainly learned this lesson. He discovered the truth that even when everything seems against us, it is possible by faith to rejoice in the Lord, for at the end of his prophecy he says:

> Though the fig tree does not bud
> and there are no grapes on the vines,
> though the olive crop fails
> and the fields produce no food,
> though there are no sheep in the pen
> and no cattle in the stalls,
> yet I will rejoice in the Lord,
> I will be joyful in God my Saviour (Habakkuk 3:17-18).

What amazing faith! Faith does not always deliver us *from* our problems. Sometimes it delivers us *in* them! *In* all these things we are more than conquerors through him who loved us (Romans 8:37). This was the great lesson learned by some of the heroes of faith in Hebrews 11. Yes, there were those who through faith

> conquered kingdoms... administered justice... gained what was promised... shut the mouths of lions... quenched the fury of the flames... escaped the edge of the sword... became powerful in battle... received their dead raised to life again (vv. 33-35)

but there were also those who

> were tortured and refused to be released... faced jeers and flogging... were chained and put in prison... were stoned... sawn in two... put to death by the sword... (vv.35-37).

Verse 39 tells us that these were *all* commended for their faith. Not just those who *escaped* the sword (v.34), but those who *endured* it (v.37). They were all heroes of faith.

But that raises a very important question for us. When we are facing problems, how do we know what to do? Should we seek to escape from them or to face up to them and endure them?

Facing problems – escaping or enduring?

The answer to this question is that more often than not we don't have to know! The choice is made for us. Our lives are in God's hands and he knows what is best. We know that in all things he is always working for our good because we love him (Romans 8:28) and, more importantly, because he loves us (vv.35-39). Our faith is in God himself, not in what he will do for us! We can trust him because of who he is, knowing that nothing can separate us from his love. If I really trust him, I don't need to know what he is doing!

When my wife is driving and I am in the passenger seat, I don't need to keep on questioning her actions – 'Why are you accelerating now? Why are you changing gear? Why are you braking? Why are you *not* braking?!' Because she is a careful and conscientious driver, I can trust her to get me to our destination. And hasn't our God promised to get us safely to our destination? More often than not we do not need to know what to do in the midst of our problems. It is enough to know that he will bring us through.

But if we do need to know, God is well able to tell us. There are times when our problems are such that, whether we are to endure them or escape from them, we need a word from the Lord to give us the faith we need. As Paul tells us in Romans 10:17

> *...faith comes from hearing* the message, and the message is heard through *the word* of Christ (my italics).

Faith through the word

The context of the verse we have just quoted from Romans 10 is the need for people to hear the gospel before they can believe and be saved. Faith for salvation comes from hearing the word, the message of the gospel. However, a more general principle is being taught here. Most things we believe we *believe* because we have *heard* them. So it is with the things of God. The Bible is God's word. It reveals to us what he is like. It tells us that he is all-powerful. Nothing is too difficult for him. As we hear the truth about God as it is revealed in his word, faith is created in our hearts.

But the Bible is not the only way God speaks to us. As we have already seen, he may speak to us through spiritual gifts like prophecy. In this way, and in many others, God can make his will known to us in any given situation. Indeed, there are times in our experience when we need a clear 'word' of this kind if we are to have faith for the situation in which we find ourselves.

Earlier in the chapter I referred to the building programme we undertook at Mattersey in the 1980s. We had nothing in the bank and we needed £600,000. The matter was so serious that the Board of Governors referred it to the Executive Council, and the Executive Council referred it to the General Council of Assemblies of God meeting in its Annual General Conference in Minehead.

The matter was discussed at length and, during the course of the debate, one of the pastors went to the microphone and asked me a direct question: 'David, have you heard from the Lord?' In all honesty I had to answer, 'No, I just know that we need this new building'. The debate drew to a close and the matter was put to the vote. To my delight, the proposition to go ahead received the two-thirds majority required by the Constitution. Now all we needed was the money!

After the vote had been carried by so large a majority, I fully expected the money to come pouring in. But very little came! Everyone seemed to be leaving it to everyone else! As the time for the signing of the contract drew near we still had very little money, and I began to be anxious. Who has to sign the contract? What happens if the money doesn't come in? Who goes to prison if the money doesn't come in?! These were serious questions that were troubling my mind, and I kept remembering the question that pastor had asked me in Minehead: 'David, have you heard from the Lord?'

Eventually, in desperation I said to Eileen, 'I need to hear from God about this. I'm going to pray all night, and if he doesn't speak to me, I'm going to phone the Board of Governors and cancel the whole thing'. So I began my night of prayer. After several hours, at around 2am, I began to feel like giving up. God wasn't speaking and I really didn't know what to do. I decided to take a break, so I sat down on the settee and picked up a copy of *Redemption Tidings* magazine.

As I opened it the title on the editorial page struck me forcibly: FAITH. So I began to read. Now if you have ever been in desperate need to hear from God and have been in a meeting where someone has brought a prophetic word which you have known was just for you, you will understand just how I felt as I read that editorial. Every single word of it came as *Thus says the Lord* to David Petts. I knew that God had spoken. I knew that we were to go ahead. I knelt down by the settee and sobbed into the cushion and asked God to forgive me for my lack of faith. Then I went to bed. From that moment I never doubted that God was behind our building project after all.

But that is not the end of the story. The next morning I went down to the College and walked into the office. Ernest Anderson, who was then a resident member of faculty, was standing there and I excitedly told him what had happened. 'That's wonderful, David', he said, 'I was praying all night too'. I thought it was strange that we had both decided independently to pray all night and I could not imagine why he had decided to do so. 'Oh', I said, 'What were you praying for?' 'I was praying for the same thing', he replied, 'I knew that unless you, as the Principal of the College, heard from God, the thing would never happen'. 'Oh, thank you Ernest', I said, 'but you could have gone to bed at 2 o'clock!'

I immediately telephoned Colin Whittaker, the editor of the magazine. 'Colin', I said, 'you have written the greatest editorial you will ever write', and I told him what had happened. Then he told me that he had known when he was writing the editorial that he was writing it for the College, but of course he could not be that explicit in print.

Jesus said that every matter may be established by the testimony of two or three witnesses (Matthew 18:16) and, although the context in which he said it was not to do with guidance, I knew beyond doubt that this matter was established. I had received faith through hearing a word from God.

As we grow in the life of faith, from faith to faith, there may be times when the need before us is too big for our present level of faith. It is then that we can only truly believe if we know we have heard from God. Perhaps that is how the gift of faith is usually communicated, by the impartation of a word from God.

This seems to be what happened with Noah. Hebrews 11:7 tells us that by faith Noah built an ark. But Genesis 6, which recounts the story, makes no direct reference to Noah's faith. It does tell us, however, that Noah walked with God (v.9) and that God spoke to Noah (v.13) telling him to build an ark. And Noah did everything just as God commanded him (v.22). It started with relationship. This led on to revelation. And Noah's obedience to that revelation from God, the New Testament calls faith.

CHAPTER THIRTEEN

Discerning of Spirits

T here has been little difficulty in understanding the basic meaning of the six spiritual gifts we have considered so far. With the remaining three gifts, however, we will discover that there is a measure of disagreement among commentators and among popular writers on the subject. In the next chapter we will consider the message of wisdom and the message of knowledge, but in this we will turn our attention to the gift that NIV refers to as 'the ability to distinguish between spirits'[123].

Our first task will be to decide on a satisfactory definition for this gift. We will then consider what we mean by the 'spirit world' and examine our relationship to it as Christian believers. We will also look at three ways of 'testing the spirits' before investigating the gift of discerning of spirits itself.

Finding the right definition

As we have already mentioned, there is some disagreement as to the exact nature of this gift. Views on the subject may be summarised as follows:

- *Seeing* into the spirit world
- *Weighing* the source of a prophecy
- *Detecting* the presence of evil spirits.

We will consider each of these briefly.

---

[123] I shall refer to it, however, as 'discerning of spirits' since this is the term that is most commonly used.

Seeing into the spirit world

Howard Carter was probably the first writer to advance this particular view. In his book *Questions and Answers on the Gifts of the Spirit*, he states that

> The discerning of spirits is a gift of the Holy Spirit by which the possessor is enabled to see into the spirit world.

He clarifies what he means by this as he goes on to say

> By this insight he can discern the similitude of God, or the risen Christ, or the Holy Spirit, or cherubim, or seraphim, or archangels or the hosts of angels, or Satan and his legions[124].

From this and from other comments he makes in the same chapter it is clear that for Carter the gift of discerning of spirits was in effect the gift of *seeing* spirits. So, whenever anyone sees God or Satan or an angel or a demon, that is the gift of discerning of spirits.

However, there are three main objections to this definition. The first is that the Greek verb *diakrino* does not mean 'see' but 'discern' or 'distinguish'. Secondly, there is nothing in the context of 1 Corinthians 12 where Paul refers to this gift to suggest that this is what he had in mind. And finally, since *all the gifts Paul lists are given to Christians for the building up of the church*, it is difficult to interpret every apparition of angels, for example, as the gift of discerning of spirits. If angels could appear to shepherds who were not yet Christians (Luke 2), and if the risen Christ could appear to the unconverted Saul on the Damascus Road (Acts 9), and if Balaam's *donkey* could see the angel of the Lord (Numbers 22:27), it must surely be wrong to include every sighting of a supernatural being as the gift of discerning of spirits!

---

[124] Both quotes from Carter, H., *Questions and Answers on the Gifts of the Spirit*, Slough, Ambassador, 1946, p. 106.

Weighing the source of a prophecy

This view is based on the fact that discerning of spirits is placed straight after prophecy and before tongues and interpretation in the list of gifts in 1 Corinthians 12:8-10. It would make sense, therefore, if it were related in some way to these vocal gifts. Furthermore, when Paul deals with the subject of prophets in chapter 14, he says that the others should 'weigh carefully' what is said (v.29) and the Greek word here is *diakrino*, which is the same as is used for the 'discerning' of spirits.

A further argument in favour of this view is that the word Paul uses for spiritual gifts in 1 Corinthians 14:12 is the same word in Greek as the word for 'spirits' when he talks of discerning of spirits in 1 Corinthians 12:10. Understood this way the gift is, in effect, the discerning of spiritual gifts, rather than the discerning of spirits.

Of course, implicit in the idea of discerning a spiritual gift is the assumption that one is also discerning the spirit that motivates the gift. This means that this view is fairly close to the one we are about to consider, that the gift is the ability to recognise what kind of spirit is at work, particularly with regard to the exercise of spiritual gifts[125].

Perhaps the major weakness of this view is that it is too narrow. The gift undoubtedly is relevant to discerning the source of a prophetic utterance, and indeed that may be why it is placed immediately after prophecy in the list of gifts. But prophecy is not the only situation where it is important to know what spirit is at work and, therefore, the view that we are about to discuss is to be preferred.

---

[125] For further discussion of this view, see Fee, G.D., *The First Epistle to the Corinthians*, Grand Rapids, Eerdmans, 1987, pp. 596-597. See also Barrett, C.K., *A Commentary on the First Epistle to the Corinthians*, London, Black, 1983, pp. 286ff.

Detecting the presence of evil spirits

This view is not as broad as the first view we discussed, but it is not as narrow as the second, which limits the gift to the area of spiritual gifts. According to this view, the gift of discerning of spirits has two main applications:

1. It detects the presence of evil spirits in the sense that it distinguishes between the activity of the Holy Spirit and the activity of demons in any given situation.
2. It discerns when an illness is caused by an evil spirit, or when 'mental sickness' is caused by demon-possession.

Understood this way, the gift imparts the ability not only to *distinguish **between** spirits*[126], but also to *discern spirits*[127].

This position is broadly in line with Harold Horton's definition of 'supernatural insight into the spirit world'[128] and in my view is probably correct. We will consider some scriptural examples of the gift later in the chapter, but before doing so will consider the nature of the spirit world.

What is the spirit world?

Ever since the dawn of history, mankind has been aware of spiritual forces at work in the universe. The acknowledgement of the reality of 'spirits' by all the major world religions provides abundant evidence of this. The fact that the outlook of the modern 'civilised' world is largely materialistic and mechanistic has

---

[126] i.e. whether a supernatural occurrence is motivated by the Holy Spirit or by an evil spirit.

[127] i.e. detect the presence of evil spirits where their activity might not otherwise be obvious.

[128] Horton, H., op. cit., p. 33.

undoubtedly had the effect of casting doubt, and in some cases disbelief, in the minds of many people as to the reality of the realm of the spirit. But it has by no means disproved it. In fact there is plenty of evidence available if only people would be prepared to examine it.

In saying this I am not suggesting that Christians should recommend enquirers to dabble with the occult in order to satisfy their curiosity. I am simply saying that those who have experienced the power of the Holy Spirit in their lives can say with assurance that they *know* what they are talking about.

The Christian life is one of constant combat. This struggle, says Paul

> ...is not against flesh and blood, but against the rulers, against the authorities, against the powers of this dark world and against spiritual forces of evil in the heavenly realms (Ephesians 6:12).

Fortunately, the Christian's knowledge in these matters is not dependent on the superstitions of the community in which he lives, (as is the case with the sadly misguided notions of the primitive animist), but on the infallible revelation of the word of God. If we want to know that truth about the world of the spirits, it is to the Bible that we must turn out attention.

The Bible makes it plain that there are both good and evil forces at work in the spirit world. We are told little about their origin, except that they were created by God:

> For by him all things were created: things in heaven and on earth, visible and invisible, whether thrones or powers or rulers or authorities; all things were created by him and for him (Colossians 1:16).

In addition to this we are told that some of them

> did not keep their positions of authority but abandoned their own home (Jude 6).

These include Satan himself and the spirits who fell with him. These are often referred to as demons, or evil spirits. Good spirits are usually referred to as angels.

Angels

A detailed study on angels is neither possible nor necessary within the scope of this book, but the outline below may prove helpful.

- They were created by God (Colossians 1:16, John 1:1-2)
- They live in heaven (Matt. 18:10; Luke 1:19, Heb. 12:22)
- They were present at the creation of the world (Job 38:7)
- They worship God (Job 38:7; Luke 15:10)
- They are joyful beings (Job 38:7, Luke 15:10, Heb.12:22)
- There are thousands and thousands of them (Heb. 12:22)
- They are stronger and more powerful than us (2 Peter 2:11)
- They visit the earth[129] (Luke 1:19)
- They are sent to be of help to Christians (Hebrews 1:14).

Demons

The New Testament makes it clear that demons may be responsible for a variety of evil activities. These include:

- **Afflicting people with sickness** [NT examples are curvature of the spine (Luke 13:11, 16), blindness (Matt. 12:22), deafness (Mark 9:25), dumbness (Matt. 12:22; Mark 9:25)].

---

[129] *Angelos* in Greek means 'messenger'.

- **Completely take over a person's personality** [demon possession (Mark 5:5; Luke 9:39) which may also be what is meant by 'tormenting' (Acts 5:16)].

- **Deceiving** [causing people to follow false doctrine and to abandon the faith (1 Timothy 4:1), and leading them astray by predicting the future (Acts 16:16)].

Now that we have briefly outlined some basic Bible teaching with regard to angels and demons, it is important for us to consider what is our relationship as Christians to this world of the spirits.

Our relationship to them

The first thing that we need to remember is that even though the demons are against us, the angels are on our side! They are 'ministering spirits sent to serve those who will inherit salvation' (Hebrews 1:14). The Bible gives some wonderful examples of this.

The angels are on our side

Jerusalem was about to be destroyed and God's people butchered to death by the invading Assyrian army. Sennacherib as a ruthless monster had devastated every nation and city that lay before the cruel might of his invincible forces. For Jerusalem there was neither help nor hope, except it should come from heaven! But the godly Hezekiah had put his trust in the Lord, and God had answered by the mouth of his servant, the prophet Isaiah:

> This is what the Lord says concerning the king of Assyria: 'He will not enter this city, or shoot an arrow here... for I will defend this city to save it...' (Isaiah 37:33-35).

God's answer was an angel. Not a legion of angels, but *an* angel. One was enough. For in vv.36-37 we read

The angel of the Lord went out and put to death 185,000 men in the Assyrian camp... So Sennacherib King of Assyria broke camp and withdrew.

Hallelujah! If GOD is for us, who can be against us? The forces of heaven are at hand to help. The angels are on our side.

It was an angel who fed and strengthened Elijah as he lay under the juniper tree wishing to die (1 Kings 19:5). It was an angel who stopped the lions' mouths for Daniel (Daniel 6:22). It was an angel who rolled away the stone from the tomb for the women on that resurrection morning (Matthew 28:2), and it was an angel who delivered Peter from prison (Acts 12:7).

Yes, the angels are on our side! But our resources are even stronger than that! For apart from angelic assistance, the Lord Jesus Christ himself has given us authority over all the forces of darkness.

We have Christ's authority over the enemy

The Christian has nothing to fear from demons. Jesus told his disciples

> 'Behold I give you power over *all* the power of the enemy, and *nothing* shall by any means hurt you' (Luke 10:19).

1 John 4:4 reminds us that the one who is in us is greater than the one who is in the world. Ephesians 1:13 tells us that we were included *in Christ* when we heard and believed the gospel of salvation. This means that all those who have believed and are saved are in Christ. And because we are in Christ, *our* position in relation to the demonic forces, which the Bible sometimes calls 'authorities and powers' (see Ephesians 6:12), is the same as *his* position!

And what is *his* position in relation to them? He is head over every power and authority (Colossians 2:10). This is because at

Calvary he disarmed the powers and authorities by triumphing over them in the cross (Colossians 2:15). Now he is at God's right hand in the heavenly realms, far above all rule and authority, power and dominion and every title that can be given, not only in the present age but also in the one to come. *All* things are under his feet (Ephesians 1:15-23).

So what is *our* position? By his grace we have been raised up with Christ and seated with him in the heavenly realms (Ephesians 2:5-6). We are identified with him. *His* victory is *our* victory. Authority over all the enemy is ours, because it derives from him who could say, '*All* authority is given unto me' (Matthew 28:19). No wonder Jesus could say, 'These signs will accompany those who believe: In my name they will drive out demons' (Mark 16:17). Demons have nothing in common with Christ (Mark 1:24). They leave his presence as quickly as they can. And Christ is in us and we are in him. We surely have nothing to fear.

Testing the spirits

Now that we have examined what the Bible has to say about our relationship to the spirit world, we need to consider three ways in which we can 'test the spirits to see whether they come from God' (1 John 4:1). The Bible says that we can test them

–   By their fruits
–   By their doctrine
–   By their attitude to Jesus Christ.

By their fruits

In Matthew 7:15-23 Jesus talks about false prophets and miracle-workers who will expect to enter heaven by virtue of the wonderful works they have performed. But Jesus says that they will be rejected because he never knew them (v 23).

Since these people clearly never belonged to Christ, the miracles they performed could not have been done by the power of his Spirit. The test for such miracle-workers as far as we are concerned is by the 'fruit' (vv. 16-20) in their lives. Here good fruit seems to refer to doing the will of God (v.21) and evil fruit is to do evil (v.23). Even if a person works miracles using the words 'in the name of Jesus', if he is not doing the will of God in his life, he is an evil tree producing evil fruit. Therefore any miracles he performs are from an evil source.

Miracles in themselves are not necessarily a mark of God's favour and blessing. Some spiritualists, for example, perform miracles and use the words 'in the name of Jesus' but they are 'evildoers' because they disobey God by seeking to contact the spirits of the dead (Isaiah 8:19-20). Men who perform miracles by the power of the *Holy* Spirit will be those who are doing the will of God and obeying the word of God.

By their doctrine

In 1 John 4:1 we are told to 'test the spirits' and in the following verses a test is given whereby we may do so. This is in respect to doctrine. John wrote his first epistle to combat a heresy which taught that Jesus Christ could not have come as a physical person ('in the flesh') because, they said, matter was inherently evil. It is in this context that the test 'Every spirit that acknowledges that Jesus Christ has come in the flesh' must be interpreted. It is essentially a doctrinal test. It is a test that distinguishes between truth and error (v.6).

In general we could say that *any* doctrine that denies the biblical teaching concerning the Person of our Lord Jesus Christ – any teaching that is anti-Christ (v.3) – is demonically inspired. 1 Timothy 4:1 makes it clear that there are 'things taught by demons', and the evil spirits who serve the father of lies (John 8:44) are busily occupied in the task of spreading falsehood and error.

Indeed it would seem the miracles they perform are only with a view to confirming man in his error, just as the miracles performed by the Holy Spirit are given to confirm the word of truth. We may test the spiritual source of a doctrine, then, by the measure in which it conforms to the biblical teaching about Jesus.

By their attitude to Jesus Christ

The final test, which in a remarkable way combines and summarises the other two, is *by their attitude to Jesus Christ.* Only a person who is inspired by the Holy Spirit can really say from the heart that 'Jesus is Lord' (1 Corinthians 12:3). This does not mean merely to utter the words with the lips – though those who are directly under the control of demon power cannot even do that – but to acknowledge the lordship of Christ in one's heart and in one's life. The doctrinal test is here and the practical test is here. He must be Lord in my doctrine. He must be Lord in my living.

True Christians gladly acknowledge his lordship both in their doctrine and in their lives. Those who deny it, like the 'Jehovah's Witnesses' in their doctrine, and the Spiritualists by their practices as well as doctrine, are not speaking by the Spirit of God. They are weighed in the balances of the criteria of Scripture and found abysmally wanting. They are found to be speaking by another spirit. They are of their father the devil. Another personal experience will illustrate what we have been saying in this section.

The witch at Chester

Some years ago I was invited by the Christian Union of a college in Chester to conduct an evangelistic mission among the students. When I arrived just after lunch on the Monday, a member of staff conducted me to the bedroom they had allocated for me.

'I hope you don't mind', he said, 'we're putting you in a room that was occupied until recently by a student we have had to expel from the college. He had been practising witchcraft'.

I was rather surprised by this, to say the least, but I put a brave face on it and said, as casually as I could, 'Oh, that's fine. No problem!' But when I entered the room, I confess I began to wonder what evil presence might be lurking there. The half-burnt candle on the windowsill didn't help. Had that been part of his devilish paraphernalia? Or had they just had a power-cut recently?!

Then I remembered what Jesus had promised to his disciples as he sent them out on the task of world evangelisation: 'Surely, I will be with you always, to the very end of the age' (Matthew 28:20). I reminded myself of other Bible verses like

'Behold I give you power over *all* the power of the enemy, and *nothing* shall by any means hurt you' (Luke 10:19)

and I began to take courage. I settled into my room and started to prepare myself for the meeting at which I had to speak that evening.

After a few minutes there was a knock at the door. Two men stood there. They had seen the light on in my room and wondered who it was that was in there. 'Are you a new student?' they asked. 'No', I replied, I've come to conduct a mission for the Christian Union'. 'That's interesting', said one of them. 'It's strange they should put you in *my* old room'.

It was the man they had expelled for practising witchcraft! He had come back to visit his friend. Of course I invited them to the meeting that evening and the 'witch' said he might come. And sure enough, when the time for the meeting came, there he was sitting in the audience.

I preached the gospel and I would like to be able to say that the man gave his life to Christ, but he didn't. Instead he came and argued with me! This went on for some time after the meeting had closed, and after about half an hour, feeling that we were getting nowhere by arguing, I decided to invite him to come to the meeting the next day.

'I think you'll be particularly interested tomorrow', I said. 'The subject is *Jesus the way to power. How real is the supernatural? Is it safe?*'

'I don't think you know the first thing about the supernatural', he replied. What a challenge to a Pentecostal preacher!

'Well, I don't know much about what you get up to when you practise your witchcraft', I said, 'but I will tell you one thing. When you come under the control of a familiar spirit, you can't say *Jesus is Lord,* can you?'

I don't know who was more surprised, him or me! I had said this on the basis of my understanding of 1 Corinthians 12:1-3, but I was not prepared for the effect it had on this young man. He went visibly pale and said, 'How did you know that?'

Taking courage by his reaction, I said, 'Because the Bible, which is God's word tells me so. And I'll tell you something else it says. You may not acknowledge that Jesus is Lord now, but the day is coming when you will have to, whether you like it or not. For the Bible says that one day *at the name of Jesus every knee shall bow, of things in heaven and things on earth and things under the earth, and every tongue confess that **Jesus Christ is Lord** to the glory of God the Father!*'

As I quoted these verses from Philippians 2:10-11 to him, he retreated out of the room!

I went to bed at around 11pm and fell asleep straight away, sleeping soundly until about 7 the next morning. While the students were having their breakfast, I went down the corridor to the washroom to shave. While I was shaving, I saw in the mirror the face of the 'witch'. He was standing right behind me.

'Good morning', he said. 'Did you sleep well?'

'Yes, thank you', I replied.

'Are you sure?'

'Yes, perfectly sure. I went to bed around 11 and slept soundly until about 7'.

'Really? I can't understand that!'

'Why? What so unusual about having a good night's sleep?'

'Well, you see', he confessed, 'I was so annoyed with what you said last night that I stayed up all night practising my witchcraft. I was trying to get a poltergeist[130] into your room to disturb you. I've done it many times before and it's never failed. That's why they expelled me from the college. I can't understand why it didn't work this time'.

'Oh', I said, 'I wish you had told me. I could have told you not to waste your time. Don't you know that Christians are immune to such things?'

Later that day he was seen leaving the college with his bag packed. 'Leaving?' said one of the Christians. 'Aren't you coming to the meeting today?'

'No', he replied, 'that fellow knows too much about the supernatural'.

I tell this story for God's glory, and to illustrate the truth of what we have been saying. Those controlled by demons cannot acknowledge the lordship of Jesus Christ, and those who are *in Christ* have nothing to fear from demons.

The three tests we mentioned earlier in this section will usually prove sufficient for the exposure of doctrines and miracles inspired by demons. These tests may be applied by any Christian. But in addition to all this there are occasions and circumstances when some Christians are given by the Spirit a *supernatural* revelation of the presence and activity of the spirit world, whether good or bad. And such occasions are manifestations of the gift of discerning of spirits to which we will now turn our attention.

---

[130] An evil spirit that makes its presence known by noises.

The discerning of spirits

We have already seen that the basic idea behind the gift of discerning of spirits is the ability to distinguish or tell one kind of spirit from another. There is therefore no reason whatsoever to include (as some have) all those occasions when angels have been seen within the category of this gift. It must surely be possible to see an angel without possessing this gift as seems to have been the case with the first part of Gideon's encounter with the angel (Judges 6:22), and conversely it is certainly quite possible to *discern* a spirit without *seeing* it.

A possible example of the use of this gift in the New Testament is the case of Paul and the fortune-teller in Acts 16: 16-18. What is interesting here is that the things that the girl was calling out after him were true:

> These men are servants of the Most High God who are telling you the way to be saved (v.17).

So how did Paul know that she had a demon? Probably through the gift of discerning of spirits[131]. It is interesting too that Paul allowed her to do so for 'many days' (v.18). He did not rush into dealing with it. Eventually, however, 'Paul was so troubled' he cast the demon out of her.

This suggests that there is a right time to deal with evil spirits. Paul did not say, 'This girl is a fortune-teller. She must have a demon. I'd better cast it out!' It seems likely that he prayed about the matter – note the reference to the place of prayer in v.16. Jesus said that certain kinds of demon can only come out by prayer (Mark 9:29). He also said that demons were to be cast out in his name (Mark 16:17) which is what we see Paul doing here (v.18).

---

[131] We should not assume that all people who are involved in fortune telling are demon possessed. However, they certainly lay themselves open to it.

Another possible example is the case of Paul with Elymas (Acts 13:5-12). However, it is by no means certain that Paul needed the gift of the discerning of spirits in his case. The very fact that he opposed Paul's preaching and sought to dissuade Sergius from becoming a Christian would have been enough to incur Paul's emphatic denunciation in verse 10. Nevertheless the case is interesting because it is a possible example of the gift of discerning of spirits being used in combination with one or other of the three 'tests' referred to earlier. Paul could have been aware of demonic influence either by the gift or by the 'test' or by both.

Finally, a word of caution is necessary in connection with this gift. When we consider the reality of the unseen spirit world around us, its importance should be obvious to all. But there is a very real danger that it can be over-emphasised. Some, imagining that they have the gift when they have not, see demons 'under every stone'.

Others, comparing symptoms with those they see recorded in biblical cases of demon-possession jump to wrong conclusions, forgetting that similar symptoms may be produced by totally dissimilar causes. (The cause might well be physical or mental, rather than spiritual). We need to remember that we are not spiritual 'doctors' diagnosing spiritual 'diseases' by observing spiritual signs and symptoms. Of course there is a sense in which the analogy is valid, but in the final analysis, the things of the Spirit are discerned by the *spirit*.

And some are far too quick to 'diagnose' demonic activity in the lives of other Christians. That Christians are subject to the attacks of the devil is undeniable both from experience and from Scripture, but there is no New Testament evidence whatsoever that a Christian can be demon-possessed. The evidence is quite to the contrary.

The gift of the discerning of spirits will be given to us if and when the Spirit will; and if he will, he will show us the purpose for which he has revealed it to us. Until that time comes, we would do well to set our minds and hearts on the things above (Colossians 3:1-2). In Scripture we read of several occasions when God's people were enabled to see the angels. Little or nothing is said about seeing demons. God has better things for us to think about! Whatever is true, honest, just, pure and lovely, let us think on these things! And if we do come into contact with demonic influences, we may rejoice that we have authority over them in the name of our victorious King, our Lord and Saviour Jesus Christ.

CHAPTER FOURTEEN

Words of Wisdom and Knowledge

word of wisdom and a word of knowledge[132] are the first
two gifts of the Spirit mentioned by Paul in his list in 1
Corinthians 12. I will be dealing with them together
because they are so closely related and have left them until last
because of the difference of opinion that exists as to what these gifts
are. One widely held view is that they are gifts of revelation
whereby God supernaturally reveals facts that would not otherwise
have been known. An alternative position is that these gifts relate
very closely to, or possibly should be identified with, the ministry
of teaching or preaching.

We will consider these views later in the chapter, but will begin
by examining the basic difference between wisdom and knowledge.
We will then proceed to look at different levels of wisdom and
knowledge before turning specifically to the gifts themselves.

A Basic Distinction

Obviously the difference between the spiritual gifts of a word
of wisdom and word of knowledge will be closely connected to the
basic difference between wisdom and knowledge in general. This
difference can be seen quite clearly by a very brief look at the
English Dictionary. 'Knowledge' is defined as 'familiarity with
facts', and to know is to be aware of a particular fact. 'Wisdom' on

---

[132] Despite the NIV translation which replaces 'word' with 'message', I
have referred to these gifts as 'words' of wisdom and knowledge because
this is the way they are popularly referred to in Pentecostal and
charismatic circles today.

the other hand is 'The possession of experience and knowledge *together with the power of applying them*'. (Oxford English Dictionary – my italics).

This means that wisdom is the ability to apply knowledge. It is one thing to be able to retain certain facts in one's memory. It is quite another thing to know how to make the best use of those facts in practical experience. Perhaps we could say that knowledge is the faculty whereby we are aware that something is true, whereas wisdom is the faculty whereby we know *what to do* in certain circumstances[133]. It will be helpful if we bear this basic distinction in mind as we now come to consider various levels at which wisdom and knowledge may operate.

Different Levels

Of course, when the dictionary gives us the meaning of the words 'wisdom' and 'knowledge' it is speaking in general terms of the wisdom and knowledge that we possess *naturally*. But as Christians we are aware that our knowledge and understanding of the gospel and the truths of God's word are not merely natural. This knowledge and wisdom would be better described as *spiritual*. But in addition to this spiritual knowledge and wisdom that are possessed in some measure by *all* Christians, there are the gifts of a word of wisdom and a word of knowledge which according to Paul are only given to *some*. By these gifts, as we shall see later in the chapter, Paul is probably referring to a wisdom and knowledge that are *supernaturally revealed*.

---

[133] If this understanding is correct, then it is clearly wrong to define a word of wisdom as revelation of facts (future) as distinct from a word of knowledge which he defines as revelation of facts (past or present). Cf. Horton, H., op.cit., p. 68.

Understood this way, there are three levels of knowledge and wisdom – natural, spiritual, and supernatural[134]. We will discuss each of these briefly before turning our attention to the different views with regard to the nature of these two gifts.

Natural Knowledge and Wisdom

On the natural level, there seem to be two main categories of knowledge and wisdom, that which is *intuitive* and that which is *acquired.*

Intuitive knowledge

Knowledge can be described as 'intuitive' or 'instinctive' when we know intuitively by immediate insight that something is true. Paul tells us, for example, that in this way all mankind is aware of God's existence (Romans 1:21). There is no need for us to argue about it. Everyone is intuitively aware that he exists, whether they admit it or not! There is no room for argument about this. The universe declares God's existence and demands that we believe in him. He *is*, and those who deny it are not only fools, but corrupt (Psalm 14:1). If they say that they do not believe in him it is not because they *can* not believe, but because they *will* not. They do not *'think it worthwhile* to retain the knowledge of God' (Romans 1:28), but that knowledge is nevertheless intuitively there.

Acquired knowledge

Acquired knowledge is the knowledge we gain either by instruction, experience or observation. Unlike intuitive knowledge, we do not possess it instinctively, but acquire it not only during the period of our formal education but by the very process of living. We simply learn that certain things are so, either by being taught them by others or by our own observation and experience.

---

[134] Cf. the three different levels of faith we discussed in Chapter Twelve.

Another aspect of acquired knowledge is *personal* knowledge – the knowledge of people, which we gain largely by experience. Of course, there is a considerable difference between the way in which we know a fact and the way in which we know a person[135]. However, I have included personal knowledge within the category of natural knowledge because it has such an important parallel in the realm of spiritual knowledge as we shall see in a moment.

Intuitive and acquired wisdom

What is true about knowledge is largely true about wisdom. If we define wisdom as knowing what to do, we might say that a baby's desire for food or our natural instinct for self-preservation are examples of *intuitive* wisdom. Without any doubt, however, most of our natural wisdom is *acquired*. In the Bible this wisdom is associated with men and women of experience, and Acts 7:22 makes clear that there is a measure in which it may be acquired by instruction, for 'Moses was learned in all the wisdom of Egypt'.

Spiritual Knowledge and Wisdom

We have already seen that mankind has a certain intuitive knowledge of God on a natural level, for the Creator has revealed himself to us through the wonderful world he has created. However, the main way in which God has chosen to reveal himself to us is through his word, and consequently it is through the word of God that spiritual wisdom and knowledge are mainly received.

Spiritual Knowledge

We find in the Bible three main forms of spiritual knowledge which are sometimes referred to as *legal, evangelical* and *personal*. *Legal* knowledge refers to our awareness of our guilt before

---

[135] Indeed in certain languages an entirely different word is used, (for example, the difference between *savoir* and *connaitre* in French).

Almighty God. Romans 3:20 and 7:7 make clear that it is 'by the Law' that we know our sin. This legal knowledge may lead to our salvation but in itself it does not save us. *Evangelical* knowledge refers to knowledge of the facts of the gospel. But only *personal* knowledge can save us. 'This is life eternal, that they might know *you'* (John 17:3). Our salvation is dependent on our knowledge of a Person, and it is the Christian's greatest desire that his personal knowledge of Jesus Christ should deepen and grow as the days go by. We can say with Paul, 'I want to *know Christ'* (Philippians 3:10).

Spiritual Wisdom

Like spiritual knowledge, spiritual wisdom is largely received from the word of God. The opening chapters of the Book of Proverbs have much to say on this subject making it clear that true wisdom is to obey what is written in God's word. Paul shows us in 1 Corinthians 2 that there is a great difference between what the world calls wisdom and the wisdom of God. True wisdom is God's wisdom. It is revealed by the Spirit in and through the word of God.

Supernatural Knowledge and Wisdom

In 1 Corinthians 1:23-24 Paul describes the message that Christ was crucified for our sins as *the wisdom of God.* It is by that wisdom that we are saved. Without it we would not be Christians at all. It follows, therefore, that all Christians must possess a measure of *spiritual* knowledge and wisdom. They could not be saved without it.

To say this, however, does not necessarily mean that all Christians receive knowledge by *supernatural* revelation in the same way, for example, as Agabus the prophet in Acts 11:28. We are not all given insight into future events as he was. There is, therefore, a dimension of knowledge and wisdom that lies, not only beyond the natural, but also beyond the spiritual. It is supernatural.

But is this the wisdom and knowledge to which Paul refers in 1 Corinthians 12:8 when he speaks of a word (or message) of wisdom and a word (or message) of knowledge? Or is it perhaps an aspect of the gift of prophecy? As we mentioned right at the beginning of this chapter, there are differences of opinion as to the nature of these gifts. And it is to the precise nature of those gifts that we must now turn our attention.

Comparing different views

The various views with regard to the gifts of a word of wisdom and a word of knowledge centre around:

1. the significance of the Greek word *logos* ('word' or 'message') in 1 Corinthians 12:8
2. whether or not all the gifts in this list are supernatural
3. the nature of the gift of prophecy
4. the relationship, if any, between these gifts and those listed in Ephesians 4:11.

With regard to (1), those who understand *logos* to mean 'message' argue that these gifts relate to *speaking* whereas those who prefer the translation 'word' emphasise the idea of receiving a word (of revelation) from God rather than passing it on by speaking.

Concerning (2), those who take the view that not all the gifts in the list are supernatural tend to see these gifts as the ability to *speak* with wisdom or knowledge. Those who believe that all the gifts in the list are supernatural either view the two gifts as different forms of revelation, or seek to combine the idea of supernatural revelation with the spoken ministry of preaching or teaching.

The nature of the gift of prophecy (3) is significant because, if *prophecy* is seen as *speaking* on behalf of God, then a word of knowledge or wisdom need not involve speaking but could be the revelation one receives from God which may, or may not, be passed on to others in the form of a prophecy.

Finally, with regard to (4), those who see a direct connection between the Ephesians 4:11 gifts and the gifts in 1 Corinthians 12:8-10 tend to suggest that the two gifts we are considering must at least be related to teaching and preaching.

Having now outlined the main areas around which differences of opinion centre, it will now be helpful to bring all these various strands of thought together by summarising briefly the various views on the subject. A word of wisdom and a word of knowledge are understood to be either

1. Flashes of supernatural revelation, or
2. Supernatural insight in preaching and teaching, or
3. The ability to speak with wisdom or knowledge in various situations.

Having now outlined the three main views on the subject it will be helpful in the next three sections to:

– Examine these different views in more detail
– Explore the strengths and weaknesses of each view
– Explain how to reach a conclusion.

Examining the views in more detail

Each of these different positions is supported by more than one writer, but for our discussion we will use Harold Horton, Donald Gee, and Wayne Grudem to illustrate views (1), (2), and (3) respectively. We will confine our discussion largely to a word of knowledge as the same principles apply to a word of wisdom.

Harold Horton

Harold Horton's book, *The Gifts of the Spirit,* has for a long time been considered a Pentecostal classic. First published in 1934 it represents the views of many of the early Pentecostal pioneers, including especially Howard Carter in whose Bible School[136] Horton served as a tutor.

Horton's understanding of the gifts of a word of wisdom and a word of knowledge was shaped by his insistence on

> ...the hundred percent *supernatural* character of each and all of the Gifts[137].

Accordingly his understanding of a word of knowledge is

> ...the supernatural revelation by the Holy Spirit of certain facts in the mind of God[138]

and, more explicitly, it is

> ...knowledge miraculously conveyed, in the same way that speaking with other tongues is utterance miraculously given. It is not the sudden or gradual discovery or accumulation of things or facts about God or man: it is a divinely granted *flash of revelation* concerning things which were hopelessly hidden from the senses, the mind or the facilities of men... It is the operation, by the Spirit, of God's faculty of Knowledge, in such a way that for a

---

[136] The Bible School at Hampstead, London, where Carter served as Principal for some 30 years later moved to Kenley, Surrey and became the official Bible College of Assemblies of God in Great Britain and Ireland under the principalship of Donald Gee, whose views we will consider next. In 1973 it moved to Mattersey Hall where the present author became Principal in 1977.

[137] Horton, op. cit., p.8.

[138] ibid., p.48. Cf. his understanding of a word of wisdom as 'the supernatural revelation, by the Spirit, of Divine Purpose' (p.67).

specific purpose man gets a temporary gleam of God's omniscience (my italics)[139].

So Horton saw a word of knowledge as a 'flash of revelation', a fragment of God's omniscience imparted to one of his people. Even though Paul calls it a 'word' of knowledge, Horton does not see it as a vocal gift. As Christ is the *Logos* ('Word', John 1:1) and as such is God's *revelation* of himself to the world, so for Horton a word of knowledge is a revelation of God's knowledge. When such a revelation is vocalised, it becomes a prophecy.

Horton lists numerous biblical cases of what he believes is a word of knowledge in operation[140], but one simple example should be sufficient to illustrate clearly what he believes the gift to be. In Acts 5:1-2 Ananias and Sapphira sold a piece of property and brought the proceeds to the apostles for the purpose of meeting the needs of other Christians (cf. 4:34-35). But they kept back part of the money for themselves without telling anyone. However, Peter *knew* that they were being deceitful and exposed their lies publicly (vv.3-5, 7-9) as a result of which both Ananias (v.5) and, later, Sapphira fell down and died (v.10). There seems little doubt that Peter only knew about their deceit by revelation from the Holy Spirit. According to Horton's view, that kind of revelation is a word of knowledge.

Donald Gee

Donald Gee was also one of the early Pentecostal pioneers and his book, *Concerning Spiritual Gifts,* expresses similar ideas to that of Horton with respect to most of the spiritual gifts[141]. However, his views on a word of knowledge and a word of wisdom differed

---

[139] ibid., p.49.
[140] ibid.; pp.54-57.
[141] Gee, Donald, *Concerning Spiritual Gifts,* Springfield MO, GPH, 1972 (first published 1928) passim.

considerably from Horton's. Gee was careful to insist, like Horton, that these gifts are supernatural, but believed that

> ...the highly important office of teacher within the church does require to be linked up with some recognised manifestation of the Holy Spirit. It is intolerable that such a vital function within the body of Christ should be viewed simply and solely as the work of purely natural ability[142].

While he acknowledged that a revelation springing from God's omniscience (cf. Horton's view) 'can justly be described as a word of knowledge', Gee argued that 'this type of supernatural revelation almost always has some connection with the ministry of prophets'[143] and that we cannot be sure, therefore, that this is what Paul meant by 'a word of knowledge' in 1 Corinthians 12:8. It is more likely to be linked to the ministry of the teacher.

In this connection it is important to note that Gee did not argue that all teaching in the church involved the gift of a word of knowledge. He wisely recognised that

> ...there is, and always must and should be, in the church an essential teaching ministry that is the result of consecrated natural ability working upon a generally accepted body of doctrine... (2 Timothy 2:2). Our Bible schools largely exist to supply it today[144].

But he insisted that

> ...there come times when the spirit of revelation is so operating through a teacher exercising an anointed ministry that we become conscious of an illumination transcending all natural ability either to gain or to impart[145].

---

[142] Ibid., p. 114.
[143] Ibid., pp. 35-36.
[144] Ibid., p.39.
[145] Ibid., p.40.

In short, then, Gee's understanding of a word of wisdom and a word of knowledge may be summarised as supernatural insight in preaching and teaching.

Wayne Grudem

Wayne Grudem, unlike Horton and Gee, is an American charismatic scholar of the present generation. Although he argues for the use of charismatic gifts today and believes that some of them are undoubtedly miraculous, he takes the view that a word of wisdom and a word of knowledge probably are not. In his *Systematic Theology* he states that there are weighty considerations against the view that these two gifts are supernatural. He offers three reasons for saying this[146].

First, he argues that the words 'word', 'wisdom', and 'knowledge' are extremely common terms in the New Testament and that they 'are not ordinarily used to denote miraculous events'.

Secondly, he states that Paul would almost certainly have included some non-miraculous gifts in his list in case the Corinthians should think that only those with miraculous gifts really had the Holy Spirit at work within them.

And finally, he argues that the New Testament already had a term to describe receiving a special revelation from the Holy Spirit and that this was what Paul calls 'prophecy'.

Grudem concludes, therefore, that it is preferable to understand these two gifts in a 'non-miraculous' way. They are simply the ability to speak with wisdom or with knowledge in various situations.

---

[146] Grudem, Wayne, *Systematic Theology*, Leicester, IVP, pp.1080-82.

234

Exploring their strengths and weaknesses

We have now outlined three different views with regard to the nature of these two gifts:

- Horton's view – that they are flashes of supernatural revelation
- Gee's view – that they are supernatural insight in preaching and teaching
- Grudem's view – that they are simply the ability to speak with wisdom or knowledge in various situations.

We must now briefly consider the strengths and weaknesses of these three positions.

Horton's view

The main strength in Harold Horton's view is its emphasis on the supernatural nature of these two gifts. In Chapter Seven I gave several reasons, based on both the contents and the context of the list, for believing that the gifts in this list are probably intended to be understood as supernatural, and there is no need to repeat them here. If I am right about this, then clearly Horton's understanding is correct at least insofar as it stresses that a word of wisdom and a word of knowledge are supernatural manifestations of the Holy Spirit.

But is Horton right in his view that they are flashes of revelation? It seems to me that this is the weakest aspect of Horton's view for two main reasons. First, it is at least possible to understand the instances that Horton cites as examples of a word of knowledge as cases of the prophetic gift in operation, as both Gee and Grudem suggest.

Secondly, although the word *logos* ('word' or 'message') can be used in a non-vocal sense, the most natural way to understand it is surely not simply that one receives a word from God, but that one passes it on by speaking it! Horton's argument that, if a revelation received through a word of knowledge is passed on as a message to someone else it requires the 'sister-gift' of prophecy, is for me extremely unconvincing!

Gee's view

Donald Gee's view that these gifts take the form of supernatural insight in preaching or teaching has two main advantages. It not only stresses the miraculous nature of these gifts but also makes room for their vocal expression without the need for an accompanying gift of prophecy.

However, his definition is rather vague compared with that of Horton or Grudem and he does not make clear how 'supernatural insight' in teaching works out in practice. Furthermore, his insistence that the ministry of teacher must be linked up with some recognised manifestation of the Holy Spirit is far from convincing. It is true that the gift of prophecy is clearly linked with the ministry of the prophet, but does that mean that all the Ephesians 4:11 gifts must have some spiritual gift to which they are linked? There is no clear teaching to that effect in the New Testament. What spiritual gift should we associate with the ministry of pastor, for example?

Grudem's view

Grudem's view makes perfect sense if one is prepared to concede that not all the gifts in the list in 1 Corinthians 12:8-10 are supernatural. However, the three arguments he offers for a non-miraculous view of these gifts are easily countered.

First, the fact that the words 'word', 'wisdom', and 'knowledge' are *not ordinarily* used to denote miraculous events in the New Testament does *not* mean that they are *never* used in this way. I shall argue in the next section that 'knowledge', at least, is sometimes used in this way.

And his second argument is equally unconvincing. Paul *does* include some non-miraculous gifts in his second list of gifts (1

Corinthians 12:28-30)[147]. So even if Grudem's point is valid that some non-miraculous gifts must be included in case the Corinthians should think that only those with miraculous gifts really had the Holy Spirit at work within them, there is no need that they be included in the list in verses 8-10.

Finally, his claim that the New Testament already had a term to describe receiving a special revelation from the Holy Spirit and that this was what Paul calls 'prophecy' really misses the point. Prophecy is not merely receiving a revelation. It involves speaking it out! If the revelation is not vocalised, it is not prophecy! It is at least possible, as Horton argues, that the revelation is what Paul means by 'a word of knowledge' and that by 'prophecy' he means the vocalisation of that revelation.

So Wayne Grudem's view appears to fare no better than those of Harold Horton and Donald Gee. No view is entirely convincing and we are left wondering if there is any way of being sure what Paul meant by these gifts. And that is the subject of the next section.

Explaining how to reach a conclusion

In the light of the differences of opinion that we have been considering and of the real difficulties posed by the various views we have examined, it would clearly be foolish to attempt a dogmatic definition of these gifts[148]. In seeking to come to a conclusion, therefore, the first thing to recognise is that nowhere does Paul clearly explain what he means by these gifts. This is precisely why there are differences of opinion on the matter. But in seeking to evaluate those opinions and to come to a decision for

---

[147] For example, 'those able to help others' and 'those with gifts of administration' (v.28) do not appear to be miraculous gifts. See Appendix for a brief discussion of these gifts.

[148] In fairness to Gee and Grudem, both these writers recognise this. Horton, on the other hand tends to assert his views more dogmatically.

ourselves, we are most likely to come to a correct understanding if we consider:

- Paul's use of *logos* (word) in 1 Corinthians as a whole
- Paul's use of *sophia* (wisdom) in 1 Corinthians
- Paul's use of *gnosis* (knowledge) in 1 Corinthians
- the immediate context of the passage in which 'a word of wisdom' and 'a word of knowledge' are set.

Paul's use of *logos* in 1 Corinthians

Paul uses the word *logos* (word) 16 times in 1 Corinthians[149] and it is noteworthy that, with the exception of 15:54 which refers to a *written* word or saying, he uses it to refer to words that are *spoken*. This is usually made very clear from the context in which each reference is set. For example, in 1:17-18, 2:1-4, and 15:2 it is used in connection with Paul's *preaching* the gospel. In 14:9 and 19 it is directly connected with *speaking* in church.

It seems highly unlikely, therefore, that in 12:8 it refers to an *unspoken* revelation as Harold Horton insists. Indeed there is no clear evidence that Paul ever uses it in this way. In the light of this, it seems likely that a correct definition of a word of wisdom and a word of knowledge will include the idea of something that is *spoken*.

Paul's use of *sophia* in 1 Corinthians

Paul uses *sophia* (wisdom) 17 times in this letter[150]. With the exception of 12:8, all the references are to be found in the first three chapters where Paul is contrasting human wisdom with the wisdom of God. Human wisdom is mentioned 10 times whereas God's

---

[149] See 1:5, 17, 18; 2:1, 4 (twice), 13; 4:19, 20; 12:8; 14:9, 19 (twice), 36; 15:2, 54.
[150] See 1:17, 19, 20, 21 (twice), 22, 24, 30; 2:1, 4, 5, 6 (twice), 7, 13; 3:19; 12:8.

wisdom is mentioned only 6 times. These are all to be found between 1:20 and 2:13.

Since 'a word of wisdom' (12:8) is a gift which comes from the Holy Spirit, it is obvious that it has no connection with the human wisdom that is foolishness in God's sight (3:19). In the absence of any clear explanation of its meaning, therefore, it seems reasonable to conclude that the 6 references to the wisdom of God might shed some light on the matter.

These references are all firmly set in the context of Paul's discussion which contrasts the wisdom of man that both rejected and crucified Christ and the wisdom of God which is none other than the message of Christ crucified. This message is sheer foolishness to the world (1:23). It is hidden from them (2:7). But to those who are called it is the wisdom of God (1:24). Indeed, Christ himself has become for us wisdom from God – that is, *our righteousness, holiness, and redemption* (1:30). This is the 'wisdom' that Paul preached (2:6) in words *taught by the Spirit* (2:13).

It seems likely, therefore, that when in 12:8 Paul talks about a *word of wisdom* as a spiritual gift, it must in some way be connected with the ability to speak the wisdom of God, the message of the gospel, and to do so with words 'taught by the Spirit'. This understanding preserves the idea that the gifts listed in 12:8-10 are supernatural manifestations of the Holy Spirit for the words spoken are taught by the Spirit himself. It relates directly to Paul's teaching about *sophia* earlier in the letter, and is consistent with his usual use of the word *logos* to mean something spoken.

Paul's use of *gnōsis* in 1 Corinthians

Paul uses *gnōsis* (knowledge) 10 times in 1 Corinthians[151]. Of these references, 5 are found in 1 Corinthians 8 where he discusses

---

[151] See 1:5; 8:1 (twice), 7, 10, 11; 12:8; 13:2, 8; 14:6.

whether Christians should eat meat that has been previously sacrificed to an idol. The 'knowledge' he refers to in this chapter is simply the knowledge that idols are nothing and that there is only one true God (vv.4-6). Paul says that this is something that we all know (v.1), so it seems unlikely that these references have any connection with what he means by 'a word of knowledge' in 12:8.

The remaining references, however, probably do relate to this spiritual gift. In 1:4-7 Paul thanks God for the grace that has been given them in Christ, for

> ...5 in him you have been enriched in every way – in all your *speaking* and in all your *knowledge* – 6 because our testimony about Christ was confirmed in you. 7 Therefore you do not lack any spiritual gift... (my italics).

The italicised words in this quotation are *logos* and *gnōsis* and so may well be relevant to what Paul means by 'a word of knowledge' in 12:8, particularly in the light of his reference to 'any spiritual gift' in 1:7. Fee[152] is almost certainly right when he takes the view that these two terms refer to the spiritual gifts mentioned in 12:8-10. However, the context gives no clear indication as to the precise nature of these gifts and we must turn to the remaining references in 1 Corinthians for clarification. These all fall within the context of the chapters in which the list of spiritual gifts is set.

The immediate context of the passage itself

It is generally recognised that chapters 11 to 14 of this letter form a section in which Paul is addressing various disorders in the worship of the Corinthian church. It is within these chapters that the remaining references to *gnōsis* are set. Apart from the reference to a

---

[152] Fee, op. cit., p.39.

word of knowledge in 12:8, the word *gnōsis* is found in the following passages:

> If I have the gift of prophecy and can fathom all mysteries and all *knowledge*, and if I have a faith that can move mountains, but have not love, I am nothing (13:2 my italics).

> Love never fails. But where there are prophecies, they will cease; where there are tongues, they will be stilled; where there is *knowledge*, it will pass away (13:8 my italics).

> Now, brothers, if I come to you and speak in tongues, what good will I be to you, unless I bring you some revelation or *knowledge* or prophecy or word of instruction?
> (14:6 my italics).

These three references indicate strongly that when Paul speaks of *knowledge* he has some form of supernatural gift in mind. In the first passage it is set in the context of *prophecy, mysteries,* and *faith that can move mountains.* In the second it is placed alongside *prophecy* and *tongues* and is seen, like them, as a spiritual gift[153] that will one day pass away. And in the third it comes between *revelation* and *prophecy.* Although none of this makes clear exactly what Paul meant by a word of knowledge it seems evident that he intends a knowledge that is supernaturally imparted.

In line with this understanding, Gordon Fee concludes:

Most likely it is a spiritual utterance of some revelatory kind[154].

---

[153] Paul clearly does not intend us to understand that *all* knowledge will eventually pass away. It is the spiritual gift of a word of knowledge that, like tongues and prophecy etc. will no longer be needed when that which is perfect has come.

[154] Fee, op. cit. p.97.

Cf. Bultmann, R., in Kittel, G. (ed.), *Theological Dictionary of the NewTestament,* Vol. 1, Grand Rapids Mich., Eerdmans, 1964, p.708.

We have now examined Paul's use of the words 'word', 'wisdom', and 'knowledge' both in the overall context of the letter as a whole and in the immediate context of the passage in which the list of spiritual gifts is set. We may summarise our conclusions as follows.

First, since the word 'word' is used almost entirely to refer to something that is *spoken*, Horton's assertion that these gifts are *unspoken* flashes of revelation is almost certainly misguided.

Secondly, whenever 'wisdom' refers to God's wisdom (as distinct from human wisdom) in 1 Corinthians, it is strongly connected with the message of the cross. It is possible, therefore, that by 'a word of wisdom' Paul may mean a message revealed by the Spirit with a strongly evangelistic purpose.

Thirdly, in 1 Corinthians 12-14 Paul places 'knowledge' in the strongly supernatural context of revelation, prophecy, tongues, mysteries etc. The knowledge he speaks of, therefore, is likely to refer to some form of revelation from the Holy Spirit.

However, we must remind ourselves that, as we have said already, Paul nowhere clearly defines what he means by these terms and it would therefore be unwise to be over dogmatic. And perhaps it does not really matter! If the Holy Spirit is giving us supernatural revelation, what does it matter if we call it 'a word of knowledge' or 'prophetic revelation'? What is important is that God's Spirit is at work in us. The testimony of one of our students will be a suitable illustration to conclude this chapter.

A phone-call from heaven?

Just a few weeks before I started to write this chapter, one of our students asked if she could share a testimony in our morning Chapel service. Emma Jayne had felt that God wanted her to go on a missions trip during the summer vacation, but she didn't have all the money she needed. So she asked the Lord to put £250 into her bank account as a sign that he really wanted her to go. A few days later her sister, who had been given permission to open Emma's mail, phoned to say that a cheque had arrived for her. It was from the Income Tax Office and was for just over £250.

Of course, Emma was delighted, but that was not why she had asked to share her testimony. Something even more remarkable was to happen. When she heard the news, she felt the Lord was telling her to phone the Tax Office and thank them for the cheque. This is not something that most people in Britain would bother to do and Emma tried to put the thought from her mind – but it would not go away. Was the Lord *really* trying to tell her to phone the Tax Office?

Emma was still unsure, but decided she had better do so in case it was the Lord who was putting the thoughts in her mind. It couldn't do any harm, anyway! So she plucked up courage and made the phone-call.

'Inland Revenue. National Insurance Number, please', said a female voice.

'Oh, no. You don't need my NI Number', Emma replied, 'I'm not making an enquiry. I just wanted to tell you about my week'.

'I'm sorry', said the voice, 'This is the Inland Revenue, not a counselling service'.

'I know', said Emma, 'but I really must tell you what has happened', and she proceeded to tell the startled woman her story.

By the time Emma had finished, the woman in the Tax Office was in tears. 'That's amazing', she said, 'I used to go to church when I was young, but I haven't been for many years, although I did go this Sunday. On my way into work this morning, I said to my friend, *I don't know. If God exists, then he will jolly well have to ring me up and tell me so!*'

Of course we were all thrilled with Emma's testimony. I don't know if that's what Paul meant by 'a word of wisdom'. It seems to fit the kind of definition I've suggested. But it could just be understood as the simple leading of the Holy Spirit which all God's children might expect (Romans 8:14). In a sense, it doesn't matter what we call it. What's important is that Emma was open to hear and do what the Holy Spirit had to say to her. That is a lesson all God's people would do well to learn.

CHAPTER FIFTEEN

Receiving Spiritual Gifts

W e have now completed our survey of the spiritual gifts listed in 1 Corinthians 12:8-10. As we saw in Chapter Seven, these gifts are of great importance both for evangelism and for the edification of the church. It is, therefore, essential that we understand how they may be received. In this connection it is vital to remember that our *only* source for faith and practice must always be the word of God. A tremendous amount of misunderstanding can arise as a result of people listening to accounts of how others have received the baptism or gifts of the Spirit if their experience in these matters is not compared with and verified by what God has revealed in the Scriptures.

As a simple example, someone with the gift of prophecy may tell us that when the Holy Spirit inspires him to prophesy, he sees the words he is to speak written out, as if on a blackboard, before his eyes. Now it would be quite wrong to suggest that a prophecy cannot be received in this way, but it would be equally wrong to imply that the gift is always imparted in such a manner. For some, it would seem, the gift comes not visually but audibly, while for others - probably the great majority - a strong impression is felt in the spirit that certain things need to be said to God's people. God seems to deal with different people in different ways, but he never acts in a way that contradicts the Bible.

In discussing how we may receive the gifts of the Spirit, then, we must be careful to say no more than what the Bible says. Once we have said that we must leave the matter to the Holy Spirit who distributes the gifts just as he determines (1 Corinthians 12:11).

This immediately raises the thorny question as to whether one Christian can be instrumental in imparting a spiritual gift to another.

Can Spiritual Gifts be Imparted?

The main basis for the view that spiritual gifts can be imparted[155] is Romans 1:11 where Paul says:

> I long to see you so that I may impart to you some spiritual gift to make you strong.

The phrase used for *spiritual gift* here is *charisma pneumatikon* and this certainly lends support to the view that Paul is referring to the same kind of gifts as he lists in 1 Corinthians 12:8-10. As we have seen, these gifts are described both as *charismata* (v.4) and as *pneumatika* (v.1). Indeed, they are the only gifts described as both *charismata* and *pneumatika* in the New Testament and so the inference is very strong that it was one of these gifts that Paul wanted to impart to the Romans.

The main objection seems to be, however, that since Paul says that spiritual gifts are given as the Holy Spirit determines (v.11) how can a man or woman be instrumental in their impartation? The answer to this question must surely be that, provided that a person is truly led by the Spirit in praying for another to receive a particular spiritual gift, there is a sense in which they may be said to have imparted that gift.

By way of illustration of this general principle we might consider the case of miraculous healings. When the sick are healed it is of course God, not man, who heals (Acts 3:12). Yet in Matthew 10:8 Jesus told his disciples to *heal the sick*. So was it God or the disciples who were doing the healing? The answer of course is both! In the ultimate sense it is God alone who can heal, but

---

[155] 1 Timothy 4:14 is also sometimes quoted in this connection.

because of the power God has graciously given his servants, they do 'heal' at his command.

A similar parallel may be drawn with the baptism in the Holy Spirit. It is Jesus who is the baptizer[156] and yet we read in Acts 8:18 that *the Spirit was given through the laying on of the apostles' hands*. There was, therefore, a sense in which Peter and John imparted the Spirit to the Samaritans. But this does not contradict the overall truth that it is God who gives us his Spirit.

In the light of this I take the view that it is perfectly proper, if you are seeking, for example, the gift of prophecy, to ask someone who already exercises that gift to pray for you that you might exercise it too. In doing so, however, you should remember that it is the Spirit himself who distributes the gifts as he determines, and therefore to give God alone the glory if you receive it. But apart from asking for prayer in this matter, what else may we do to receive spiritual gifts? The answer to this is that it will certainly help if we understand what they are and if we have a right attitude towards them. This will lead to right actions, particularly if we worship in a church where the atmosphere is conducive to their use.

A Right Attitude

In seeking for spiritual gifts it is obviously important that we have a right understanding of them and a right attitude towards them. In this connection it will help us to realise that:

- They are gifts
- They are supernatural
- They are manifestations

---

[156]See Matthew 3:11, Mark 1:8, Luke 3:16, John 1:33.

We will deal with each of these in turn.

They are Gifts

In 1 Corinthians 12:4 Paul refers to these gifts as *charismata*[157]. We have already noted that this comes from the word *charis* which means 'grace' and that the word *charisma* is also used in Romans 6:23 where the word refers to *the gift of God* which *is eternal life in Christ Jesus our Lord*. We know that we certainly cannot earn this gift by our own human merit but must gratefully receive it by faith. It is a *charisma*. It springs from God's grace. And just as we cannot earn our salvation we must recognise too that we cannot earn spiritual gifts. They are not given us because of our own righteousness or holiness. They are given because of God's grace.

The Corinthians are a clear example of this principle. They were not lacking in spiritual gifts (1 Corinthians 1:7), but this was certainly not because they were particularly holy. Paul calls them *worldly* (3:3) because of their jealousy and quarrelling, rebukes them for tolerating immorality (5:1-12), and accuses them of drunkenness at the Lord's Supper (11:21). Their example, although of course not one to be followed, illustrates very clearly that spiritual gifts are not given because of human merit but because of God's wonderful grace.

Now from this we can learn two very important lessons. First, we should not assume that a person who is used in the exercise of spiritual gifts is necessarily more holy than other Christians. Sadly the opposite is sometimes the case. And secondly, we should not hold back from seeking spiritual gifts for ourselves because we are conscious of our own shortcomings. Of course we should seek to live holy lives, but we will never be holy enough to merit God's gifts. If he has been gracious enough to save us from our sin, if he

---

[157]This is the plural form. The singular is *charisma*.

has been gracious enough to baptise us with his Spirit, then he will surely not withhold any good gift which will bless us or make us a blessing. *All* his gifts spring from his grace.

They are Supernatural

But these gifts are not only *charismata*. As we saw in Chapter Seven, they are also *pneumatika* (v.1). This is what distinguishes them from the natural *charismata* mentioned elsewhere. These particular *charismata* are supernatural. Speaking in tongues, for example, cannot possibly refer to natural linguistic ability. It is, rather, as Acts 2 makes perfectly clear, the ability to speak a language one has never learned through the supernatural inspiration of the Holy Spirit.

From this we may learn two more important lessons. First, because these gifts are supernatural there is no limit to what God may accomplish through them. Through the gifts of the Spirit the church of Jesus Christ has available to it the miracle-working power of the true and living God! And, equally wonderfully, because the gifts are supernatural there is no limit as to the persons God may give them to. They may be exercised by male and female, weak and strong, rich and poor, able and less able, young and old alike! They are not received in accordance with our natural ability. They are supernatural endowments from the Spirit.

They are Manifestations

Finally, in 1 Corinthians 12:7 the gifts are referred to as *manifestations*. The Greek word *phanerosis* which is used here literally means 'a clear display, an outward evidencing of a latent principle'. Just as the light which shines from the light-bulb is an outward evidence of the electricity at work within it, so spiritual gifts are an outward display of the Holy Spirit at work within us. We may speak a language we have never learned because the omniscient Spirit lives within us. Miracles are possible because the Almighty fills our being. And the word *energemata* which in v.6 is translated 'workings' conveys the same idea. It literally means the things that God works *in* us.

Once again we can learn two lessons from this. The first is that spiritual gifts do not come from God far away in heaven. They come from God living within us. They are well within our reach! And then, of course, if we are expecting to manifest these gifts from the Spirit, we must keep filled with him. If the light is to shine, the electricity is to be kept flowing.

To summarise then, if we are seeking spiritual gifts, we need to understand what we're asking for. We need to remember that they are *gifts* that come as a result of God's grace. We cannot earn the right to possess them. We should remember, too, that they are *supernatural* gifts that come from the Holy Spirit. We therefore need to keep full of the Spirit. As we are full of him the Spirit will *manifest* himself through us in ways that please him.

To this we should probably add that we need to bear in mind the purpose for which the gifts are given. As we saw in Chapter Seven, the main purposes for which these gifts are given are for confirming the gospel message or for the edification of our fellow-believers. If we examine our motives to check that we want the gifts for these reasons, we may expect the Holy Spirit to give us what he knows is best, for the gifts are distributed as the Holy Spirit determines (1 Corinthians 12:11).

But of course, that does not take away our responsibility in the matter. The gifts are not some optional extra for which we may pray if we happen to be interested! We are told to desire them eagerly![158] And of course if we really desire something eagerly we will do all

---

[158] 1 Corinthians 12:31, 14:1, 12.

that we can to get it! So what can we actually *do* to receive spiritual gifts? We will try to answer this question in the next section.

Right Actions

Again, in this connection it is good to remind ourselves that we must be careful not to say more than the Bible itself teaches us. And, as we examine the Scriptures, we discover three main principles:

- We should pray
- We should believe
- We should act.

We should pray

In 1 Corinthians 14:13 Paul tells us that those who speak in tongues should pray for the gift of interpretation. Although he mentions only one specific gift here, it seems to me that if prayer is encouraged as a means of obtaining one gift it must also be appropriate to pray for the others. Besides, if we eagerly desire these gifts, as Paul tells us we should (1 Corinthians 12:31, 14:1), it would only seem natural that we should ask God for them (cf. Matthew 7:11).

But how do we know what to ask for? I find this is a common problem with people seeking spiritual gifts. If the Holy Spirit gives gifts just as **he** determines (1 Cor. 12:11), how can I know that I am praying for the right one? The answer to this, I believe, is that you don't, but you should pray anyway! Pray for whatever gift you feel is right. God is not going to be angry if you ask for a gift he does not plan to give you! He is delighted that you are asking at all.

Let's suppose, for example, that you would love God to use you in healing, but that the gift he has for you is not healing, but prophecy. However, you, of course, don't know that, so you start asking for the gifts of healing. What's going to happen? Let me suggest three things.

First, even if healing is not a gift in which God intends to use you greatly, you may experience a measure of success in praying for the sick. This is because God is gracious and sees the desire of your heart.

Secondly, we need to remember that the gifts are given so that the church might be built up. This means that when you are praying for a gift, you are not just praying as an isolated individual, but you are praying as a member of the body of Christ in which you fellowship, your local church. It is possible, therefore, that God may give the gift you are asking for to another member of the body, rather than to you. The important thing is not so much that *you* should exercise it, but that *someone* does so that the church might be blessed. We should be big enough to rejoice when God answers our prayers in this way!

Finally, as you persist in prayer, the Lord will soon turn you in the right direction. If prophecy is the gift he has for you, rather than healing, you will soon find that the Lord is giving you words with which to edify and encourage the church. So don't hold back from praying because you don't know what to pray for. God wants you to eagerly desire spiritual gifts, so pray for whatever gifts you desire, and see what God does.

We should believe

The next thing to realise in our search for spiritual gifts is that we not only need to pray, but we must pray in *faith*. This is a basic requirement if our prayers are to be answered with regard to any area of our Christian lives (cf. James 1:5-8) and it certainly applies to our prayers for spiritual gifts. For example, Jesus promised that signs like tongues and healings would accompany *those who believe* (Mark 16:17,18) and Paul encouraged those who prophesy to do so *in proportion to their faith* (Romans 12:6). In practical terms, this often means stepping out in faith believing that God will not let us down if we put our trust in him. But that leads us to the next important factor. We need to act.

We should act

We must not only *ask* for the gifts in prayer, *believing* that God will give them, but we must also *put our faith into action*. This often means having the courage to lay hands on that sick person, or to speak out a word in the meeting. But how do I know *when* to do so? Can I be sure that it's God's will for *me* to do so rather than someone else? These are important questions. We must not act presumptuously. The exercise of spiritual gifts is a serious matter and we want to get it right. And to get it right we need quite simply to be led by the Holy Spirit.

But how can we know when the Spirit is leading us? We need first to remember that it is our privilege as the children of God to be led by the Spirit of God (Romans 8:14). This means that we can *expect* God to lead us by his Spirit. It should not be a strange thing for us to know his leading. It might help you to think of how God has led you in the past. It may well be that he will lead you in a similar way again.

Secondly, we should always bear in mind the fact that the Spirit will never lead us contrary to the teachings of the word of God. He inspired the Scriptures in the first place and he will not contradict himself. This means that Paul's teaching on the use of spiritual gifts in the local church (see 1 Corinthians 14, for example) gives us clear guidance on when and how gifts like tongues, interpretation, and prophecy should be used[159]. This teaching is sometimes enough

---

[159] Consider some of the principles we taught in Chapters 8 and 9 of this book.

to get us started in the use of these gifts. I personally first started interpreting tongues because the Bible says that tongues should be interpreted and nobody else was doing so! The 'leading' I had from the Spirit was directly from the teaching of the Bible.

Lastly, it is noteworthy that the Bible says nothing about the need to 'feel the anointing' before we exercise spiritual gifts. Although this is commonly taught in some circles, there is no clear scriptural evidence for it. It is true that some people feel an intense pressure from the Spirit just before they exercise spiritual gifts, but it will help us to remember that the Spirit does not always come as a rushing mighty wind. His movings are often as gentle as a dove. As we grow and mature in the exercise of these gifts we will learn to recognise even the most gentle prompting of the Spirit. We do not need to be shaking from head to toe before we prophesy! But we do need to have some sense of leading from the Spirit.

The Right Atmosphere

Finally, if we are really serious in our desire to make progress in the realm of spiritual gifts, we will make sure that we worship in a suitable fellowship or church – one that makes room for the moving of the Spirit. The gifts are given for the edification of the church, and it seems unlikely that any gift would be manifested in a church that denies their validity or underestimates their importance. Church leaders have a great responsibility here. In my experience the gifts of the Spirit will flourish in a church where the leaders follow the following five principles.

First, it is vital when people become Christians they are encouraged to receive the baptism in the Holy Spirit as soon as possible after their conversion (Acts 2:38). This gives them an early introduction into the charismatic dimension of life in the Spirit. And of course they must be taught to keep on being filled with the Spirit on a daily basis (Ephesians 5:18, 2 Timothy 1:6).

Secondly, leaders should give clear teaching on spiritual gifts. Jesus said that it is the truth that sets us free (John 8:32). People enter into the liberty of genuine spiritual experience when they are taught the truths of God's word. It is also important that we give clear guidelines for the use of the gifts (as Paul did in 1 Corinthians 12-14). This way the people feel the security of knowing how and when they may be appropriately exercised.

Thirdly, we must encourage people to exercise the gifts and lovingly correct them where necessary. The gifts are not infallible, and because we are human, people will make mistakes. But if these are corrected lovingly and sensitively, the whole congregation will feel secure under a firm but caring leadership, and those who are beginning in the gifts can learn to excel so that the church might be built up (1 Corinthians 14:12).

Fourthly, leaders must provide the right environment for the gifts to flourish. If they seek to create an atmosphere of love (rather than criticism) in the church, people will not be afraid to move forward in faith. They should also ensure that the church meetings make room for the gifts to be exercised. Large churches need to provide smaller meetings which give opportunity for a greater number of members to start to get involved in the use of the gifts.

Finally, those who lead should lead by example. Some of the fastest growing churches in the world are churches where the leadership sets the example in the use of spiritual gifts. To summarise, in the right kind of spiritual atmosphere spiritual gifts flow naturally and easily. It is not difficult to have the faith to prophesy in a fellowship where believers love each other and want to edify one another and where the leaders will sympathetically encourage us and, if necessary, lovingly correct us as we seek to move forward in faith.

APPENDIX

Other Gifts

In the table on page 10 we mentioned five lists of gifts. The two lists I have chosen to deal with in this book are those found in Ephesians 4:11 and 1 Corinthians 12:8-10. We argued that these two lists were unique because the gifts in Ephesians 4:11 are *people* and those in 1 Corinthians 12:8-10 are *supernatural*. The three lists that we have not examined so far are:

- Romans 12:6-8
- 1 Corinthians 12:28-30
- 1 Corinthians 13:1-3.

We will deal with these briefly now. As we do so, we will notice that some of the gifts in these passages have already been discussed as they are also mentioned in 1 Corinthians 12:8-10 or in Eph. 4:11.

Romans 12:6-8

In the NIV the gifts mentioned in this passage are *prophesying, serving, teaching, encouraging, contributing to the needs of others, leadership,* and *showing mercy.* We have already discussed *prophecy* (see Chapters 3 and 9) and *teaching* (Chapter 6). This leaves:

- Serving
- Encouraging
- Contributing to the needs of others
- Leadership
- Showing mercy.

Serving – *diakonia* – deacons?

The Greek word that Paul uses here is *diakonia* from which we get our English words 'deacon' and 'diaconate'. However, this word is used in the New Testament in a general sense to refer to any kind of service for the Lord as well as in the specific sense to refer particularly to the work of a deacon. Usually the context makes clear which sense is intended, but there is some debate as to its precise meaning in Romans 12:7. Some argue that the general sense of serving is intended while others believe that Paul has in mind the work of a deacon.

In my opinion, the latter view is to be preferred because of the overall context of the passage. In verse 4 Paul argues that our physical bodies have many parts but these parts or members *do not have the same function*. So, in the church, there are many members, but *we have different gifts* (v.6). The list that follows provides examples, therefore, of the *different* kinds of function that various church members have. This clearly rules out the possibility that *diakonia* here refers to serving in the general sense, as *all* Christians are expected to serve in some way. Paul undoubtedly intends us to understand a specific form of *diakonia* which is fulfilled by some Christians and not by others. It seems highly likely, therefore, in the absence of any further clarification, that by *diakonia* here he means the work of deacons. The following notes may be of some value in understanding what the New Testament teaches about the role of deacons.

Identification

Deacons are sometimes confused with elders but that there is a difference is clear from Philippians 1:1 and 1 Timothy 3 where deacons and elders are mentioned separately. As we have already seen, the function of an elder is pastoral leadership. Deacons were not present at the Council of Jerusalem (Acts 15) but elders were. A deacon's role is that of practical service.

Qualification

The following qualifications for deacons are to be found in Acts 6 and 1 Timothy 3:8ff. A deacon must be of good reputation, full of wisdom, full of the Spirit, temperate in the use of wine, not greedy, of a clear conscience, married to only one person, managing household and children well.

Function

I have assumed that Acts 6 is a description of the appointment of the first deacons – although *diakonos* is not found in the passage, the verb *diakoneo* is (v. 2). If this assumption is incorrect, then we have no description of the role of a deacon in the New Testament. Assuming it to be correct, however, the function of deacons included such responsibilities as:

– supervising the distribution of charity to the poor (Acts 6:1)
– serving at tables (Acts 6:2).

This has been extended in many churches today to cover responsibility for the financial affairs of the church, the upkeep of church premises etc.

Appointment

In Acts 6:2-3 the apostles told 'all the disciples' to 'choose seven men'. Following this model, deacons are chosen by the church membership not by the leadership, though 'whom we may appoint' (literal translation, end of v.3) may indicate that the apostles needed to approve the choice. Indeed, the fact that they laid their hands on them (v.6) clearly indicates their approval of the choice.

In my view deacons should be chosen by the membership but leadership should exercise a power of veto. There is much wisdom (as there was in Acts 6 in the light of complaints that had been received) in letting the members appoint those who handle the church finances. Indeed in England today the Charity Commissioners would expect such people to be democratically elected.

However, we cannot be sure that the Seven appointed in Acts 6 were 'deacons' in the sense referred to elsewhere in the NT. But, even if they were not, Acts 6 is still a good illustration of:

- how a growing church adapts its structure to facilitate more growth (see v. 7)
- how those with spiritual ministries should not become over-burdened with mundane matters
- how important it is to learn to delegate
- how appointments to similar jobs may be carried out today [160].

Two extraordinary deacons

Although the office of deacon is essentially that of a servant, this does not limit individual deacons having ministries that extend far beyond the role of deacon. Stephen (Acts 6:8-7:60) and Philip (Acts 8) are wonderful examples of this. Note, however, that there is no suggestion that Philip's role as an evangelist (cf. Acts 21:8, Acts 8:4ff) was in any way related to his part in the diaconate, or that he 'graduated' from being a deacon to being an evangelist. A person may fulfil two distinct roles without those roles being essentially connected.

---

[160] In other words, even if these men were not the first deacons, it seems to me that this manner of appointment is well-suited to the appointment of deacons today.

Encouraging

The Greek verb Paul uses here is *parakaleo*. This is found over one hundred times in the New Testament and usually means 'exhort', 'beseech', 'comfort', 'urge', or 'encourage'. It is closely related to the noun *paraklesis* meaning 'encouragement', 'exhortation', or 'consolation' which Paul also uses in Romans 12:8.

Although the general sense of what Paul is saying here is clear, it is difficult to define with any certainty exactly what Paul understood this gift to be. The word is used in such a wide variety of contexts that any one of them might be what he had in mind. For example, the word is used of:

- Peter preaching the gospel on the day of Pentecost (Acts 2:40)
- Barnabas encouraging the Christians at Antioch (Acts 11:23)
- Paul and Barnabas encouraging the new disciples at Lystra etc. to remain true to the faith (Acts 14:22).

But it was not just the apostles who were expected to encourage. The writer to the Hebrews tells us to 'encourage one another daily' (3:13), and to do so 'all the more as we see the Day[161] approaching' (10:25). From this it seems clear that all Christians are expected to encourage in some measure, but that some are especially gifted at this. As we saw earlier, all God's people should evangelise but not all are evangelists. Similarly all should encourage, but some, perhaps like Joseph whom the apostles called Barnabas which means 'Son of Encouragement' (Acts 5:36), are especially gifted to do so. Note also that there appears to be some overlap between this gift and the gift of prophecy, as Paul tells us in 1 Corinthians 14:3 that encouragement is part of the purpose of prophecy.

---

[161] i.e. of the Lord's return.

Contributing to the needs of others

The Greek word Paul uses here is *metadidomi*. Its basic meaning is 'give', 'impart' or 'share'. It has been suggested that this gift also refers to the role of the deacon who distributes to the poor on behalf of the church. However, it is more likely that it is used here to mean giving of one's *own* possessions. This is how it is usually used elsewhere in the New Testament, as for example when John the Baptist tells the person who has two tunics to give to the person who has none (Luke 3:11, cf. Ephesians 4:28).

It seems, therefore, that some Christians have a special ministry in giving to others and those who have it are to exercise it *en haploteti* (Romans 12:8). NIV translates this 'generously' but the sense of the Greek is more probably 'without ulterior motive'. We are all expected to give to those in need (James 1:27, Ephesians 4:28 etc.), but some are especially used in this way. To have sufficient to be able to share it with others, and to be willing to do so, Paul sees as a *charisma* from God. 1 Corinthians 13:3 is also a possible reference to this gift, but see my comments later in this connection.

Leadership

The word used here is *proïstemi* meaning to 'lead' or 'go before'. From this basic idea it comes also to mean 'direct', 'preside', or 'govern'. It can also mean 'protect' in the sense that a person going ahead of another shields them from danger. There can be little doubt, therefore, that in Romans 12:8 it refers to the role of elders. In Chapter 5 we argued that *poimen* (shepherd, pastor), *episkopos* (overseer, supervisor), and *presbuteros* (elder) all refer to the same leadership role in the church. We also saw that these people were charged with the responsibility of leading and protecting the flock. Furthermore, *proïstemi* is used in 1 Timothy in direct connection with *episkopos* (3:5) and with *presbuteros* (5:17), and in 1 Thessalonians 5:12 Paul is surely referring the eldership team when he says:

> Now we ask you, brothers, to respect those who work hard among you, who are over you (*proïstemi*) in the Lord, and who admonish you.

In the light of the fact, therefore, that the meaning of *proïstemi* matches what is taught about the role of elders elsewhere in the New Testament, and indeed because it is used with direct reference to them, we may be confident that 'leadership' (Romans 12:8, NIV) is a reference to the work of the pastoral team.

If this conclusion is correct, then it is clearly mistaken to see 'leadership' as a separate gift in the church as some suggest. In my view such ideas spring more from modern business practice than from the New Testament itself.

Showing mercy

The Greek verb *eleeo* means 'to show mercy' or 'to take pity' on someone. In the New Testament it is mainly used of Jesus taking pity on the sick or of God having mercy on sinners. In the parable of the unmerciful servant, however, it is clear that we are expected to have mercy on others even as God has had mercy on us (Matthew 18:33).

This means that all Christians are to be merciful, but the reference in Romans 12:8 indicates that some are specially gifted in this respect. Since there are many different ways of showing mercy, and since Paul does not clarify the matter, it is possible that this gift may be expressed in a wide variety of forms. However, it seems likely that it is connected with *eleemosune* or alms-giving. Paul's instruction to do it 'cheerfully' would certainly be appropriate to this understanding. Perhaps Tabitha (or Dorcas) would have been thought of as having this gift as she was 'always doing good and helping the poor' (Acts 9:36). If this explanation is correct, the gift is clearly closely connected to 'contributing to the needs of others, which we discussed earlier.

1 Corinthians 12:28-30

In the NIV the gifts listed in this passage are *apostles, prophets, teachers, workers of miracles, gifts of healing, those able to help others, those with gifts of administration, tongues, and interpretation.* Most of these gifts have already been discussed in some detail earlier in this book. The two remaining gifts are:

– those able to help others
– those with gifts of administration.

Those able to help others

1 Corinthians 12:28 is the only place where *antilempsis* is to be found in the New Testament. Its basic meaning is 'help' and NIV paraphrases this as 'those able to help others' which, although it appears to be its meaning in this passage, is rather vague. However, any attempt to define it more precisely is at best a guess and we should beware of dogmatism. Nevertheless it is at least possible that Paul has in mind a function not far removed from that of deacon, especially bearing in mind that the next word in the list, despite the NIV translation, may well refer to elders. See below.

Those with gifts of administration

The NIV translation is rather misleading here. Valuable though administrative skills certainly are in the church today, this is hardly what Paul had in mind. The Greek word, which occurs in the New Testament only here, is *kubernesis* meaning 'the ability to steer a ship'. The people Paul has in mind, therefore, are 'helmsmen'. But what is the ship that they are steering?

If we understand it to be the individual lives of Christians, then the ability to give guidance or counselling might be what is intended. However, it is unlikely that the New Testament church knew anything of the 'counselling' that is offered to Christians today, helpful though that sometimes may be. It is far more probable that the 'ship' that is being steered by these helmsmen is the local church. If that is the case, then we are in order if we understand Paul to be referring to the eldership[162].

In saying this, however, we need to recognise that models of local church leadership in the New Testament period were by no means static. Even the Book of Acts reveals a fluidity of development from time to time and from place to place. Terminology may well have varied from one church to another and from one period to another. Viewed this way we should have no difficulty in understanding that Paul might have adapted his terminology in accordance with local usage. Thus the *episkopos* of 1 Timothy 3 could well be the *proïstamenos* of Romans 12:8 and the *kubernesis* of 1 Corinthians 12:28.

1 Corinthians 13:1-3

The gifts mentioned in verses 1-2 are *tongues, prophecy, knowledge, and faith.* These we have already discussed at length. We now need to consider briefly the gifts (?) referred to in verse 3. These are:

- Giving to (feeding) the poor
- Martyrdom (?)

---

[162] The view that *antilempseis* and *kuberneseis* refer to deacons and elders respectively is supported by H.W. Beyer in Kittel, G.F. (ed.), *Theological Dictionary of the New Testament*, Vol.3, Grand Rapids Mich., Eerdmans, 1965, p. 1036.

Giving to (feeding) the poor

At first sight this gift appears to be the same as 'contributing to the needs of others' in Romans 12:8. There certainly seems to be a connection in thought. However, the precise meaning of the Greek in this verse is unclear. It literally reads

> If I feed (*sc.* to others) all my belongings...

The verb that is used is the same as in Romans 12:20, where Paul says that if our enemy is hungry we should *feed* him. So perhaps a better translation would be:

> If I give all I possess to feed (*sc.* the hungry)...

It is possible, then, that this is a gift which Paul saw as closely connected with contributing to the needs of others, but which was specifically associated with *feeding* the hungry. In the absence of any further clarification, this seems the most likely interpretation.

However, it is questionable whether Paul intends us to understand this as a 'gift' at all. It certainly comes immediately after a mention of the gifts of tongues, prophecy, knowledge, and faith. But Paul's purpose in 1 Corinthians 13 is not to provide a list of spiritual gifts. Rather it is to point out the supremacy of love. Whatever gift we may have, indeed whatever we may do, is without value unless motivated by love. If feeding the hungry is intended to be understood as a gift – and there is no reason why it should not be – the emphasis is not on the gift itself but on the extravagance of its expression[163]. What Paul is stressing is that even if I give *all I possess* (to feed the hungry), without love it is pointless. So feeding the hungry may be a gift or it may not. Paul may have moved beyond the gifts to demonstrate further that without love nothing we

---

[163] Cf. how he refers to the other gifts in vv.1-2 in the same extravagant way.

may do is of any value. But that leads us to the so-called gift of martyrdom.

Martyrdom

As I pointed out in the Introduction to this book, it is highly unlikely that Paul intended us to understand this as a gift. Apart from the fact that the Greek text is uncertain (cf. NIV footnote) and the verse may not refer to martyrdom at all, even if it does, it need not necessarily be viewed as a gift. Paul's point is simply that even if I go as far as dying for the sake of the gospel, it is of no value unless I do it because of love. And, as I mentioned earlier, if martyrdom is a gift, by definition we could exercise it only once!

Gifts not mentioned in the NT?

We have now concluded our study of gifts in the New Testament. It remains only to ask if God sometimes gives gifts that are not mentioned there. In my view the answer to this question depends on which kind of gifts you are talking about. I think it likely that in 1 Corinthians 12:8-10 the complete range of *pneumatika* (supernatural gifts) is covered and it would be unwise to seek supernatural manifestations that are not revealed to us in God's word.

It is also quite likely that the Ephesians 4:11 gifts are a complete description of the people gifts that equip God's people for works of service. That is not to say that today they will always take exactly the same form as they did in the New Testament, but that all such equipping functions will most likely fall under the category of one or other of the gifts listed there.

But in the more general sense of Paul's use of *charismata* it is clear that there are many gifts that are not recorded in the New Testament. Every gift from God, whether natural or supernatural, comes from his grace and is, therefore, a *charisma*. How grateful today we are for the ministry of musicians! And how we notice if a musician is 'gifted' or not! Nowhere does the New Testament call musical ability a *charisma*, but it undoubtedly is, and we should thank God for it.

Of course there are many other gifts that could be mentioned. The list would be endless. But whatever gift we may have received by God's grace, the important thing is to recognise with gratitude and humility that it was God who gave it to us, and to use it in love for benefit of others.

INDEX

eternal life, 8, 9, 188, 196, 248
euaggelion, 57
euaggelistes, 57
euaggelizo, 57, 58, 60
eunuch, 64, 67
evangelism, 58, 67, 113, 114,
    115, 159, 178, 245
evangelist, 2, 6, 32, 33, 57, 58,
    59, 60, 61, 63, 64, 65, 66, 67,
    68, 69, 70, 73, 90, 98, 173,
    174, 184, 259
evangelists, 8, 10, 20, 57, 59, 60,
    61, 64, 65, 66, 67, 68, 70, 73,
    100, 104, 166, 174, 182, 260
evil spirits, 164, 212
faith, 4, 7, 10, 15, 45, 66, 70, 83,
    98, 99, 105, 113, 116, 130,
    134, 135, 146, 150, 153, 154,
    155, 156, 160, 165, 166, 167,
    168, 178, 181, 182, 183, 185,
    186, 187, 188, 189, 190, 191,
    192, 193, 194, 195, 196, 197,
    198, 199, 200, 201, 202, 203,
    204, 205, 206, 213, 226, 241,
    245, 248, 252, 253, 255, 260,
    264, 265
Father, 15, 24, 25, 26, 38, 90,
    97, 100, 113, 155, 219
feeding the hungry, 265
financial support, 33, 34, 35, 36,
    38
foretelling, 138
foundation, 33, 34, 36, 37, 38,
    53, 54, 55, 93
fruit, 4, 186, 188, 189, 190, 216,
    277
gift, 1, 3, 4, 6, 7, 8, 9, 10, 11, 12,
    16, 18, 30, 39, 42, 43, 44, 45,
    46, 47, 48, 56, 57, 66, 68, 69,
    70, 71, 74, 86, 89, 90, 91, 93,
    94, 105, 107, 109, 110, 112,
    113, 115, 117, 118, 120, 121,
    123, 124, 125, 126, 127, 128,

129, 130, 131, 133, 135, 136,
    137, 138, 139, 140, 141, 142,
    143, 144, 145, 146, 147, 148,
    158, 160, 166, 170, 171, 172,
    174, 175, 176, 181, 182, 183,
    185, 186, 187, 188, 189, 190,
    191, 192, 193, 194, 206, 207,
    208, 209, 210, 220, 221, 222,
    229, 232, 233, 235, 236, 239,
    240, 241, 245, 246, 247, 248,
    249, 251, 252, 254, 260, 261,
    262, 265, 266, 267
gifts, 1, 3, 4, 5, 6, 7, 8, 9, 10, 11,
    12, 14, 16, 17, 18, 19, 20, 21,
    40, 45, 46, 51, 65, 68, 86, 89,
    90, 98, 100, 101, 104, 105,
    106, 107, 108, 109, 110, 111,
    112, 113, 114, 115, 116, 117,
    118, 129, 133, 134, 135, 136,
    137, 139, 141, 142, 143, 144,
    145, 149, 150, 152, 153, 157,
    158, 159, 160, 169, 170, 171,
    172, 175, 182, 183, 186, 187,
    189, 190, 191, 194, 203, 207,
    208, 209, 210, 224, 225, 226,
    229, 230, 231, 232, 234, 235,
    236, 237, 239, 240, 242, 245,
    246, 247, 248, 249, 250, 251,
    252, 253, 254, 255, 256, 257,
    263, 264, 265, 266, 267, 277
gnosis, 238
gospel, 2, 31, 32, 34, 54, 55, 57,
    58, 59, 60, 62, 63, 64, 66, 69,
    79, 98, 114, 122, 152, 159,
    173, 175, 177, 178, 180, 181,
    203, 214, 218, 225, 228, 238,
    239, 250, 260, 266
grace, 8, 9, 12, 15, 18, 20, 45,
    62, 63, 106, 188, 196, 215,
    240, 248, 249, 250, 266, 267
healing, 4, 7, 8, 10, 27, 32, 65,
    83, 112, 149, 150, 151, 152,
    153, 154, 155, 156, 157, 158,

Matthias, 28, 31
medical profession, 150
mental sickness, 210
metadidomi, 261
minister, 20, 78, 86
ministers, 1, 14, 20, 147
ministry, 1, 2, 6, 19, 20, 23, 25,
26, 27, 28, 29, 30, 31, 32, 33,
35, 36, 38, 39, 40, 43, 46, 47,
48, 50, 51, 55, 56, 57, 58, 59,
60, 61, 63, 64, 65, 66, 67, 68,
69, 70, 73, 77, 78, 80, 85, 89,
90, 92, 94, 95, 96, 98, 99,
100, 101, 116, 136, 138, 142,
143, 151, 152, 155, 173, 174,
224, 229, 233, 236, 261, 267
miracle, 4, 98, 155, 159, 170,
171, 172, 173, 177, 178, 179,
180, 183, 185, 186, 192, 215,
216, 249
miracles, 4, 7, 8, 10, 27, 28, 32,
41, 51, 65, 66, 68, 70, 96,
105, 111, 114, 116, 152, 160,
167, 170, 171, 172, 173, 174,
175, 176, 177, 178, 179, 180,
181, 182, 183, 185, 186, 191,
192, 193, 194, 216, 217, 220,
263
miraculous, 10, 34, 38, 65, 66,
105, 109, 114, 122, 170, 171,
172, 173, 174, 175, 179, 181,
191, 193, 234, 236, 237, 246
miraculous powers, 10, 170,
171, 174, 175
missionary, 33, 35, 47, 54, 60,
182, 195
Moses, 39, 40, 42, 43, 47, 138,
194, 196, 227
musical ability, 267
mysteries, 120, 128, 140, 191,
241, 242
name of Jesus, 152, 219
natural talent, 93, 95

Noah, 206
overseers, 2, 71, 72, 73, 74, 75,
76, 81, 83, 84, 85, 86, 88
parakaleo, 260
paraklesis, 260
pastor, 7, 71, 72, 73, 74, 75, 76,
81, 86, 87, 88, 89, 91, 92, 94,
98, 134, 183, 204, 236, 261
pastors, 6, 8, 10, 20, 71, 72, 73,
74, 76, 77, 79, 80, 81, 84, 85,
86, 87, 88, 89, 91, 92, 96,
104, 147, 184, 204
Paul, 1, 6, 7, 8, 9, 12, 14, 15, 16,
18, 19, 21, 22, 23, 28, 29, 30,
31, 32, 33, 34, 35, 36, 37, 38,
39, 45, 46, 47, 48, 49, 50, 51,
52, 53, 54, 55, 56, 59, 60, 66,
69, 73, 74, 77, 79, 82, 83, 85,
92, 93, 95, 96, 100, 101, 105,
106, 107, 108, 109, 111, 113,
114, 115, 116, 120, 121, 122,
123, 124, 125, 126, 127, 128,
129, 131, 132, 133, 137, 138,
139, 140, 141, 145, 146, 148,
150, 152, 161, 163, 167, 168,
170, 172, 173, 175, 181, 182,
183, 188, 189, 190, 191, 193,
195, 196, 197, 203, 208, 209,
211, 221, 222, 224, 225, 226,
228, 229, 232, 233, 234, 236,
237, 238, 239, 240, 241, 242,
244, 246, 248, 251, 252, 253,
255, 257, 260, 261, 262, 263,
264, 265, 266
Paul's thorn in the flesh, 167
Pentecost, 6, 19, 27, 31, 32, 37,
42, 43, 44, 46, 47, 48, 49, 58,
66, 90, 108, 109, 110, 111,
118, 119, 122, 128, 136, 172,
175, 177, 260
Pentecostal, 7, 104, 108, 109,
112, 127, 130, 132, 219, 224,
231, 232, 276

Pentecostal Movement, 7
personal sickness, 162
personal sin, 156, 162, 163, 164,
    165
Peter, 28, 30, 31, 32, 34, 59, 66,
    67, 68, 72, 74, 76, 79, 82, 83,
    144, 152, 157, 158, 164, 172,
    175, 176, 177, 182, 183, 189,
    193, 194, 212, 214, 232, 247,
    260
phanerosis, 249
Philip, 6, 32, 58, 59, 61, 62, 63,
    64, 65, 66, 67, 68, 69, 70,
    152, 174, 182, 259
pistis, 188, 189
plurality, 2, 76, 77, 78, 79, 86
pneumatika, 12, 106, 107, 115,
    171, 246, 249, 266
poimaino, 73, 82
poimen, 72, 73, 261
Pool of Bethesda, 163, 168
power, 27, 32, 42, 44, 64, 66,
    68, 70, 107, 108, 114, 116,
    118, 121, 149, 150, 151, 152,
    154, 157, 166, 171, 172, 173,
    174, 175, 176, 177, 178, 180,
    181, 182, 189, 191, 192, 211,
    214, 216, 217, 218, 219, 225,
    247, 249, 258
powers and authorities, 166, 215
praise, 123, 127, 129, 132, 153
pray, 68, 112, 115, 119, 123,
    124, 125, 126, 130, 147, 153,
    154, 155, 157, 204, 205, 247,
    250, 251, 252
prayer, 42, 83, 123, 124, 127,
    130, 131, 134, 147, 153, 155,
    166, 184, 204, 221, 247, 251,
    252, 253
preaching, 4, 32, 58, 60, 63, 66,
    69, 79, 80, 83, 90, 94, 98,
    114, 122, 134, 137, 141, 142,
    143, 159, 160, 175, 177, 180,

181, 184, 195, 222, 224, 229,
    230, 234, 235, 236, 238, 260
prediction, 4, 47, 49, 137, 138,
    143
presbuteros, 75, 80, 84, 261
Priscilla, 93, 95
proïstemi, 261
prophecy, 1, 5, 7, 8, 10, 11, 17,
    18, 35, 43, 44, 45, 46, 47, 48,
    49, 55, 56, 64, 69, 105, 109,
    116, 124, 125, 126, 127, 129,
    133, 136, 137, 138, 139, 140,
    141, 142, 143, 144, 145, 146,
    147, 148, 190, 191, 201, 204,
    207, 209, 229, 232, 234, 236,
    237, 241, 242, 245, 247, 251,
    252, 253, 256, 260, 264, 265
prophesy, 20, 42, 44, 45, 52, 93,
    100, 122, 136, 142, 144, 146,
    147, 148, 183, 245, 252, 254,
    255
prophet, 1, 6, 18, 24, 39, 40, 42,
    43, 44, 46, 47, 49, 52, 54, 55,
    56, 90, 95, 98, 136, 138, 140,
    142, 195, 213, 228, 236
prophetes, 39, 138
prophets, 1, 6, 8, 10, 17, 20, 33,
    39, 40, 42, 43, 44, 45, 46, 47,
    48, 50, 51, 52, 53, 54, 55, 56,
    73, 100, 104, 136, 138, 142,
    148, 209, 215, 233, 263
qualifications, 2, 3, 75, 76, 84,
    87, 91, 93, 258
repentance, 66, 70, 159, 178
resurrection, 27, 29, 30, 37, 43,
    156, 214
revelation, 4, 34, 47, 49, 50, 52,
    53, 55, 136, 137, 138, 139,
    140, 141, 143, 145, 206, 211,
    220, 224, 225, 228, 229, 230,
    231, 232, 233, 234, 235, 237,
    238, 241, 242, 277
righteousness, 9, 178, 239, 248

Samaria, 27, 44, 59, 61, 63, 64, 69, 70, 174

Samaritans, 67, 68, 152, 193, 247

Sapphira, 232

Satan, 64, 107, 121, 164, 166, 171, 174, 176, 208, 212

satanic, 150, 164, 165, 166, 174

Scripture, 52, 55, 62, 65, 67, 110, 142, 144, 145, 146, 217, 222, 223

semeia, 177

serving, 10, 134, 200, 256, 257, 258

shepherd, 2, 72, 73, 74, 75, 82, 83, 85, 86, 87, 88, 96, 261

shepherds, 6, 72, 73, 74, 81, 82, 83, 84, 87, 208

showing mercy, 10, 256, 262

sick, 4, 26, 63, 77, 83, 149, 150, 152, 153, 154, 155, 157, 158, 159, 160, 161, 162, 163, 165, 166, 168, 246, 252, 253, 262

signs, 32, 33, 34, 38, 65, 66, 70, 98, 114, 115, 122, 159, 160, 172, 173, 174, 175, 176, 177, 178, 181, 190, 215, 222, 252

Silas, 46, 47, 54, 182, 183

singing with the spirit, 123

Son, 8, 15, 24, 26, 35, 46, 90, 188, 196, 260

sophia, 238, 239

spirit, 5, 112, 120, 122, 123, 124, 125, 128, 130, 131, 144, 164, 182, 207, 208, 209, 210, 211, 215, 216, 217, 219, 220, 221, 222, 233, 245

Spirit, 3, 8, 9, 15, 19, 25, 27, 34, 41, 42, 43, 44, 45, 47, 50, 53, 54, 55, 64, 65, 66, 67, 68, 80, 87, 98, 103, 104, 108, 109, 110, 111, 112, 113, 114, 118, 119, 120, 124, 128, 129, 130,

135, 136, 139, 140, 143, 144, 145, 147, 148, 154, 158, 169, 172, 173, 180, 181, 182, 183, 186, 187, 188, 189, 191, 192, 208, 216, 217, 220, 222, 224, 228, 231, 239, 242, 244, 245, 246, 247, 249, 250, 253, 254, 258, 277

spirit world, 5, 207, 208, 210, 211, 215, 220, 222

spirits, 5, 10, 25, 52, 63, 65, 105, 115, 164, 207, 208, 209, 210, 211, 212, 213, 215, 216, 221, 222

spiritual gifts, 7, 20, 106, 111, 112, 153, 171, 190, 209, 240, 247, 248, 249, 251, 252, 253, 254, 255, 265

spiritualists, 216

supernatural, 3, 6, 7, 8, 9, 11, 12, 17, 46, 65, 66, 104, 105, 106, 107, 108, 109, 112, 114, 115, 118, 120, 126, 137, 139, 140, 141, 143, 150, 151, 154, 170, 171, 172, 174, 189, 190, 191, 193, 208, 210, 219, 220, 226, 228, 229, 230, 231, 233, 234, 235, 236, 239, 241, 242, 247, 249, 250, 256, 266

teacher, 3, 7, 18, 89, 90, 92, 93, 94, 95, 96, 97, 98, 99, 100, 101, 142, 143, 233, 236

teachers, 3, 8, 10, 20, 46, 51, 73, 81, 83, 84, 89, 90, 91, 92, 93, 94, 95, 96, 98, 99, 100, 104, 263

teaching, 3, 10, 14, 16, 18, 34, 59, 65, 71, 79, 80, 82, 83, 89, 90, 91, 92, 93, 95, 96, 97, 98, 99, 100, 101, 108, 112, 131, 132, 142, 144, 145, 153, 167, 173, 199, 213, 216, 217, 224,

Select Bibliography

Allen, D., *The Unfailing Stream*, Tonbridge, Sovereign World, 1994

Barrett, C.K., *The First Epistle to the Corinthians*, London, Black, 1971

Bennett, D. and R., *The Holy Spirit and You*, Eastbourne, Kingsway, 1979

Bittlinger, Arnold, *Gifts and Ministries*, London, Hodder & Stoughton, 1974

Burton, W.F.P., *Signs Following*, London, AOG, 1949

Bridge, Donald, *Signs and Wonders Today*, Leicester, IVP, 1985

Bridge, D., and Phypers, D., *Spiritual Gifts and the Church*, London, IVP, 1973

Canty, George, *The Practice of Pentecost*, Basingstoke, Marshalls, 1987

Carson, D., *Showing the Spirit*, Grand Rapids Mich., Baker, 1987

Carson, H., Are *Spiritual Gifts for Today?* Eastbourne, Kingsway, 1987

Carter, Howard, *Spiritual Gifts and their Operation*, Springfield MO, GPH, 1968

Carter, Howard, *Questions and Answers on Spiritual Gifts*, London, AOG, 1946

Fee, G.D., *The First Epistle to the Corinthians*, Grand Rapids Mich., Eerdmans, 1987

Fee, G.D., *God's Empowering Presence*, Peabody MA, Hendrickson, 1994

Gee, Donald, *Concerning Spiritual Gifts* Springfield MO, GPH, 1972

Gee, Donald, *The Ministry Gifts of Christ* Springfield MO, GPH, 1930

Grudem, W., *Are Miraculous Gifts for Today?* Leicester, IVP, 1996

Harper, M., *These Wonderful Gifts*, London, Hodder & Stoughton, 1989

Harris, R.W., *Spoken by the Spirit,* Springfield MO, GPH, 1973

Hathaway, W.G., *Spiritual Gifts in the Church*, Clapham Park, Elim, 1933

Horton, Harold, *The Gifts of the Spirit*, Nottingham, AOG, 1976

Horton, Stanley (ed.), *Systematic Theology*, Springfield MO, GPH, 1994

Horton, Stanley, *What the Bible says about the Holy Spirit*, Springfield MO, GPH, 1976

Hubbard, Ray, *Gifts of Grace*, Bromley, New Life Press, 1971

Kay, William K., *Prophecy!*, Nottingham, Lifestream & Mattersey Hall, 1991

Lim, David, *Spiritual Gifts - a Fresh Look*, Springfield MO, GPH, 1991

Linford, Aaron, *Spiritual Gifts*, AOG, London, Undated

Menzies, W.W. and Horton, S.M., *Bible Doctrines, a Pentecostal Perspective*, Springfield MO, GPH, 1993

Pearlman, Myer, *Knowing the Doctrines of the Bible*, Springfield MO, GPH, 1937

Petts, David, *The Dynamic Difference*, Springfield MO, GPH, 1976

Petts, David, *The Holy Spirit – an Introduction*, Mattersey, Mattersey Hall, 1998

Petts, David, *You'd Better Believe it!* Mattersey, Mattersey Hall, 1999

Pytches, David, *Come Holy Spirit*, London, Hodder, 1985

Pytches, David, *Prophecy in the Local Church*, London, Hodder & Stoughton, 1993

Rea, John, *The Holy Spirit in the Bible*, Marshall Pickering, 1990

Riggs, R., *The Spirit Himself*, Springfield MO, GPH, 1949

Rosser, Ivor, *Grace Gifts*, Risca, Rosser, Undated

Schatzmann, S., *A Pauline Theology of Charismata*, Peabody MA, Hendrickson, 1987

Turner, Max, *The Holy Spirit and Spiritual Gifts – Then and Now,* Carlisle, Paternoster 1996

Wagner, C.P., *Your Spiritual Gifts Can Help Your Church Grow,* Bromley, Marc, 1985

Warrington, K. (ed.), *Pentecostal Perspectives,* Carlisle, Paternoster, 1998

Wigglesworth, Smith, *Ever Increasing Faith,* Springfield MO, GPH, 1924

Williams, J. Rodman, *Renewal Theology Vol. 2*, Grand Rapids Mich, Zondervan, 1990

Articles in Periodicals/ Journals

Carlson, G. Raymond, 'The Interpretation of Tongues', *Paraclete,* Vol. 11, No. 2 (1977)

Hadden, A., 'Gifts of the Spirit in Assemblies of God Writings', *Paraclete,* Vol. 24, No. 1 (1990)

Holdcroft, L. Thomas, 'Spiritual Gifts we may fail to recognise', *Paraclete,* Vol. 3, No. 2 (1969)

Holdcroft, L. Thomas, 'The Gift of the Gifts of Healings', *Paraclete,* Vol. 2, No. 2 (1968)

Hoy, Albert L., 'The Word of Knowledge', *Paraclete,* Vol 2 No 2 (1968)

Rainey, Chris, 'Harold Horton', *Paraclete,* Vol. 28, No. 2 (1994)

Also by David Petts:

'You'd Better Believe It!'

20 chapters on basic Christian doctrine from a Pentecostal perspective.

Introduction: The Importance of Doctrine
Why We Believe in the Bible
The Nature of God
The Life of Christ
His Substitutionary Death
His Bodily Resurrection
His Triumphant Ascension
His Abiding Intercession
His Second Coming
The Fall of Man
Saved through Faith
The Blood of Christ
The New Birth
Water Baptism
Breaking of Bread
The Baptism with the Holy Spirit
The Gifts of the Holy Spirit
The Gifts of Christ
Divine Healing
Holiness
Heaven and Hell

Published by Mattersey Hall
4th edition 1999, 142pp.
£6.99   US$10.99   10.99

Also by David Petts:

'The Holy Spirit – An Introduction'

In this clearly written and easily readable book Dr David Petts answers questions like:

Who is the Holy Spirit? How can I answer the Jehovah's Witnesses who say that the Holy Spirit is only an impersonal force? Should we worship the Holy Spirit? What is our answer to those who deny the Virgin Birth? What is the blasphemy against the Holy Spirit? How can I help someone who believes they have committed the unforgivable sin? What role does the Spirit play in the work of conversion? Can the Holy Spirit help me live a holy life? What is the Baptism in the Holy Spirit? How do I know if I've received it? How can I receive and maintain the fulness of the Spirit? Do I have to be baptized in the Spirit to manifest the fruit of the Spirit? What are the gifts of the Spirit and how can I receive them and use them? What's the role of the Holy Spirit in the life of the church? What's the connection between the Holy Spirit and the age to come?

Written from a distinctly charismatic perspective this book will both inform you and inspire you. The author's balanced approach, with his insistence that our experience of the Spirit must be understood and evaluated in the light of biblical revelation, gives the reader confidence that the writer is familiar with the Holy Spirit's work not only from his study of the Word of God but also from personal experience.

Published by Mattersey Hall, 1998, 140pp.
£6.99   US$10.99   10.99